Animal Rights, Human Rights

This book is dedicated to Ann,
who pulled me through,
and the memory of John Bradbury,
my friend and colleague, who
convinced me that it
needed to be written.

Animal Rights, Human Rights
Ecology, Economy and Ideology in the Canadian Arctic

by
George Wenzel

University of Toronto Press
Toronto • Buffalo

First published in North America by
University of Toronto Press 1991

Reprinted 1992

ISBN 0-8020-5961-9 (hb)
    0-8020-6890-1 (pbk)

Canadian Cataloguing in Publication Data

Wenzel, George W.
    Animal rights, human rights

    Includes bibliographical references and index.
    ISBN 0-8020-5961-9 (bound) ISBN 0-8020-6890-1 (pbk)

    1. Inuit – Canada – Hunting.* 2. Sealing. 3. Inuit –
    Canada – Cultural assimilation.* 4. Animal rights.
    I. Title.

E99.E7W46   1991   306'.089'9710719   C91-093377-4

CONTENTS

List of figures   vi
List of tables   vii
Acknowledgements   viii

Introduction   1

1. Traditional people in the modern world   11
2. Animal rights, the seal protest, and Inuit   35
3. The culture of subsistence   56
4. Clyde Inuit and seals: ecological relations   64
5. The Clyde Inuit economy   97
6. Seals and snowmobiles: the modern Clyde economy   106
7. Ideological relations and harvesting   134
8. The seal protest as cultural conflict   142
9. A blizzard of contradictions   162
10. The controversy today   173

Appendix: Notes on Inuktitut   185
Bibliography   187
Index   203

LIST OF FIGURES

1.1 Canadian Arctic islands and selected communities   12
1.2 Seasonal complexes and conditions of Inuit seasons   17
4.1 Clyde English place names   65
4.2 Socio-territorial areas, 1920–45   67
4.3 Clyde Inuktitut place names   68
4.4 Sealskin process, 1955–83 (Clyde River)   71
4.5 Ringed seal harvest, 1955–83 (Clyde River)   72
4.6 Sealskin trade volume, 1955–83 (Clyde River)   73
4.7 Clyde winter activity areas, 1970–89   78
4.8 Clyde summer activity areas, 1970–89   79
5.1 Extended family food allocation, 1984 (Clyde River)   102
6.1 Suluak camp composition, 31 May–5 June 1985 and Nuvuktiapik
     camp composition, 19 June–26 July 1985   127
6.2 Eglinton Fjord summer camp grouping, May–September 1972   128

LIST OF TABLES

2.1 Events in the anti-sealing campaign   46
4.1 Correlation of physical and biological conditions in the Clyde
     environment   76
4.2 Estimated Clyde River harvest, 1979   80
4.3 Clyde Inuit diet by season, 1979   81
4.4 Clyde harvest by edible weight per species, 1981–83   82
4.5 Time allocation in three winter hunt samples   86
4.6 Strike–retrieval ratios in Clyde seal hunting   88
5.1 Material-sharing parameters of the Clyde economy   105
6.1 Clyde HBC fur purchases, 1935–45   107
6.2 Clyde HBC Operations Record, 1935–44   107
6.3 Clyde fur sales, 1947–60   112
6.4 Equipment depreciation, Clyde River, 1985   116
6.5 Clyde harvesting costs, 1971–2, 1975–6, 1984–5   117
6.6 Clyde wild products cash income, 1979–80   118
6.7 Clyde one-day sample menu, 1984   119
6.8 Clyde edible harvest levels and frequency, 1979   120
6.9 Nutrient comparison of seal meat and beef   121
6.10 Inuit seasonal wild food consumption, Broughton Island,
     N.W.T.   121
6.11 Net rate of profit from harvesting as compared to store food
     purchases at Clyde River, 1984   122
6.12 Clyde ringed sealskin sales, 1979–80 to 1984–85   124
6.13 Clyde harvesting cost comparison in dollars ($) and sealskin
     units (SSU), 1975–76 and 1984–85   125
6.14 Clyde seasonal seal harvest, 1981–83   126
6.15 Clyde harvester survey, 1981–84   130

ACKNOWLEDGEMENTS

Any work in which the research spans almost a decade and the final writing two years is indebted to more people than can ever be fairly acknowledged. This is especially true when the original intent was a short note in a scientific journal. Now, after spending thousands of hours in 'field sites' as different as the winter ice of Baffin Bay and an office of a US Congressman, it is sometimes difficult to recall who made that particularly salient comment that opened my eyes to another aspect of the sealing controversy. Therefore, I must immediately apologize to all those whom I am about to overlook.

Perhaps the place to start is with the agencies and organizations that supported various aspects of my research. Foremost is the Social Science and Humanities Research Council of Canada which, through its Independent Scholars Programme, provided the only funds I received that were fully dedicated to the Inuit–animal rights controversy. They supported the whole of my work in Greenland, as well as making it possible for me to travel to Washington, DC, Vancouver, and Toronto to meet with animal rights representatives. They also supported twenty-two months of my work, from 1985 to 1989, in Clyde River, N.W.T. In addition, small grants were received from 1981 to 1984 from Indian and Northern Affairs Canada and the Canadian Ethnology Service to study, respectively, the economics of Inuit harvesting at Clyde and at Holman Island and Inuit demographic and settlement patterning on eastern Baffin Island. I also wish to acknowledge the invaluable opportunity that the Royal Commission on Seals and the Sealing Industry in Canada provided for me to immerse myself in this question during part of 1985.

It is hard to thank fairly all the many Inuit from communities in the N.W.T., Quebec, and Greenland who so cooperatively contributed to this book for they are far too numerous to acknowledge individually. I extend my thanks generally to the people of Holman Island, Kangir-suk, Pangnirtung, Iqaluit, Salluit, and Lake Harbour for their generous help at various times and to members of the Home Rule Authority during my stay in Nuuk, Greenland.

It is easier to express my gratitude to the Inuit of Clyde River since the wholehearted help and good humor they have extended to me has been constant since 1971. It is a shock to realize that, in some cases, men and women who were just born when I first appeared in their community are now adults and that some of the people who helped me most during my first years at Clyde are no longer living.

A short list of Clyde Inuit to whom I owe the greatest debt leads me to thank first the elders who 'taught me the rules' and always kept me on track. To Iqalukjuak, Killaq and Inuraq, Piungnituq, Qammanuk, Sippora, Inutiq, Qillaq, and Ashivak, I offer my respectful gratitude. Then there are the 'younger' people with whom I travelled and camped, who often fed and housed me, and who assisted every phase of my research. I especially thank Sam, Jamesee, Isa, Uttuvaq, Mikiyuk, Leah, Sakiasse, Limiki, Joe, Sara, Iga, and Mo – without your kindness and help this book might not have been completed. I hope it helps your children.

Last, there are the many southerners who at least gave me information, but more often good counsel and encouragement. Among people in the seal protest, I offer my thanks particularly to Vivia Boe, Michael O'Sullivan, George Grandy, Paul Watson, and Steven Best, all of whom accepted my inquiries with courtesy and patience.

Among the many colleagues and friends who contributed in so many ways, I can only single out a few. My thanks to Tiger Burch, Dave Damas, Marc Hammond, Peter Usher, Kristen Borre, Peter Holland, Toby Morantz, Ludger Muller-Wille, Arlene Stairs, Bob Wooley, Mary Tapsell, and Oran Young, all of whom gave generously of their wisdom and help, and especially, Sherry Olson, who did all that and voluntarily proof-read a most tedious first draft. Any and all errors in this work are solely my own.

Finally, I must also thank the many students who sat through long lectures at the Center for Northern Studies and at McGill as I worked through various ideas. There are two McGill graduate students who deserve special mention: Jacques Critchley, who contributed his cartographic skills to this book, and Michelle Dupuis, who offered invaluable bibliographic assistance and helped me keep the citations straight. Without the assistance of all these people, this book never would have been completed.

INTRODUCTION

Inuit and the seal controversy

On 27 September 1985, the Council of the European Economic Community met in Luxembourg to discuss trade and commercial issues of relevance to its member states. One item under discussion was of special interest to Canada's northernmost people, the Eskimos, or Inuit, of the Northwest Territories, Arctic Quebec and Labrador. This was whether the EEC would extend the provisions of Council Directive 83/129/EEC, first enacted in October 1983, beyond the two-year period set out in the original order.

Directive 83/129/EEC forbade the importing of commercially hunted sealskins and products manufactured from them into any part of the European Community. Its general intent was to address the ecology and conservation reservations of the EC's members with respect to the effects of hunting on the world's populations of harp and hooded seals. The directive's stated aim was to close the single most important fur fashion market, Western Europe, to sealskins. Left unspoken, but just as clear, was the intention that the directive serve notice to Canada (and to a lesser extent Norway) that the European Community would, in good conscience, no longer tolerate any form of environmental behavior that its citizens perceived as inhumane and immoral with respect to wildlife, even when those actions occurred outside the borders of the European Community.

In the mind of the European public, this was exactly the circumstances of the Northwest Atlantic, or Canadian, harp seal hunt. To the governments, politicians, and citizenry of Europe, the harvesting of the seal pups was just such an outrage. The EEC's 1985 decision to renew the ban on seals confirmed Council Directive 83/229/EEC for what its most vocal opponents, the fur industry, feared it was – the loss of a lucrative market and the most impressive victory ever achieved by the international animal rights movement. To Inuit, however, who had gone virtually unnoticed in the general furor of lobbying in the preceding days, it represented not simply the loss of a market but the real problem of maintaining the fabric of their culture in the face of increasing southern domination.

The most surprising aspect of the extension was its timing. Canada was at the mid-point of a detailed investigation, conducted through the Royal Commission on Seals and the Sealing Industry in Canada, into the scientific, environmental, social, and economic ramifications of sealing. It was the Canadian hope that this body of 'hard scientific data' would convince the EEC of the environmental integrity and socioeconomic importance of at least some aspects of sealing. The day the boycott was extended, news programs showed satisfied EEC representatives, crestfallen Canadian officials, and jubilant animal rights activists. None mentioned its meaning for 25,000 Inuit.

The 1985 EEC decision, coming as it did before the completion of the Royal Commission's report and before recommendations could be completed and presented, underlined a key aspect of the entire seal controversy. This was that the general perceptions fixed in the minds of southerners about the seal issue, that sealing was cruel, ecologically imprudent and even immoral, outweighed objective examination.

Equally disturbing was the fact that the boycott renewal came on the heels of the Royal Commission's visit to Inuit communities in Nouveau-Quebec and the Northwest Territories. Here the Commission heard testimony from scores of Inuit on the importance of sealing to their subsistence and their culture. True to the pattern followed throughout the seal controversy, the early decision meant that their voices would remain unheard.

On the day the boycott renewal was announced, I was buying supplies at the Hudson's Bay Company store in Clyde River, Northwest Territories, a small Inuit community on the east coast of Baffin Island. I was there on behalf of the Seal Commission as one member of a team of anthropologists investigating the social, nutritional, and economic effects of the sealskin ban on Canadian Inuit culture. I was in the village *on route* to the Inuit summer camp further up the coast that was the focus of my own research.

I was surprised and shocked by the EEC's precipitous action. My surprise came because this new decision essentially pre-empted our efforts to collect the scientific and social information that Europeans said was missing in 1983 (see Malouf 1986a). The announcement also shocked me because it meant that the EC had opted to keep Europe's markets closed to sealskins long before any information on the effects of the ban over the last two years on Inuit could possibly be prepared for presentation to Europe's policy-makers and public.

I discussed the news with Jamassie, a close Inuk friend. Jamassie was one of a number of Clyde hunters who had allowed me to monitor his harvesting, travel, and economic activities for nearly six months. Our friendship, however, extended back nearly twenty years to my earliest research work in Clyde.

I introduced the topic of the European Community's boycott extension and asked him his thoughts. Jamassie said that he had not heard about it as he had been helping his father repair his canoe, but that maybe it would be repeated on the late night radio news. He was sorry that European *Qallunaat*, White men, still did not understand why seals were important to Inuit, but it was not really surprising as Whites were often too impatient. Accompanied by his fourteen-year-old son, he was going hunting for *natsiq* (ringed seal) that evening, although the sea was rough for boat travel and there was still broken ice along the coast. Caribou had been hard to find in recent weeks – they were far inland this year – and so fewer than usual were being caught. Besides, his father wanted to have seal meat and it was important for Inuit to eat *natsiq*.

Jamassie said he regretted what the new decision might mean. Hudson's Bay Company prices for ammunition and spare parts were high, gasoline was always expensive. Did Europeans understand that hunting was costly? Without sealskins it would be hard to get money for these things. Maybe he could get some work, but then he would not be able to hunt much. In any case, he would continue hunting for seals as he always did, they were the best food and Inuit had always hunted for the animals they needed.

This introduction typifies the dimensions of the Canadian seal controversy, an issue with two parts and two stages. To most people living in *Qallunaat nunangit*, the places where non-Inuit reside, the Canadian sealing controversy raised intense matters of conscience about the moral basis of seal hunting. From Berlin to San Francisco, the anti-sealing campaign waged a public relations and political battle using direct mail appeals, thirty-second television vignettes, and glossy photographs of protesters clutching baby seals amid scenes of pools of blood staining crystal pure ice, all of which decried man's callous slaughter of seals. After all, as Brian Davies of the International Fund for Animal Welfare once put it, the seal protest was a war for the capture of southern hearts and minds. The milestones of this war were recorded by the contributions that reached the campaign coffers and the bags of pre-printed IFAW and Greenpeace postcards that inundated the desks of politicians.

The other part of the seal controversy, a part which to most southerners was little more than a sideshow, is the Arctic, where the consequences of southern publicity battles are now being lived. This is the region, with its dozens of Inuit camps and villages spread from Bering Strait to northern Greenland, where seals and seal hunting mean sustenance. Among all the seal debate participants, the politicians, protestors and businessmen, Canadian Inuit were the most at risk and have felt the greatest impact.

Canada's Inuit did not choose to be involved in the sealing controversy. To Inuit it was an issue between *Qallunaat* – those Whites who took sealskins for money alone and those to whom this was wrong. It was not what Inuit did and it was not for them to interfere among Whites.

It was only in 1982, when Inuit had an opportunity to speak to European parliamentarians, that they discovered their involvement. In Europe, Inuit stated their feelings with sincerity and honesty. They did not defend the harp seal hunt, they simply stated what seal hunting meant in their lives. Inuit did not debate or rationalize these points. For them, ecology, hunting, and culture are synonymous. Sealskins, in a northern world colonized and ruled by Euro-Canadians, provide a

3

small measure of independence from mines and oil wells, bureaucracy and good intentions.

In stating this position, Inuit were hampered by their geographic isolation, small numbers, few financial means, and the dictates of *Qallunaat* economic and political concerns. Most debilitating of all, however, was a paternalism, itself a trenchant example of the *Qallunaat*-Inuit relations colonialism that had made sealskins a part of the northern economy, that could not accept the contemporary realities of Inuit and the concerns they voiced.

The seal controversy: relating wildlife, politics and history

The seal controversy, through its long unfolding, has widely come to be seen as an animal rights cause. Brian Davies (CBC 1985), founder of the International Fund for Animal Welfare, has stated that animal rights have always been the issue, although strategic reasons mitigated against their direct presentation during most of the seal protest. To Davies and other activists, the heart of the controversy was the morality of humans exploiting seals and whether the rights of animals are superior to human interests.

Inuit, too, have stated that the issue is one of rights. To them, wildlife harvesting, whether of seals or other species, is a right that predates the rules and regulations of European philosophy and law. This right is based on the fact that Inuit have demonstrated a clear interest in the natural environment that surrounds them and have done so for at least four thousand years. Few other peoples, not least New World Europeans, can claim such a consistent tradition of occupancy and use of the land.

This is not to say that Inuit have been strangers to environmental, technological, economic, and even social change. However, the constancy of their use and occupancy of the Arctic and its resources has continued from the proverbial time immemorial. The land, sea, and ice, with all their fish and game, have formed the base for the practice of Inuit culture. As an Inuk resident of Tuktoyaktuk told the Mackenzie Valley Pipeline Inquiry (1976, Vol. C44: 4234):

> Just like you white people work for wages and you have money in the bank, well my bank was here all around with the fur and whatever kind of food I wanted. If I wanted caribou I went up in the mountains, if I wanted fox I went up in the mountains, in the Delta I got mink and muskrat. I was never a big trapper, I just got enough for my own use the coming year. For the next years those animals are going to be there anyway, that's my bank.

Inuit take the use of these lands and resources for granted. This has occurred not through a callousness caused by slaughter and profit, but through the knowledge that birds, seals and caribou are a part of being Inuit. Hunting as a right has, for Inuit, its foundations in their customary and consistent acknowledgement of the environment as an active element of their day-to-day lives. This acknowledgement embodies within it the belief that animals also posses rights – the right to refuse Inuit hunters, to be treated with respect, to be hunted and used wisely.

The reason why the seal controversy is directly an issue of Inuit rights is that, as well as expressing an expanding environmental consciousness on the part of European and North American urbanites, it also brought into the open a new mode of thought about Inuit and all North American Natives. In the words of one anonymous opponent of sealing, 'To me, Inuit culture is a dying one. I see my job as helping it go quickly'.

In the history of Euro-North American colonial encroachment into the Arctic, there has never been a southern challenge so directly aimed at the physical and biological base critical to Inuit culture. To Inuit, sealing is central to their way of life. In its sweep, the fact that Inuit seal hunting came to be so easily included in the scope of a protest ostensibly directed at commercial sealing, with foreign ownership and steel factory ships, suggests that it was not Inuit sealing, but Inuit culture that was the object of militant assault. Other kinds of Inuit harvesting – caribou, beluga whales and birds – are now seen as legitimate targets for attack. The seals were the first skirmish in a war that continues in the North to this day.

The conflict between Inuit and the animal rights movement reflects the antipathy the movement feels for Inuit explanations of why wild-life harvesting is important. Inuit emphatically state that hunting is their means of subsistence, their history, their culture. In reply, opponents state that Inuit claims on seals for subsistence veil a commercial economy based on profit. History 'proves' that fur traders and government services have transformed Inuit from an independent aboriginal people to consumers in a cold climate, and that Inuit opposi-tion to the seal protest is proof of collusion with the fur industry and gives the lie to claims of subsistence and cultural need.

Inasmuch as Inuit do invoke *their* history as a claim for the legitimacy of wildlife harvesting as a culturally rooted right, history itself forms an important facet of the northern seal controversy. In fact, history, and especially the question of whose interpretation of history is valid, has affected the entire forum in which aboriginal rights have been debated in Canada (see, for example, Mahoney 1979) and has by no means been limited to the animal rights question.

What is similar between earlier Inuit-*Qallunaat* conflicts and the present one is the effort that is being made to deconstruct Inuit inter-pretations of their place in the ecosystem, history, and present-day northern development. Just as historical deconstruction has sometimes been a tool wielded against Inuit by government and industry, so is the movement using it to deprive Inuit of their past and any claim to the future.

The animal rights movement has redefined Inuit culture and, more importantly, what measures are applicable to its analysis. In so doing, it has found Inuit to be a former aboriginal people who are now just like us. This is so because the artefacts that made Inuit what they were are no longer a part of the visible present. Images of dogteams and snowhouses, harpoons and predator–prey ratios, and wardrobes of 'traditional' sealskin clothes are established and then compared to the snowmobile and rifle that equip Inuit today.

In this anthropology, the word 'tradition' becomes a semantic telescope that is used the wrong way round. What is distant is good; what is contemporary is bad because it has been tainted by modernity.

Where rights, history, and anthropology meet in the seal controversy is through the attempts southerners, on both sides of the animal rights question, have made to rearrange Inuit culture and social history to support their own arguments. When these transformations are complete in the mind of the public, then the matter of aboriginal harvesting as a right to which Inuit have a moral claim will become moot and the northern theatre of the seal war will become silent.

The anthropology of Inuit

Charles C. Hughes, who studied processes of modernization in North Alaskan Eskimo (or, more properly, Inupiaq) communities, once remarked (1963: 452) that 'rarely has so much been written by so many about so few'. I do not know whether Hughes was referring solely to scientific writing on Eskimos, or if he also was including the popular works of his day. In either interpretation, his comment rings true.

Systematic anthropological interest in Eskimos dates back well into the nineteenth century. Since that time, several thousand articles and monographs have been published on topics ranging from kinship and family relations to ethnographic descriptions of hunting technology. The literature on Canadian Inuit is fully as rich.

In the first detailed study, *The Central Eskimo* (1888), Franz Boas presented a description that has become almost a formula for describing the 'traditional' Eskimo - snowhouse villages, harpooning seals, and environmental hardship. While much of what anthropologists have had to say about Inuit over the last twenty-five years has dealt with their adaptation and adjustment to technological, social, and economic change, the image lives on of the traditional Eskimo, as a *qajaq* hunter and igloo dweller.

Until the end of the Second World War, Canadian Inuit maintained a mode of life not so different from Boas's time. The reasons for this continuity are important. But it is also the case that the changes that have been introduced into the North, from firearms to satellite television, appear to have reduced the traditional relationship that existed between Inuit and their environment to one of snowmobiles, alcohol, and social welfare. Newspapers, if not anthropologists, have made this side of northern life known.

This book is about traditional Inuit in the modern world. There may seem to be a contradiction in the idea of Inuit maintaining their traditional culture in a setting that includes television, high-powered rifles, wages and welfare. The contradiction arises from the limited perspective available to most observers. If the measure of a culture is its artefacts and the artefacts Inuit use are those familiar to the observer, then the observer is not likely to look much beyond his own cultural interpretation of these objects. This has certainly been the case in the Inuit seal controversy. Since 1976, animal rights advocates have argued that because the tools Inuit use in hunting are modern, because Inuit sell sealskins, and because they spend these dollars at the Hudson's Bay Company store, then the meaning they attach to wildlife cannot claim to be 'traditional'.

Studies about Inuit, like anthropological research in general, are almost always set in the wider context of a theoretical framework. Descriptive studies of artefacts and culture history are rare today. Instead, research is directed toward the understanding of Inuit ecology, of inter-cultural relations, and so forth. This is done because the objective of anthropology is not simply to describe habits, customs, and history, but to provide some measure of analysis to interpret what is inherently foreign and unfamiliar. The objective is to gather 'inside' information as it is explained or more often, lived by Inuit, and then to test these data against what we think we know about how Inuit hunters live and change.

This book has its origins in work I began in 1971 on the way Baffin Island Inuit organized their ecological activities. My original intent was to apply certain ideas about the way their choices affected the capture of animals. This work included experiencing the environment, as well as observing and speaking to the people.

I soon discovered that an important part of Inuit hunting was who hunted with whom and how animals were divided between men, their families and whole communities. In effect, I learned that Inuit hunting involved social, as well as ecological, choices. And while I continued the explicitly ecological part of my study, I gained an increasing respect and appreciation for the social aspects of what I initially assumed was a simple 'search, kill, and retrieve' operation. My first reports dwelt heavily on the cultural information Inuit shared to harvest successfully. Years later, as I continued my research, I also realized that it was these shared social values that make wildlife a unique part of Inuit culture.

This book, therefore, deals principally with the values that underpin Inuit hunting. My argument is that it is these values of mutual security and support that are the essential link between Inuit culture present and past. This value structure is not limited to hunting, but pervades all areas of Inuit life. As such, they are truly cultural, not narrowly economic, in their scope.

A second argument concerns the handling of modern technology as evidence of cultural change. Artefacts, like rifles, snowmobiles, and outboard motors, so often cited as proof of the demise of Inuit tradition, must be re-examined in the context of Inuit experience with *Qallunaat*. To date, most analyses have been confined to a narrow historical framework like the fur trade, or have been unabashedly ahistorical, ignoring the social setting of new technology. It is argued here that the animal rights movement is itself a part of a continuing colonial process in the Canadian North.

Finally, this book is concerned with a succession of stereotypes – a falsely romantic stereotype of Inuit which has been manipulated to create a second one that is also false and more dangerous. Inuit were first portrayed as a people in natural harmony with the Arctic environment. Today they are increasingly presented as knowingly and willingly participating in the destruction of their own culture and the harmony of the ecosystem. Carried to its logical conclusion, the new image will have the effect of denying to Inuit their past and a voice in their future.

This work, if it must be categorized, might be best described as advocacy anthropology. While I know of no such 'official' designation, there is, in fact, a history of such activity by anthropologists dating from at least the wave of decolonization that began immediately following the Second World War. Organizations like the International Work Group on Indigenous Affairs and Cultural Survival Inc. are examples of the united efforts of scientists to work for the rights of Native peoples.

The general thrust of advocacy anthropology has been to intercede on the side of indigenous groups against the efforts of national governments and industrial interests to 'civilize' aboriginal peoples by expropriating their lands and resources. Certainly, anthropologists in Canada have tried to contribute in the James Bay hydroelectric dispute (see Salisbury 1986), to name one example.

In the seal controversy, the state and industrial developers are only tangentially involved. They are important, but only nominally, at this moment. The seal controversy typifies the willingness of the animal rights movement to exercise a self-ascribed moral imperative toward Inuit and other aboriginal peoples. In the case of Inuit and the seal protest, this has meant painting a new portrait of Inuit as hunters whose sole motivation is monetary profit. Inuit culture, as presented by the movement, is as one comprehensible exclusively in the context of the marketplace. By implication, Inuit cannot possess any intrinsic moral right or claim to the northern environment nor, indeed, to their own heritage.

This denies Inuit not only their past and present, but also a cultural future. Since 1970, Inuit in Canada, Greenland, and Alaska have assumed increasing leadership on northern environmental and political issues. They have done so by demonstrating the connectedness between themselves and the northern ecosystem. Yet the image that has been projected by the animal rights movement undermines those prerogatives. In the vision of animal rights advocates Inuit culture is shaped by the market and, in the words of Steven Best of the International Wildlife Coalition (1984), 'Inuit are just like us'.

Advocacy on the part of anthropologists for Inuit is, therefore, not directed at the revival of commercial sealing and European markets. The fundamental issue is the right of Inuit, and Cree and Dene Indians, to retain control over their cultures. In order to understand the northern seal controversy, a new, realistic perspective is needed. In the first instance this means understanding Inuit sealing within the whole of Inuit society. Second, it is necessary to contextualize the anti-sealing campaign if only to ask: have some animal rights advocates sought to deny and deculturize the relationship between Inuit and animals? These are the objectives of this book.

The present study

Anthropology, like any specialized field of study, possesses its own language, or jargon. The same is true of ecology or engineering. The purpose of these terminologies is to help specialists more easily communicate among themselves. It may also appear the case that such usage at times appears expressly designed to confuse 'outsiders'. I shall keep the use of anthropological terminology to a minimum, or at least explain it when it cannot be easily avoided. The same will be the case with ecological and other specialized references.

Another specialized language will also be used from time to time. Because Inuit are consummate hunters of seals and practitioners of northern living, it is appropriate that Inuktitut words and terms be used in order to express aspects of the relationship between Inuit, their land, and the animals they interact with on a daily basis. These terms are highly relevant to the theme and spirit of this discussion. Naturally, explanations of this terminology will be provided.

Much of the data that appear here on Inuit harvesting and culture have been derived through twenty-two years of research, and especially nineteen spent with the people of Clyde River, Baffin Island. Other villages also provided me with valuable opportunities to observe, participate, and interview Inuit about hunting, animals, and ecological relations. In the N.W.T. and Quebec, residents of Holman Island, Resolute Bay, Kuganiuk (Creswell Bay) on Somerset Island, Iqaluit, formerly Frobisher Bay, Pangnirtung, and Aqviqtiuq, Salluit (Sukluk) and Kangirsuk (Payne Bay) all assisted me. In addition, hunters and officials of *Kalaalit Nuna* provided me with data on the situation in Greenland. Inuit in all these places generously spoke and travelled with me and often fed, clothed, and housed me.

Data on the animal rights movement also include original, as well as secondary, sources. In 1984, I began a series of interviews with the spokespersons of organizations active in the anti-sealing campaign. Most allowed me to record their comments on tape. In addition, correspondence received from members of the protest and published animal rights material have been used in analysing the seal campaign with regard to Inuit.

The organization of this work, at least for presentation, has not come easily. The need to present two sides of this complex issue makes this task inherently difficult. Overall, these materials are presented in four sections. The first two chapters form a broad introduction to the northern seal controversy. Here the concern centers on the culture and history of both Inuit and the animal rights movement. These chapters offer basic descriptions of these two entities and the imagery that surrounds them in the seal debate.

The second section is an analysis of seal hunting as part of Inuit subsistence culture. As part of this analysis, a systematic examination of Inuit hunting as a cultural, social and economic endeavor is offered. This depth of examination is necessary if the basic relationship of seals, and other animals, to Inuit is to be appreciated in the cultural context meaningful to Inuit themselves. Inuit subsistence, I shall argue, is not a part of Inuit culture; it is Inuit culture since it encapsulates a self-image and identity shared by all Inuit.

The third section concentrates on the analysis of the animal rights movement specific to its conflict with Inuit. In this discussion, while sealing certainly is taken as the initial motivator, the discussion is expanded to all Inuit use of wildlife. Here the concern is as much on the animal rights movement's perception of Inuit, as representatives of 'aboriginalness', as it is on the linked issue of seals and the relationship between human beings and the natural world.

The last section discusses both the immediate and wider ramifications of the present sealing crisis for Inuit. Its purpose is to broaden the study's framework to include the socio-political and socioeconomic reverberations that have occurred during the last six years on Inuit society and community. The final chapter enters into the large issue of Inuit aboriginal rights and their meaning in the face of the seal protest. The intent is to draw some conclusions from the experience of Inuit in their recent adversarial relationship with opponents of sealing and what this may mean in terms of future relations between Inuit and *Qallunaat*.

1 TRADITIONAL PEOPLE IN THE MODERN WORLD

Arctic impressions

Inuit means 'The People'. It encompasses all the Eskimos of Canada, Greenland, and northern Alaska. All are speakers of *inuktitut*, the eastern dialect of the Esk-Aleut language, and all live along the rim of Arctic North America from the Chukchi Sea to Scoresbysund, East Greenland.

Today, some twenty-five thousand Inuit, nearly one-third of all *inuktitut* speakers in the world, live on the coast and islands of Canada (Figure 1.1), from the Northwest Territories to northern Quebec and Labrador. Like all Eskimos and Aleuts, they are descendants of Asiatic hunters who crossed the Bering Strait near the end of the last glaciation. Their forebears, known to archaeologists as Palaeoeskimos (see McGhee 1978), colonized the Canadian Arctic almost five thousand years ago.

In the 1600s, when Europeans began searching for a north route to India and China, they were met by a culture more than adequately adapted to the rigors of Arctic life. Where Europeans struggled, Inuit lived with efficiency. Only when men like C.F. Hall and John Ross adopted Inuit methods of dress, travel and diet were Europeans able to survive the Arctic.

A product of the contact between Europeans and Inuit was the growth of public and scientific interest about Inuit. The ability of 'The People' to live, and live well, in the polar environment spawned a literature, both popular and scholarly, of its own.

Perhaps because of the harsh starkness of the northern ecosystem, these writings have come to embody a degree of idealization so large that the basic attribute of Inuit survival, their remarkable and innovative culture, has been obscured and replaced by a Rousseauian image of natural man tenuously holding primeval nature at arm's length. With 'primitive', if superbly crafted, tools of stone, skin, and snow Inuit outperformed the wooden boats, cloth clothes, and iron technology of explorers and whalers. The tools used by Inuit, igloos, *qajaq*, caribou parkas and harpoons, as much as their inventors, captured the imagination of southern audiences.

The image of Inuit as a people possessed of unsurpassed ingenuity and survivability in a climate and landscape only slightly less formidable than the moon's remains today. Ninety years ago, Robert

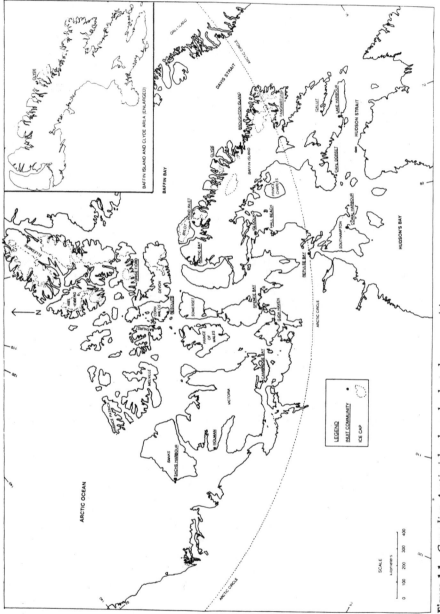

Figure 1.1 *Canadian Arctic islands and selected communities*

Peary wrote and lectured in this vein about the Polar Eskimo. The books of Farley Mowat and James Houston do so now. Added to this is a catalogue of Inuit customs and social behaviors so mythologized that a popular 'anthropology' exists for Inuit as for no other aboriginal people. The film adaptation of Houston's 'The White Dawn' brought southern audiences the same images that Robert Flarety's 'Nanook of the North' did nearly fifty years ago. So pervasive is this popular image that it is still possible to be asked whether Inuit rub noses or leave the elderly on the ice when they grow too weak to travel.

The combination of a complex technology and exotic behavior has been distilled into a portrait of a people who are environmentally adept, yet live only for the moment because of the unpredictability of weather and food. This image is by no means dispelled when all but the most recent experience of Europeans in the Arctic has been one of scurvy, frostbite, lost ships, and vanished expeditions.

The problem is that it says nothing about Inuit culture, either past or present. Rather, the South has created a stereotype about Inuit and the Arctic in order to make people and place comprehensible. There is a dual romanticism in which the North is a frontier for us, yet a homeland to Inuit. Arctic expeditions make elaborate military preparations, but Inuit survive through arcane customs and skills that fascinate and repel us all in one. As was once remarked, Inuit serve as an allusion to a world inconceivably more difficult than the privileged one we know.

Seeing an Inuit community

The initial impression of a visitor to a modern Inuit community on Baffin Island or in the Mackenzie Delta might be disappointing. After flying over the immensity of the Arctic in a small piston-driven airplane to get to Gjoa Haven or Repulse Bay, the first glimpse from an unpaved landing strip is down a dusty road (almost all visitors come in summer) to a cluster of lights and rising smoke four or five kilometres distant. The only easy way there is by 'taxi', usually the town dumptruck.

Once at the hotel, the visitor sets out to walk around the village. There are no sealskin *qayaq* or snow houses, no soapstone seal oil lamps and no one is wearing caribou skin clothing. Instead of the expected dogteams, snowmobiles zoom between wood houses connected by a power line to a power station at the end of the village. Besides snowmobiles, or ski-doos, there are also trucks, motorcycles, and bulldozers moving slowly over unpaved dirt roads. The largest buildings are garages and warehouses, the school, a nursing station, and the government office complex, all constructed from aluminum trailers. Along the beachfront, there are canvas-wood canoes and skiffs drawn up among fuel drums and partially disassembled outboard engines. On an overlooking hill sits a satellite receiving dish. Returning

13

to the hotel, the visitor realizes that at no time during his or her's two-hour walk was there a moment when the sound of a motor or the hum of electrical lines could not be heard.

In fact, close up, the community looks little different than most southern Canadian rural towns. Although there are no trees, lawns or pavement, men and women are moving to and from work and the store or standing in the street talking, while children play and go to school. A visitor might easily conclude that Inuit, except for the cold climate, strange-style clothing and ubiquitous snowmobiles, have become assimilated Canadians.

The contrast between this reality and the image most visitors arrive north with are light years in time from each other. A few decades ago, only the most intrepid sportsman or journalist and the odd scientist visited even the fringe of the Arctic. Today, a single 'Midnight Sun' jet passenger tour to Resolute Bay (latitude 75°N) deposits a hundred travellers from Chicago, Toronto, and Atlanta well above the Arctic Circle for a half day and then whisks them back.

The arctic image implanted by Freuchen, Mowat, and *National Geographic* appears to relate only to a far distant past. Headlines about alcoholism and oil discoveries seem closer to the truth for the modern arctic. The only news that fits the 'real' North concerns treks by Japanese, American, or British adventurers to the Pole, expeditions from which Inuit are notably absent.

The question soon arises, 'where is the real Arctic?'. In 1986, Barry Lopez's *Arctic Dreams* became a Book of the Month Club choice and stayed on the *New York Times* list of bestsellers for months. Lopez described for his readers a northern wilderness that is almost beyond human scale. The animals, the power of the frozen sea, the arctic wind and weather are mindboggling. In only one way does *Arctic Dreams* differ from the literary tradition that began with the explorers: until the epilogue there is hardly a reference to Inuit. My surmise is that Lopez, in his travels through North Alaska and the High Arctic, found Inuit too ordinary. He confines himself mainly to stories of scientists and school teachers, southerners who provide 'scale' to the environment. For Lopez, the real arctic is a place of challenge – not bulldozers, decked-over canoes, or Inuit political organizations. So, too, is it the case for the tourist, although he or she rarely goes beyond the boundaries of the modern village 'into' the Arctic.

Yet every Inuit settlement, small or large, is joined to the environment, not by roads and power lines but through 'The People'. The motorized canoes that line the beach are for hunting and travel. In winter, ski-doos, with long sleds called *qamutiik*, move hunters and their supplies in and out of the village. Much of this is not apparent to the visitor who is too shy to visit Inuit homes or who keeps a southern activity schedule. The office and service people seen during the workday can only begin their 'Inuit' activities after 5 o'clock. Men hunt seals for a few hours just a few kilometres from town. Women sew *kamik*, sealskin boots, and prepare 'country' food, which may only mean placing a frozen arctic char on a board where it is available to anyone who wishes to eat.

The visitor has probably overlooked many signs of Inuit life. The snowmobile parts, wood-drying racks, bits of bone and antler, and spent cartridge casings that litter the ground in every village are signs of a people who live close to the land. Close inspection of the houses reveals stretched sealskins against walls, racks of meat on roofs, soapstone carvings in various stages of completion, and all the tools and parts that hunters need to keep their equipment in repair. Almost nothing is wilfully discarded, from pieces of cargo pallet useful for sled cross-pieces to dogskins that become parka ruffs.

In this context, the absence of a snowmobile and sled is certain evidence that the men of the household are away hunting. When the weather is clear, even during the deep cold and long dark of the arctic winter, some men are always away hunting, often for several weeks travelling a thousand kilometres.

The astute observer, contrary to what may be read or heard, has found that Inuit are neither assimilated nor in cultural confusion. While many tools and settlement jobs are 'White', it is also apparent that much of local life is Inuit. Reality is that Inuit are far from cultural demoralization: they are a people adapting southern artefacts, institutions, and ideas to their present ecological and historical situation.

This thought bridges the difference between expectation, the shock of initial impressions, and what is really happening. Although the boundary between the village and the arctic environment has not been physically crossed, there is for the first time a feeling of the connectedness between Inuit and the land.

Environment and ecology

Perhaps more than any other place on earth, the rhythm of life in the Arctic, human, plant and animal, is affected by the seasons. Winter is a time of such intense cold and darkness that it is hard to believe that serious activity can occur beyond the walls of snug shelters. Summer often seems only slightly less strenuous. Yet it is to the extremes of this environment that Inuit have adapted so successfully.

It is hard to imagine the sensations of the arctic winter. Most people know that it is a time of 'cold, snow and ice, and that it is dark', but these words do not begin to convey the feel of that cold. On northern Baffin Island, from October to May winter dominates biological life. The sea is frozen not into a smooth stable plain, but into lively ripples and mountains. Constant, sometimes howling, wind reduces the effective temperature for animals and men by 1.2°F for every mile per hour of force. Air temperature averages − 35°C. The days are short - in December and January only an hour or so of twilight can be seen at noon - and snow, the element we most associate with winter, is glassine and in constant movement, not falling but driven literally into 'white-outs' by the wind. The land and sea share the same apparent white emptiness.

The principal concern of all life at this time is thermal regulation, or maintenance of body temperature. Plants cease their growth, while most animals either migrate south or settle into dormancy. The land is motionless except for the snow. The tundra's lemmings and hares are dormant, ptarmigan stir only as necessary, and the caribou and musk-ox have either moved southward or forage in protected inland areas. Pregnant polar bears stay in deep dens. Only ravens display any energy.

But even at the time of deepest cold, when the land is still, there is movement on and below the ice, which is most active, while the land is near still. Dunbar (1968) has calculated that in winter Arctic waters remain much more productive than the terrestrial ecosystem. The marine food chain is unaffected by the winds and cold. Plankton feed shrimp, the shrimp are eaten by polar cod that are in turn eaten by ringed seals. The visible signs of this maritime activity are the domed tops of the breathing holes that ringed seals (natsiq) keep open from the start of the freeze-up. The overlapping footprints of polar bears and arctic foxes are the only signs of these openings.

The second season, spring–summer–fall, begins some time in May as the sun sets off a slow melting of the snow and ice. It is very bright and on the best calm days, when the air is at −15°C, it is possible to be out with only a light jacket for a few hours. Female polar bears, with their cubs, move to the ice and ringed seals pup in snow lairs.

With the warmth, rivulets of fresh water begin running across the land and ice. The domes of agluliit, breathing holes, collapse, and ice cracks that are present through the winter because of the dynamic effects of stress and currents now form open channels. Ringed seals bob in open water or bask on the ice in the long daylight, and by June narwhal investigate these leads.

Summer brings life to the land and air. Microtines, especially in the peak population years, are literally underfoot. Peregrine falcons and snowy owls are perched on every boulder watching for small rodents and snow buntings. Large mammals also reappear. Barren ground caribou (Rangifer tarandus) of the mainland Bluenose, Kaminuriak, and George River herds move across the tundra toward their calving grounds, while on Baffin Island and the Arctic Islands these herbivores leave their inland winter ranges for the coast.

By the time the land is free from snow and the ice is gone from the sea, the final summer visitors appear. Colonies of seabirds occupy cliffs and snow geese saturate the tundra. The last wave to appear is the marine mammals, open ocean herds of harp seals and pods of narwhal, beluga and bowhead whales.

While simplified, this description provides some idea of the annual ecological pattern (for more detailed examinations see: Freeman 1984; Peterson 1976; Remmert 1980). It also presents northern ecology in the framework most often used by the casual non-Inuit observers – as simply two seasons.

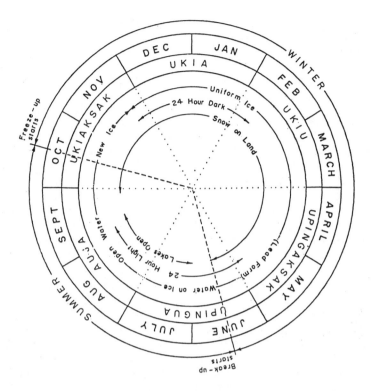

Figure 1.2 *Seasonal complexes and conditions of Inuit seasons*

Inuit offer a much more complex interpretation of the Arctic 'seasons' (see Figure 1.2). Each of these seasons correlates with a set of ecological events that are significant to the intimate users of the North. This detailed calendar is important to the structuring of Inuit movements and use resources. For the moment, however, Inuit activities will be discussed in terms of the simple winter-summer format.

Winter days

Family and community activities are centered in winter around the villages in which Inuit have resided since the 1960s. Adults who are employed follow a 9 to 5 routine much like people outside the North. They works as clerks, truck drivers and labourers, interpreters and teachers. Children spend their days in the community school. The single notable difference is that these northern wage earners drive snowmobiles or walk to their places of work. In recent years, the language of workplace and school has increasingly become Inuktitut as Inuit have come to fill positions in teaching and municipal government. Yet other activities, rarely visible to the casual observer, form the heart of winter settlement life.

In winter, when almost all village members are in residence, one can begin to gain an understanding of two important aspects of contemporary Inuit life. The first is that more than half of each community is under the age of eighteen. Classrooms are crowded and the nursing station's best-attended clinics are those on pre-natal and neo-natal health.

The other feature is revealed by a tour of the offices, garages and warehouses, and school. This is that only one-fifth of the adult population is actively working for wages. This takes some little time to discern because of the short daylight of winter. Hunting, shopping, family care and visiting are not structured as they often are in the South. This leads to the initial impression that 'nothing happens' during winter in Inuit settlements.

Village residents who are neither workers nor students spend their days in more traditional activities. Men, if they are not already out on the land, prepare their snowmobiles and equipment for hunting. Only the windiest weather, when the visibility nears zero and the effective temperature falls to −40°C, prevents hunting. Once repairs to snow-machines (a constant need) and other preparations are complete, hunters, by twos and threes, set off in search of ringed seals within a day's trip of the village. For these day hunts, each *qamutik* is packed with a stove, rifles and ammunition, engine parts and tools, a caribou parka and sleeping skin, fuel, along with a snowknife and harpoon. Even on a short trip, a man carries nearly 50 kg of gear and fuel in case of a mechanical or weather emergency. Longer winter journeys, for caribou or polar bear, are made by parties of up to five hunters and carry enough fuel and equipment to be self-sufficient for a month.

In winter, the hunting day, even for *natsiq*, is long and hard. Men begin leaving the village by 8 a.m., several hours before the twilight of midday, for the nearest breathing hole area. Here, the ten or twenty hunters who have travelled out to the ice, some riding the sleds of other men, begin to search for active holes. Each ice hummock is examined for signs of seal activity. In a short time, each hunter is positioned at an *aglu*.

The basic technique used in winter *aglu* hunting has often been described (see Boas 1888; Nelson 1969). For all its regional variations, it is apparently simple, if tedious. On North Baffin, once an Inuk locates an active hole, he carefully checks to see if there is sufficient snow around it to ensure that he cannot be seen through the ice by a rising seal. He then places himself so that neither his shadow nor scent passes over the hole. The hunter assumes a stiff-legged, bent-at-the-waist stance alongside the dome and stands nearly motionless, with a harpoon or rifle cradled in his arms. In this position, the man will wait, relieving his tension by occasionally glancing about, alert to actions of other hunters and wary of polar bears.

If a seal does enter the *aglu*, the hunter is warned first by the slop of water and then by the seal's first exhalation. He then aims his rifle or harpoon over the direct centre of the hole's opening and strikes as the animal takes it second or third breath. If the animal has been struck with a harpoon, the hunter holds the line in one hand and clears the ice dome away with the ice-chisel butt of the harpoon shaft. If a rifle is used, the man slips a gaff into the hole and then uses the chisel to free the seal.

Only one of every four or five such waits in a day is likely to yield a *natsiq*, but even one animal can provide some 30 kg of meat and edible organs. The work of winter sealing is hard, from driving a snowmobile to fighting off the cold while motionless, but the reward is large. Borre (1986), in modelling the energetics of sealing, has found that a man who uses some 3,000 calories a day in hunting can catch one seal every six days and still avoid starvation. In other words, the energy provided by a seal will sustain one adult Inuk for six full days.

The routine of *aglu* hunting is broken only when men move to new holes, sometimes meeting on the ice to brew tea on stoves shielded from the wind by a *qamutik* runner, or when it appears that the weather is worsening. Otherwise, after eight or ten hours of active hunting, men begin the one – or two – hour return trip to their homes, hopefully with at least one seal lashed to each sled.

For women, winter is a time of less outdoor activity, but just as busy and productive as that of the hunters. They rise with the men, help prepare hunters for the day, as well as their children for school. After schoolchildren and the men have left the house, the women begin their own day.

A dozen women leave their homes to work at the village store, the school, and government offices, but most work cooperatively with other women. They share infant care, process meat, preparing the skins of seals, polar bear and caribou, shop at the Hudson's Bay Company store or Co-op, and sew winter clothes and boots.

As with male sealing parties, women's activities are done in groups and almost always with people who are joined by kinship. This grouping for activities is, however, more than social; it also allows the knowledge and skill of older generations to be passed to the young and reinforces bonds of solidarity and security among kin.

The preparation of animal skins is a constant activity because such work is time-consuming and each type of pelt requires a particular kind of handling. Ringed seal and caribou are the skins that women work with on a daily basis. In the past, nearly every sealskin that came in from hunting was scraped, stretched, dried and washed by the women so that they could be used for clothing or 'fixed' for sale. In most communities today, even though there is no cash market, a majority of sealskins still undergo basic processing.

The process of preparing a *qlissik* (sealskin) so that it can be sold or used for the manufacture of boots and clothing takes from six to ten hours of a woman's labour. The first stage after butchering is to flense all remaining fat and flesh from the inside of the pelt with an *ulu*, or half-moon-shaped woman's knife. The skin is wet and elastic and care must be taken not to damage it. The skin is soaked in bleach to clean it and help break the tough fiber.

Once this stage is completed, the pelt will be stretched tightly over a wooden frame and placed outside to dry. This procedure is followed immediately after scraping if the skin is to be sold or used with the hair still on, as in mittens or pants. If it is to be waterproof, however, then all the hair is shaved with an *ulu* before it is dried. Once the pelt is placed on a stretching frame, it must be tightened and retied two or three times during the drying process. Only then can it be used for *kamiit* (boots) or the other items Inuit use everyday.

In the evening, long after twilight has gone, hunters return from the ice and families gather at the homes of elder kinsmen to share the day's harvest, eat, and talk. Most of the social gatherings in Inuit communities occur in the houses of the oldest extended family (*ilagiit*) members who provide leadership and advice to the young. People eat what they want, infants are passed among adults, and older children come and go from house to house.

The village stays awake until midnight or so as children ride bicycles over the snow and adults make repairs to equipment or mend parkas. Even later, snowmobiles can be heard as a few wage earners return from hunting long after their official job at the garage or office ended.

The summer pattern

To the forty-odd Inuit communities spread across the Canadian North, summer comes at different times. If the break-up of sea ice marks the onset of summer, then southerly villages, like Eskimo Point and Nain, Labrador, begin the season sometime in May or June, while Grise Fiord and Pond Inlet may have ice well into July. In all the communities, summer means open water, warming temperatures and near round-the-clock daylight.

Now the focus of Inuit life shifts outdoors and, in many cases, completely away from the settlement. Tents appear beside many of the village houses. But much of the settlement population leaves town for summer camp. Even families who have an employed member go a few kilometres so that a commute between camp and town by snowmobile or boat can be made with hunting along the way.

Since most families do not have the tie of village employment, many move into semi-permanent summer camps at greater distances from their home villages. From June to September, these families will move as much as 300 km to important caribou hunting and char fishing sites, often in areas where they had lived before resettlement. From most communities, one-half to two-thirds of the residents are absent a month or more.

Each family lives in a home-made octagonal canvas tent large enough to hold eight to twelve people. Cooking is done on a camp stove or outside over an open fire fuelled with *kiuktaaq*, heather abundant on the tundra. All the normal activities of people at home are carried out – food is prepared, clothes and dishes are washed, equipment is repaired, tents are swept clean daily. Families sleep on a prepared gravel bed covered with several thicknesses of caribou skin mattresses. Work and food are shared and children play, eat, and sleep where and when it pleases them. Each camp becomes a microcosm of a social life that predates Europeans. The families who camp together are all related by blood or marriage and are one *ilagiit*. Men and women elders provide the direction to summer camp as they do to the winter settlement.

Unlike the situation in winter, summer allows each person to set his or her own rhythm. To a visitor's eyes, day and night blend. Daylight allows outdoor activity at all times. Inuit children are much in evidence, both night and day, in village or camp at every hour. For them, it is a time to play, pick berries and fish, begin to learn or hone the skills of adults: to become Inuit.

More important, however, is the reversal Inuit make in their 'normal' schedule. The partition that time provides in winter, with night and formal work hours, appears to be gone. Through the 'day' camps sleep; no one, except a few children, is about at 9 a.m. Instead, life starts around 3 p.m. The reason for this is that, although it is not dark, the westering sun brings cooler, more comfortable working temperatures. This is especially important when ice is still present because the watery surface refreezes with 'night'. Camp tasks begin in earnest and hunters start their searching travel some time between 6 p.m. and midnight, only returning near 6 a.m. Until then, the 'night' belongs to children and their mothers.

Summer hunting has a decidedly different character from that of winter. It is a time of movement. There are no concentrations of *agluliit*. Game is randomly distributed in the sea and on the land. Caribou can graze wherever there are lichens and sedges, ringed seals are free-swimming, no longer limited to a few holes for surface access, and arctic char have migrated from inland lakes to the sea. The patience and endurance of the cold *aglu* wait must now be turned to remaining alert through many hours of numbing boat travel or walking. The animals are everywhere, but they are also sparsely distributed along the coasts and across the tundra.

Summer harvesting focuses on four or five main activities, depending on the area of the North in which Inuit live. To Inuit everywhere caribou are an important food resource, one much missed in winter. Hunting them is the hardest work because they must be sought on foot far from camp and from where boats can travel. The rewards are meat, *tunuk* (fat), and thick pelts suitable for winter parkas, mittens and socks. Even caribou antler is valued as a medium for Inuit sculpture. Caribou hunting commences as soon as herds are located and continues until they move to their winter ranges.

Seal hunting, primarily for ringed, but also harp and bearded seals is also important. While caribou are much sought as food, the fact that ringed seals remain close at hand through the summer means that they are the second most important camp resource.

In early summer, while the ice remains usable, *natsiq* are hunted at collapsed breathing holes and in ice leads. At this time, bearded seals (*Erignatus barbatus*) also begin to appear and are sought especially for their thick hides which are used to make sealskin rope, which is strong and durable. Hunting is done by snowmobile and when an active hole is found a hunter hides to one side and shoots or harpoons the seal when it surfaces.

Once the ice is gone, Inuit enter the poorest time of the seal hunting cycle, when hunting is restricted to rifles and boats and *natsiq* have only a thin layer of blubber and do not float well. Through most of the year, ringed seals will float for at least several minutes, but in open water, when they are fat-poor and the salinity of inshore waters is low, they often sink quickly. Consequently, more seals are lost, more ammunition and gasoline used so that the cost of hunting is higher. Sealing is still done because there is no guarantee of other food, but is discontinued when other resources are available.

This is also the time when a few Canadian Inuit communities have the opportunity to hunt herds of mature harp seals (*Phoca groen-landicus*) that summer in northern waters. This is open ocean hunting, mainly in Cumberland and Jones Sounds, by Inuit from Pangnirtung and Grise Fiord. The season rarely lasts more than a month.

Two other major summer hunts occur from mid-August into September when arctic char (*Salvinus alpinus*) return from the sea to freshwater and small whales (beluga, *Delphinus leucas*, and narwhal, *Monodon monocerus* – adults of both species weigh as much as one and one-half tons) enter shallow bays and fiords before the move to ice-free winter waters. Whaling is better known to southerners, but fishing, where it is possible, provides Inuit with a valuable food surplus for autumn when new ice, wind, and bad weather limit harvesting.

Whaling, whether for beluga at the mouth of the Mackenzie River or narwhal at the ice edge of Lancaster Sound, is arduous and, at times, dangerous. When whales are in bays and close to shore, several boats herd the animals at high speeds and try to isolate individuals. Harpoons, with plastic or sealskin floats (*avvataq*), are used to secure the whale, but guns are the main killing tools. Accidents among the hunters are infrequent, but drowning, either through collision with an animal or capsizing during a turn, is a real possibility.

Around northern Baffin Island, narwhal hunting, in years when ice persists through the summer, must often take place at the floe edge, where the open sea meets continuous ice. Here, whale camp consists of several canoes, each with two to four hunters, who sleep, eat and seldom venture more than a few metres from their boats because of the danger of weak or spalling ice. A watch is kept around the clock for pods of whales swimming along the floe. The narwhal sometimes pass so close to the ice edge that they can be touched with a hand.

When a narwhal is struck with a harpoon and float, a boat is launched to retrieve the animal before it can sink.

After a beluga or narwhal is hauled to the beach or on to the ice, it is butchered for its skin (*maktaq*). (In most areas, beluga meat is also taken to be air-dried for later use. Narwhal meat, however, is eaten less frequently.) *Maktaq* is widely sought and the return from a successful hunt is shared through the camp and taken back to the settlement, while the ivory of narwhal tusks is used to produce carvings. Although the whaling season is brief and not very reliable, Inuit invest more time and equipment pursuing whales than in any summer activity but caribou hunting.

Arctic char fishing is brief, but very productive, at least during the fall run. Today, gill nets up to 10 m are set in rivers to produce large yields, but as late as 1970 several camps on Baffin and Somerset Islands maintained *saputit*, stone dams, to facilitate spearing. These three-pronged spears, or *kakivak*, are still used in winter ice fishing.

Fishing involves women and older children as well as men. Women easily maintain the nets while men are away from camp for whales or caribou. During the height of the run, yields may reach several hundred kilograms in a day from one or two nets, so nearly everyone in camp is kept busy retrieving fish from the nets, repairing torn nets, and splitting and hanging char for air drying. Fish, boiled and raw, become the staple food for the duration of the run. The end of the fish run is the time when many families decide to return from months in camp to the government village.

In all but a few parts of the High Arctic, migratory birds, especially eider ducks and geese, are important. In the Mackenzie Delta, along the coasts of Hudson and Ungava Bays, and on southern Baffin Island, their arrival is a biological marker of summer's start. Hunted on the wing and on the water, during the time of their moult, and sought for eggs and down, nearly every major summer bird species, from goose to sea gull, is used by Inuit.

By the end of summer, each extended family has gathered a large store of meat and fish to be taken back to the settlement. Much of this supply is shared with kinsmen and elders unable to spend much, if any, time on the land.

With September, school begins once again for the children and, by the end of the month, the pace of life shifts back toward that of winter. Days are shorter and each morning the skim of ice along the beach grows out a little more. As the sea mammals, birds, and caribou return to their wintering areas inland or far to the south, for the first time in nearly three months all the Inuit are back in the settlement to their jobs and preparing for freeze-up and winter seal hunting.

Economics and history

The ecological relationship between Inuit and the natural environment is one that has been repeatedly emphasized in the long history of European studies about Inuit. As has been mentioned, what we deem a special man–environment relationship is what seems to set Inuit apart.

Yet the ecology of contemporary Inuit includes artefacts, a pattern of settlement, and an economy that appear to be tied to Europeans and distinctly distant from the Inuit past. To many observers, Inuit remain hunters, a vestige of a former lifestyle, now dependent on southern machines, houses, and money.

Anthropologists have long linked the ecological and economic patterns of hunting societies. This connectivity was established early on by Forde (1934), Kroeber (1939), and Steward (1955) as cultural ecology and so began the theoretical development of what is termed today ecological anthropology. Ellen (1982: xi) has provided one of the best explanations as to the appropriateness of applying the term ecology to the study of culture. In his words (ibid.):

> It is *ecological* in the sense that it is broadly concerned with the interplay between human population behavior and environmental variables, in terms of spatial and temporal relations involving the exchange of energy, material and information. It is *anthropological* (rather than narrowly *cultural* or *social*) in contrast to an ecology focussed on physiological and genetic relations.

For several reasons hunter-gatherer peoples, and especially Inuit, became focal for research into human ecology. The first reason was that hunters were perceived as having relatively 'simple' relations to the environments in which they operated. By definition, ecology is the study of the complex web that connects living organisms, communities, and populations to all the other living and non-living features in an ecosystem. Hunting cultures appeared to offer the most straightforward setting for studying man–environment relations. Their activities, unlike those of most other societies, were intimately tied to natural events in the ecosystem, like the seasons and the cycles of animals and plants, and hunters invested little, if any, effort in attempting to modify the environment.

A second reason was the technology employed by hunters. The hunter-gatherer tool kit was generally homecrafted from materials obtained directly from the environment. It is the sophistication of their traditional tool kit, along with a forbidding environment, that have solidified the place of Inuit in anthropological lore.

Finally, hunter-gatherers, because of their dependence on an unmodified environment, were assumed to be essentially in an equilibrium state with the ecosystem around them. Without the technological ability to increase their harvesting capabilities, as farmers do by applying fertilizers and selecting for higher yields, hunters were hypothesized as simply maintaining a balanced energy exchange with

24

their environment. These reasons, taken together, made it appropriate to apply the term subsistence to the seemingly self-contained or limited activities of Inuit and other hunters.

Such a working characterization of hunting as an adaptation, particularly when it is based on special tools and steady-state use of energy, fits no society better than the Inuit. It is also deceptive because by the time some of the strongest analyses of pre-contact Inuit ecology were produced (see, for example, Spencer 1959; Gubser 1965; Damas 1969a, b; Balikci 1970), these studies were reconstructive. The commercial fur and whaling industries had introduced guns and other items several generations earlier. As well, after the Second World War the Canadian government imposed a policy of population relocation on Inuit.

In fact, while anthropologists were reconstructing pre-European patterns of Inuit adaptation, Inuit themselves were adapting to an environmental situation that was greatly influenced by the North's newcomers – teachers, nurses and administrators. Before traditional patterns of Inuit land use could be adequately studied (see Freeman 1976) Inuit were already responding to public health programs, compulsory education, scientific wildlife conservation, and wholesale population resettlement.

Therefore, it is necessary to discuss Inuit subsistence today as an adaptive response not only to the exigencies of the natural environment, but also in regard to the social and economic constraints to which Inuit have been exposed. Undeniably, the effective environment in which Inuit currently operate is one composed of unchanged natural elements, plus a number of European-introduced technological and economic introductions.

Inuit have always been included in the margins of arctic history as written by Europeans. But it is clear that a footnote presence in the exploration accounts does not do justice to a people who were living in the Arctic 4,000 years before Frobisher, Hudson, and Baffin sailed northward.

Northern history, as read from the era of neophyte exploration to the present, is distinctly flavored by a tone of adventure that highlights the struggle of southerners to colonize the North. It is indexed with reference to events that are of significance only to Europeans. When Inuit are mentioned, it is either to note the civilizing benefits of the south (see Dyson 1979) or to decry its demoralizing effects (Hall 1988). In either case, Inuit are depicted as having passively received the good and the bad with little power or will to influence their lives.

The view presented here is that Inuit are as actively involved in a cross-cultural relationship as they are with the Arctic's natural environment. Northern history, with Inuit as its subject rather than its object, projects them into a dynamic environmental role and presents the southern reader with a distinctly different perspective. Here the process of adaptation is central, and environment is itself a dynamic factor. This is the perspective that is needed in addressing the sealing controversy.

Before Europeans

Martin Frobisher, Sir John Franklin, and other early explorers were met by Inuit descended from Thule whaling culture, the last pre-European migrants to enter the Canadian Arctic. From the Alaska coast between the Chukchi Sea and the Mackenzie Delta, these archaic Inuit swept across Canada to Greenland between AD 1000 and 1300. With an eco-logical adaptation based on the bowhead whale (*Balaena mysticetus*), Thule Culture placed a stamp on the Canadian Arctic that was still visible when Europeans arrived.

Thule Inuit did not, however, even at that early date, enter an environment empty of people. They encountered, and assimilated, members of Dorset Eskimo Culture, itself an indigenous outgrowth of the first Palaeoeskimo, or Pre-Dorset, migration into the Canadian Arctic nearly 3,500 years earlier (see Maxwell 1985). Dorset Culture established itself along the central Arctic coast as early as 800 BC (ibid.: 121).

This last Palaeoeskimo Culture appears to have been centered around small, very mobile bands of hunters. The archaeological record is too scant to speculate about Dorset population size, but their villages and encampments are found from the Mackenzie Delta to Baffin Island, and from Port-au-Choix, Newfoundland, to the High Arctic Islands. Dorset hunters tapped a broad spectrum of seasonal maritime and terrestrial wildlife resources, such as caribou, ringed and harp seals and walrus, but apparently not bowhead or other large whales. Archaeologists (McCartney 1979; McGhee 1978) suggest that this ecological repertoire may be linked to cooler climatic conditions at the time. With annual temperatures 3°C lower, a summer season that may not have been ice-free could have closed the Canadian Arctic to these whales.

The development of Thule Culture along the shores of the Beaufort Sea was, like so much that is pertinent to arctic adaptation, related to a warming across the North. In fact a 'warm window', known as the Neo-Atlantic Period, with annual mean temperatures above those of today, existed from circa AD 900–1350. This warming set off a series of important ecological changes in the arctic environment that led to the Dorset–Thule transition in the Canadian Arctic.

Most important was the change in the summer ice regime around the pole. Much of Baffin and Hudson Bay, the eastern Beaufort Sea, and Lancaster Sound and Barrow Strait (the so-called Northwest Passage) that had been frozen nearly all year round were now clear of ice for three to four months. This ice-free condition allowed bowheads and other whales, herds of harp seals, and, perhaps, walrus to extend their summer ranges into waters that had been closed for a thousand years. In turn, Thule Culture, already adapted to bowhead whaling in North Alaska, was able to expand eastward, hunting these animals along the northern coast and islands of Canada.

The precise nature of Thule–Dorset Culture relations remains to this day unclear. Inuit legends speak of feuding between Thule *Inuit* newcomers and indigenous *Tunit*; more recently, a scattering of archaeological evidence (see O'Bryan 1953; Plumet 1979; Wenzel 1979; also Taylor 1960) suggests that Dorset peoples were at least partially absorbed into the fabric of Thule society. This is plausible when one considers that the indigenous Dorset Culture possessed an important asset which early Thule immigrants lacked – an intimate knowledge of the local environment.

The role of the bowhead whale in Thule Culture, and, therefore, the importance of the Neo-Atlantic and following Neo-Boreal climatic episodes, cannot be too strongly stressed. For Thule peoples, whaling was an industry, providing products that were used in everything from houses to harpoons. Many of these cultural elements, like the dogteam and the *umiak*, an open skin boat still used in Alaska, survived the end of Thule whaling and were still in use when Europeans intruded into the Canadian Arctic.

The relevance of this brief review of pre-European Inuit culture lies in the evidence it provides of Inuit adaptiveness to changing ecological and cultural circumstances. The image of Inuit as 'traditional', it must be remembered, is drawn from the accounts of explorers, traders, and missionaries who observed a Thule-derived adaptation.

Inuit culture was, first, a blend of Thule technology and maritime specialization with Dorset environmental knowledge. It reflects adaptation to a radically changed physical environment, a time when 'the Little Ice Age' removed the bowhead whale from its place in the Inuit resource system. It is therefore appropriate that we recognize Inuit history as a process of ecological and cultural adaptation, rather than as a set of European-related events. Adjustments to climatic and resource constraints are not the only aspects of traditional Inuit culture that have been carried into the present; adaptation to new technologies and social features have also been a part of the Inuit cultural dynamic for at least one thousand years.

Explorers and merchants (c. 1600-1945)

Although the Norse explored the fringe of North America, briefly colonizing south Greenland, the base for present European–Inuit relations lies in the waves of explorers, merchants, missionaries that began in the late 1600s. When Frobisher and Baffin first sailed north, they met Inuit and so began a process of cultural contact that eventually affected Inuit material culture, demography, and economy.

Arctic history is replete with names familiar to the general reader – the Hudson's Bay Company, Sir John Franklin, Christian missions (Roman Catholic and Anglican), commercial whalers and fur traders, and the Royal Canadian Mounted Police – so familiar that they run together. In nearly three and one-half centuries, Inuit figure in only a very few episodes. It is only after the mid-nineteenth century, when Europeans accepted indigenous environmental knowledge and abilities,

27

that Inuit are referenced in the works of specialized northern historians.

The importance of this condition is not in what it says about past contact, but rather that it still forms the basis for White–Inuit relations today. What has happened in the seal controversy is not new. It is part of the Euro-Canadian historical tradition. Our task here is to restate the problem in the context of Inuit adaptation.

Europe's nineteenth-century search for a northern route to Asia led immediately to the acquisition of alien materials and goods by Inuit. Whether these transfers were deliberate, through gifts and trade, or accidental as in the cases of the Franklin and McClure expeditions (see Neatby 1984; Figs. 6 and 7; also Hickey 1984), Canadian Inuit rapidly added items, as tools and amulets, to their culture. Parry (1821: 286), who made the first recorded contact with North Baffin Inuit, noted that they had, '. . . an instrument for chopping . . . of which the iron was part of an old file', presumably a gift or discard from an earlier whaling party.

It appears, therefore, that long before formal commercial trading was established, Inuit had begun to incorporate 'exotic' artefacts and materials into their own system. This willingness to absorb new items appears to be best explained in terms of the overall need of Inuit to maintain adaptive efficiency in a most rigorous environment. Efficiency in this case means investing the minimum amount of energy for the greatest possible return. This is sometimes referred to as a minimax strategy (see Lee 1968; Sahlins 1968, 1972), so-called because optimizing models consider the least amount of energy expenditure for the greatest return to be the most efficient. For Inuit, the presence of new, more durable materials and tools meant less time spent in the manufacture of artefacts and more time for resource and social activity. Indeed, this acquisition of European materials is a 're-run' of the cultural transfer that occurred between Thule and Dorset peoples five centuries earlier.

Enduring economic contact between many Canadian Inuit groups and Europeans began in earnest around 1870. It was at this time that the whaling industry, although present in northern waters for two hundred years, initiated the practice of overwintering, to be shortly followed by land-based whaling stations. This practice, unlike those of all but a few exploration parties, brought Inuit into more or less daily contact with southerners. Inuit served as crew for small chaser boats, supplied meat and fur clothing to the ice-locked ships and land stations, and socialized with the whalers. As bowhead whale stocks shrank, these 'informal' economic relations slowly gave way to an active trade in furs and ivory. Such free trading was short-lived as the Hudson's Bay Company established itself across the Canadian North.

The fur trade is an especially important period in Inuit history because it established a new relationship between Inuit and Europeans quite different from the relationship of Inuit to the explorers and whalers. It calls for critical examination because of conclusions drawn by the animal rights movement that the fur trade initiated an inevitable decline of Inuit culture. The fur trade was certainly exploitative of Inuit, but I shall argue that this perspective of 'decline' belies the 'environmental' resilience that is an Inuit hallmark.

The nearly 250 years that preceded the fur trade were dominated by exploration and the whale fishery, both of which were of very limited extent. Inuit saw *Qallunaat* but once or twice in a generation. Even wintering ships or shore stations were highly localized. While over-wintering whalers initiated the fur trade, they were a far from reliable source of imported tools and goods. It was only when whaling began to decline that a trade developed for narwhal and walrus ivory, fox pelts, and even musk-ox and bird skins (see Burch 1977; Damas 1988; Ross 1979, 1985).

The dimensions of the fur trade, especially after the Hudson's Bay Company established its control, initiated a far more complex relation-ship between Inuit and southern culture than is usually acknowledged. Conventional analyses, including those of anti-sealing and animal rights representatives, have summarized this era as one of overwhelm-ing negative effect on Inuit society and culture. Most often identified at the root of this cultural and economic erosion are the introduction of European hunting technologies, firearms, the steel trap, wood boats and fish nets. In this perspective, 'modern' hunting tools led to severe depletion of wildlife and led to greater dependence on Europeans for food and clothing. This view, as it is now voiced (see Best 1985, 1986), is only an echo of earlier comment.

Hantzsch (1977), during his travels on southern Baffin Island between 1909 and 1911, noted what seemed to him a growing dependence by Inuit on missionary and trading posts. A.P. Low (1906: 10), who surveyed the Keewatin area at the turn of this century, said, '. . . whalers may be taken as beneficial to the Eskimos . . . there is no doubt many would perish should the whaling stations be closed . . .'. This is a particularly disturbing statement from a government agent who bore no love for the American whalers who then dominated the Hudson Bay fishery.

There is no doubt that Europeans damaged Inuit culture during the whaling-trading period, but what exactly were the damaging elements? Hunting technology has been singled out as the prime cause in the destruction of arctic wildlife and Inuit culture. But this is not entirely convincing. We must consider, for instance, the limitations of firearms available at the time. We may note that trade guns were relatively simple and did little to alter Inuit ecological adaptation. Also, guns were scarce and ammunition more so. Up to the end of this period, and even into the 1960s in some areas, Inuit continued to employ customary tools, like the toggle harpoon in breathing-hole sealing, because of the distinct limitations associated with firearms. Certainly guns offered advantage, enabling hunters to operate effectively at longer ranges for species like caribou and walrus, but they did not replace native technologies.

There is no evidence that the pattern of Inuit land use was altered by these introductions. Rather, these patterns were affected by poles of long-term European activity, like whaling stations and missions, which offered Inuit opportunities to obtain desired tools, foods, and raw materials.

Is there a contradiction here? Imported tools were scarce, yet trading stations were attractive. This paradox tells us something about Inuit perceptions of the utility of European goods. While firearms were useful, at least as important was wood for sleds, metal pots and cans for cooking, cloth for garments and steel needles for sewing. All of these mundane items represented for Inuit substantial savings in manufacturing time and durability. It would be surprising if Inuit had not taken advantage of these goods. Here are signs of a developing dependence, one which arises from Inuit adherence to a minimax deployment of their time and energy. This same strategy of 'adoption' characterizes Dorset–Thule integration.

Leaving aside technology and the dependence it is said to have bred, we can identify two other factors, one biological and the other cultural, that impinged on Inuit society. The first was the introduction of diseases previously unknown to Inuit, and the second was European institutional structures.

From the moment Inuit encountered Europeans, they were exposed to diseases for which they possessed neither resistance nor immunity. Schaefer (1971), among many, has detailed the health effects of these introductions. The impact of new pathogens among Inuit was observed and reported as early as Boas's time. While working in 1882-3 at Cumberland Sound, an area of intensive whaling, missionary, scientific and trading activity, he estimated (Boas 1888: 426), that the Inuit population had declined from 1,600 people in 1840 (when they were visited by a Royal Navy expedition) to 500-600. He explained that this downward change over just forty years was, '... undoubtedly to be found in the diseases ... taken thither by the whalers'. While the impact of disease on Canadian Inuit may seem slight compared to the epidemics that struck other Native groups, the effect was magnified by the pattern and social intensity of Inuit community life. Inuit bands were vulnerable because they were so small, often only thirty to fifty members. Almost all community activities were cooperative and, with all band members in contact daily, a whole village might succumb in a single episode.

The cultural ramifications of the waves of disease go beyond sheer population depletion. These offer insight into what Low and Hantzsch saw as 'cultural dependence' on Europeans. First, Inuit who survived these outbreaks were often left in a weakened state and could only carry on harvesting and household tasks at a reduced level. Second, disease and illness sometimes removed whole cohorts of adults without whom critical activities could not be sustained. Gilberg (1974-5, 1984) reports that the Polar Eskimo of Northwest Greenland lost all knowledge of the *qajaq* because '... a disease exterminated all the old people, and the people who survived were too young to have learned this craft'. This kind of human and cultural loss had the effect of crippling ecological activities. In all cases where severe disease effects were felt, the possibility of famine and further infection increased.

While the impact of disease is immediately perceivable, as important at that time are the institutions, most notably the determination of economic relations, imposed by Whites. Following the whalers among Inuit were missionaries and fur traders, the latter dominated by the Hudson's Bay Company, and, finally, the Canadian government established itself.

The first missions among Canadian Inuit took hold in Labrador in 1771. Here the Moravian Church provided spiritual, educational, and economic service to the people. The Anglican Church began its activities in Cumberland Sound in the 1880s and the Catholic Church, while active in the Mackenzie Valley, did not enter the Eastern Arctic until the early part of this century. By the 1920s, a string of Christian missions stretched from Makkovik, Labrador, to the Mackenzie Delta.

The reach of the Hudson's Bay Company developed more slowly. The HBC began in 1670 under Royal Charter from King James II by establishing posts around James Bay and the southern shores of Hudson Bay. Through much of the North, however, it was only in this century that 'The Bay' established an institutional hold with Inuit, achieving economic hegemony by the 1930s. By this time, the HBC had absorbed almost all its northern commercial competitors. The HBC controlled almost the entire flow of southern manufactures reaching Inuit and built its trade on the export of arctic fox (*Alopex lagopus*) to the fashion markets of Europe and North America.

The Hudson's Bay Company and the Christian churches are usually seen as the main agents of Inuit economic and social change. (Some historians also include the Royal Canadian Mounted Police (RCMP) as part of what is referred to as the northern 'trinity'.) This is the case, but it must be remembered that The Bay and churches each presented Inuit with sometimes contradictory tugs, especially with regard to the patterning of local land use and settlement.

The missionaries encouraged Inuit to establish residency near or at missions whenever possible. Their efforts were to instil the values of Christianity in place of indigenous social and spiritual customs, but each of the three main northern churches, the Moravians in Labrador and the Anglicans and Catholics in Arctic Quebec and the Northwest Territories, also provided basic medical and educational services, as well as some amount of economic relief to sick and hungry Inuit bands. For instance, the Inuktitut writing system, or syllabary, still in use today by a majority of Canadian Inuit, was developed by the Anglican Peck.

The Hudson's Bay Company, because of its interest in the fox trade, encouraged Inuit to maintain residence on the land. This was done in order to maximize trapper productivity and discourage dependence on resources of the local store for economic aid. HBC records from Eastern Arctic posts provide evidence of this. At Clyde River (Hudson's Bay

Company n.d.a.) the post factor wrote that two Inuit who had arrived on 21 April 1932, '. . . also left today as they got no encouragement to hang around . . .'. In 1934 (Hudson's Bay Company n.d.b.), the store diary entry for 19 January reads, 'Owing to tales of hunger . . . Kautuk's camp are unwilling to go to Home Bay. But this shall not be, for they will be taken down there as soon as possible . . .' As the single source of tools and goods, the HBC was able to enforce its own norms for Inuit economic behavior.

While traders and churchmen, as well as the RCMP, were an important aspect of Inuit life, it is easy to forget how little contact many Inuit did have with *Qallunaat* until the post-war stage of arctic colonization. Until the Second World War, there were probably fewer than 200 Whites living above the 60th parallel. On all of Baffin Island in the 1930s there was approximately a score of non-Inuit in any year. In a very real sense, Inuit continued to set the cultural pace of their own lives.

Despite the commercial importance of fox, ringed seal, or *natsiq*, formed the foundation of Inuit adaptation during the fur trade, just as in other areas. Inuit maintained close ecological relations with their environment. Inuit settlements remained scattered across the land and along the coasts. These villages were semi-permanent, being used in winter while summer found the people constantly moving as they pursued seasonally mobile resources. The rules of everyday life were Inuit rules, although mission and fur post influenced decisions. For most bands, the only intrusion by Europeans came once or twice a year when the nearest missionary or policeman visited on his annual patrol.

The interplay of arctic fox trapping and ringed-seal hunting at this time is important. Fox formed the basis of Inuit–European commercial relations, while *natsiq* held the key to subsistence. This contrasts with animal rights commentators (see Best 1986), who, following Calvin Martin's (1978) analysis of the Indian fur trade, have suggested that massive cultural change among Inuit began because of the ecological incompatibility of the fur trade's demands for fox with the traditional ecology of Inuit culture.

It is certainly the case that fox trapping appears to have played only an incidental role in pre-contact Inuit harvesting. While not unknown archaeologically, it is unlikely that fox contributed significantly to the Inuit diet (see also Degerbol and Freuchen 1935). On the other hand, as has been discussed, ringed seals were critical, at least through the winter, to most Inuit groups. Seemingly, therefore, analyses suggesting that the fur trade altered Inuit subsistence practices, causing economic dependence on imported goods and foods, are correct.

As today, the winter ecology of Inuit during the fur era focussed almost exclusively on the sea ice and *aglu* sealing (see Freeman 1976, 1984). In winter, Inuit become sea ice hunting, if not sea ice living, beings. Like polar bear, Inuit hunt *natsiq* at their breathing holes, and the arctic fox follows to scavenge the remains of these kills. It is during the eight months that men, seals, and fox are on the sea ice, the one consistently productive winter ecological niche, that their lives intermesh.

Fox trapping, therefore, fits neatly with Inuit winter sealing. Land use maps of Inuit harvesting from about 1920 to 1975 (Freeman 1976) demonstrate the coincidence of winter sealing and fox trapping across the Arctic. Only on the Barren Grounds, west of Hudson Bay, is this pattern different. There the Inuit lived inland and depended on caribou. Analyses, à la Martin (1978) and Best (1986), which conclude that commercial trapping and subsistence sealing were essentially divergent activities appear to be in error. It would appear that through the heydays of the fur trade, from 1910 to 1945, Inuit had no option but to continue a pattern of customary subsistence.

The last four decades

Modern Canadian Inuit history begins with the end of the Second World War. To southerners, the interval since 1945 has been marked by the recognition of the North as having special strategic, political, and potentially economic significance to Canada and all the nations of the northern hemisphere. Signs of change include militarization of the North through the Distant Early Warning System, or DEW Line; perennial Euro-Canadian hopes of a northern oil 'boom'; and the emergence of 'southern' towns like Iqaluit (formerly Frobisher Bay) and Inuvik, where the majority of residents are *Qallunaat*, not Inuit. (The last few years have produced other signs of progress. One is that a traveller can board a jet in Montreal in the morning and be in Clyde River the same evening. In 1971, my first trip to Clyde meant spending over a week waiting in Iqaluit for the only airplane to reach Clyde for the next two months.)

Inuit also have markers of 'modernity', signalled by daily clinics at the village nursing station and a satellite receiving dish on the hill above each community. They experience an increasingly bureaucratized village and encounter the problem of earning enough money to travel out on to the ice to seal hunt.

The last forty years, which might well be termed the government era, are best explained though a detailed village case study (not the intent here), but meanwhile more must be said about this recent period if the conundrum of the vitality of Inuit tradition in a world of satellite communications, $120 a night hotels, and the European market for sealskins is to be deciphered.

In the fifteen years following the war, Inuit experienced the most disruptive series of events in the history of their contact with Europeans. The collapse of the fox market destroyed a century of economic relations with non-Inuit. Introduced diseases, from tuberculosis to syphilis, had become endemic. Last, the well-meant but disruptive relocation by the Canadian government of nearly all Inuit from their home villages to planned settlements strained ecological and social relations. The immediate post-war years can be said to be marked by government-inspired institutionalized relations.

Yet from 1960 until the EEC sealskin boycott, Inuit culture adapted itself to an environment that was being increasingly modified by demands of Euro-Canadian society. While Whites came North as teachers, nurses and administrators, Inuit remained joined to the land, but in a conceptual setting that was increasingly formed by southern colonization. Margaret Lantis described the situation exactly when she said (1975: 126): 'Eskimos are trying just as hard today to adapt as they did 500 or 900 years ago; the difficulty is that they are adapting not to the Arctic but to the Temperate Zone way of living.'

In an environment of sea ice and white-outs, *natsiq* and caribou, Euro-Canadians introduced and made facts of Inuit life money, satellite communications, compulsory education and social welfare, high-quality health care, airports and hotels. The thing the *Qallunaat* see as necessary for northern living have become part of the Inuit Arctic.

Inuit have adapted 'Temperate Zone' artefacts to meet these new environmental parameters, just as they did in Dorset–Thule times and during the fur trade. The best example of recent innovation and adaptation is the snowmobile.

The utility of snowmobiles relates to the post-war resettlement of Inuit. As customary camps gave way to the present arrangement of government settlements, Inuit hunters found that these new sites imposed severe time and distance constraints on harvesting. The ski-doo provided a means for hunters and communities to overcome these problems and thus maintain their links to the land and wildlife.

The snowmobile example also illustrates the overall difference in the way Europeans and Inuit each see northern history. To Whites, the snowmobile exemplifies the erosion of traditional Inuit culture; after all, the dogteam was replaced by a noisy, gasoline-fed machine. By most outside measures, this shift appears to typify negative change. The situation for Inuit, however, has been, and is, one of recognizing adaptive opportunities offered by their natural and cultural milieu. Inuit history is a continuum understood only when events connect to process and artefacts to adaptation. Too often, as Malaurie (1973: xi) puts it, Europeans mistake Inuit adaptation 'as mere techniques for living . . .' and thereby justify 'cultural, religious and economic assimilation'.

The seal protest and EEC sealskin ban combine as the strongest example of this kind of interpretive error to be found in recent Inuit–*Qallunaat* relations. The practical argument, apart from the underlying moral position of the animal rights movement, is that modern hunting technology and economic practices have so altered northern life that Inuit harvesting is neither essential nor linked to cultural tradition. In essence, Inuit adaptation has given way to southern technological and economic assimilation.

This position appears to differ little from that of generations of northern administrators, missionaries, and developers. However, in one aspect there is a crucial difference. The animal rights movement has acted to dissociate contemporary Inuit from their own culture, history and ecology.

2 ANIMAL RIGHTS, THE SEAL PROTEST, AND INUIT

Introduction

Millions of people living in the United States, the United Kingdom and Western Europe now hold as an article of faith that the preservation of seals in Canadian waters, and hence the cessation of Canadian seal hunting, is a moral test of the relationship between human beings and the other animals on this planet. A perception of this test as critical has been built by three decades of strident argument, invective, and protest. Canada has been the focus of the campaign against seal hunting because it is the only industrialized nation carrying on widespread commercial sealing activities. For many Americans and Europeans, the Canadian seal controversy comprises everything they know about seals, animal rights, and environmentalism. The place and importance of seals in Inuit culture is certainly far less well known.

The nature of this debate is encapsulated in two photographs that appeared in a direct mail pamphlet opposed to Canadian sealing. The first picture shows a newborn, or whitecoat, harp seal. The pup's coal-black eyes stare serenely into those of the viewer. Except for those calm eyes, the animal is almost pure white and behind it is pristine and glittering ice. The second photo is of a terrified pup facing a roughly clothed man who looms over it. In his hands is a spiked club poised to strike. The background is no longer unsullied ice; rather the whole surface is mottled with pools of blood that stretch into the far distance. The front cover of this brochure thoughtfully warns that its contents may be disturbing.

Until a few years ago, these two photographs offered a powerful statement (see Coish 1979; Wright 1984) about economic reality for generations of Canadian fishermen. Each spring, for some two hundred years, the men of Newfoundland and the Gulf of St. Lawrence turned to harp sealing as a source of income. Without sealskins, loans were unavailable for fishing.

Today these pictures carry an entirely different meaning. They draw a battle line between the harmony and stability of nature and the wanton disregard of man toward our planet; nature is benevolent, man is cruel. The harp seal pup has become a symbol for environmental awareness and for a social philosophy that has come to be generally known as the animal rights movement. These photographs also present

35

the clash between Inuit and animal rightists because the movement perceives Inuit use of seals in the same terms.

Although animal rights appears to be a product of the last thirty years, its roots run considerably deeper (see Mighetto 1988). Where it differs from its historical antecedents, both philosophically and ethically, is that, while the ethos of respect and rights for animals has long been a matter of individual conscience, the modern animal rights movement seeks militant economic and political solutions to end what it refers to as speciesism, the dominance of all other animals by man.

It has become alarmingly commonplace to paint a whole spectrum of opinion and viewpoint, and hence organizations, as 'animal rights advocates'. As a general label, the animal rights appelation is misleading (see Morgan 1983; also Kellert 1981). In fact, it has, at times, been placed on groups as different in philosophy and intent as the Wilderness Society and the RSPCA, the radical ecologists, anti-vivisectionists, as well as self-proclaimed animal rightists. The *mélange* is often contradictory. (In similar fashion, 'the fur industry' has become a catch-all for animal activists that includes within its sweep the Hudson's Bay Company, designers of fur fashions, mink ranchers, Inuit and Indian hunter-trappers, and even wearers of fur.)

Confused and loose application of the animal rights label can, at times, also be related to the way the movement has attempted to portray itself. For instance, some animal rightists have selected a patchwork of ideas from orthodox ecology, conservation, and wildlife management theory. Ideas have been 'borrowed' from the works of naturalists like Leopold and Muir, often free from any original context, to legitimize the protectionist perspective. In the process, the separation between conservationist and animal rights points of view has become blurred. In a similar manner, the seal protest brought together a mixture of radical and mainstream ecological thought to serve its specific needs and objectives.

The other side of this coin is the willingness of pro-sealing forces, the 'fur industry', to respond to virtually all criticism of its position by labelling critics as 'animal rightist'. In the end, both sides' rhetoric reflects hardening attitudes (see Lee 1988).

While such terms as the 'fur trade' and the 'animal rights movement' are retained here, an important goal of this discussion is to look beyond the generalizations attached to the buzzwords of the seal debate. They are part of a jargon that must be examined in depth. My use here of the term animal rights is with specific reference to groups who have based their opposition to Inuit sealing on moral and ethical grounds which can, in my view, be related to their own belief that Inuit hunting no longer possesses any cultural foundation.

In this light, for example, the activities of Greenpeace (from 1975 to 1984), the International Fund for Animal Welfare, or the International Wildlife Coalition strike me as differing markedly from those of wildlife conservation organizations and management agencies over the past twenty-five years. Whereas management and conservation interests have, at times, impinged deeply on Inuit harvesting (most recently and notably in the case of polar bears (see Lentfer 1974; Wenzel 1983a)), these intrusions have occurred only after extensive scientific research and have acknowledged and even deferred to Inuit views on the importance of wildlife in their culture.

Opponents of sealing, on the other hand, appear disposed to attack Inuit hunting in light of their own values and thus interpret Inuit activities as being motivated by market demands and economic wants. They have, in my view and as analysed in Chapters 8 to 10, judged Inuit harvesting to be without cultural or moral value.

The animal rights perspective is culture-specific. It takes a position on the issue of Inuit consumptive use of wildlife based in its own ideological evaluation of Western philosophy and ethics and its assumptions about the relationship of Inuit culture to southern society. In this regard, it deserves analysis and challenge.

The roots of the seal protest

Opponents of sealing hold the premise that animals, because they are sentient beings, have the right to live free from human exploitation (Singer 1975). Such views have appeared in various philosophical and ethical traditions, especially those of the East. The seal debate brought together two distinct voices, animal rights ethicists and radical or 'deep' ecologists, as a potent political, economic, and social force.

The seal controversy is often described by combatants on both sides as an animal rights issue. But it is more than this. It is a debate over the rightness or wrongness of Inuit hunting and especially the right of southerners, of any philosophical stripe, to dictate the nature of Inuit culture.

Discussion of the moral value of human actions towards animals predates the rhetoric and activism of the modern animal rights movement. Concern over the moral dilemma presented to us by our treatment of animals can be traced to at least the time of Plutarch (see Lecky 1911). Henry Salt, in his 1894 treatise on the rights of animals, quotes Porphyry to demonstrate the incongruity of man's generalized cruelty toward animals. Concern for the rights of animals led nineteenth-century Britain to form the first animal welfare organization, the Royal Society for the Prevention of Cruelty to Animals. Over the past thirty years, a new view, which ostensibly extends beyond the humane society model, has developed a place in the conscience of North Americans and Europeans.

While the fundamental issue of animal rights can be said to be very old, its appearance as a source of major debate among modern philosophers, lawmakers, and general public appears to correlate closely with the onset of industrial-urban society and the emergence of intensive animal husbandry and agricultural practices in nineteenth-century Europe. Regan (1983) and Thomas (1983) note that the question of animal rights appears to have been of only slight import in earlier European philosophical discourse. Regan (1983), for instance, in presenting his extensive case for accepting animal rights, nowhere suggests that a coherent view on this topic existed much before the last century. Rather, the prevailing view toward non-human fauna from Classical times through the Enlightenment and into the Industrial Revolution was differentiated between the interests of man, which were accepted as pre-eminent, and those of animals.

Pre-Christian Western thought portrayed animals as no more than 'lawless beasts' (ibid.: 2). Among the Classical thinkers, Aristotle argued that nothing in nature was without purpose, plants were created for the sake of animals, and animals for the sake of man, who was unique among all forms of life (see Thomas 1983: 30). This uniqueness was founded in the rational or intellectual element of the human soul (ibid.), whereas the soul's other parts – the nutritive and the sensitive – were shared with animals and plants.

This view of man as separate and unique among all life persisted and was strengthened through the Middle Ages as scholars, especially Thomas Aquinas, fused the Classical view of man as a superior animal with the Judaeo-Christian precept that man alone was created in God's image and likeness. Theologians pronounced man to be the Supreme Creator's highest accomplishment; a fact that was to be celebrated and which established the role of animals as man's servants.

The penetration of the Church into all phases of medieval European secular and spiritual life left little room for disputation of this anthropocentric perspective on man's place on earth. Drawing breath from Genesis 2:19 concerning the special position of man in God's framework, the Church enjoined Christians, in the words of the Old Testament, to replenish the earth and subdue it. Man, made in God's image, shared to a degree in His divine transcendence over the lesser of the earth's creatures.

Besides the effect of Christian dogma, the near total dependence of man on the energy of animals for work, in the fields and for transportation, as well as for sustenance reinforced the moral, and hence ethical, distance between men and animals. Human beings harnessed animals to work for them. Neither wind, sun, water, nor mechanical means were readily available for agriculture and manufacturing. Without the labour of beasts, only already heavily taxed human resources could substitute. The movement interprets subsequent Cartesian rationalism about man and the 'animal machine', elaborated by Descartes (1960) in his *Discourse On Method And Meditations*, as a secular rendering of earlier Church-based anthropocentrism. Rather than offering a new perspective, it provides just further systematic rationalization for the exploitation of animals.

Perhaps the most elaborate and careful rejoinder to both the Cartesian and Judaeo-Christian perspectives on animals has been offered by Tom Regan. Regan argues throughout the opening chapter of *The Case For Animal Rights* (1983) that the Cartesian view of animals as mere automata must be challenged and refuted. This he does by examining what Descartes meant by his denial of consciousness, meaning thought, in non-human animals. In so doing, he also makes clear the grounds for rejecting biblical and New Testament claims over animals. Regan's rights argument is based on a conception of animal awareness, or sentience (Wright 1990).

Descartes, as quoted in Regan (1983: 3), wrote to a seventeenth-century contemporary:

> I am speaking of thought, not of life and sensation. I do not deny life to animals, since I regard it as consisting simply in the heat of the heart; and I do not deny sensation in so far as it depends on a bodily organ.

Like many animal rights critics (see Rosenfeld 1968; Singer 1975; Regan and Singer 1976; see also Herscovici 1985), Regan attacks Descartes's construction as a denial of thought and also of any affective sensation, whether pain or pleasure, among animals. Hence the repeated emphasis by these critics on the administering of beatings by Cartesian experimenters to helpless dogs, who all the time avowed that the creatures were no more than clocks.

Since animal rightists have made the refutation of the Cartesian separateness of humans and animals, we need to consider the exact meaning of Descartes's use of reason and mind. Regan states that Descartes's denial that animals 'have thoughts' is at the same time a denial of 'any conscious awareness of anything' (Regan 1983: 4). Animal rightists have taken the Cartesian declaration that animal sensations are nothing more than 'the immediate affection of a bodily organ by external objects' as a denial that animals can experience pain.

In constructing his counterargument to Descartes, Regan uses words like thought, mind, consciousness, awareness and sensation in ways that are interchangeable. He also makes use of evolutionary biology, citing D.R. Griffen (ibid.: 19–20) to support the role of consciousness in animal adaptation and behavior.

Regan concludes his refutation of Cartesianism by presenting a 'cumulative argument for animal consciousness' (ibid.: 28). The five tenets of this argument are: (1) that attributing consciousness to certain animals is part of humanity's common-sense view of the world; (2) the attribution of consciousness to animals is in harmony with the ordinary human use of language; (3) this attribution does not rely on the fact nor imply that animals have immortal souls; (4) animal behavior is consistent with human views of them as conscious; (5) an evolutionary understanding of consciousness provides the theoretical base for attributing awareness to animals other than humans. It is by virtue of these five points that Regan postulates that animal awareness equals animal cognition and that it is this cognition that establishes the inherent right of animals to be free from human-induced pain and suffering (Regan 1982). The argument extends to all consumptive use of animals.

Regan's case for animal rights is important because it incorporates

39

within it a rejoinder to Western religious and rational claims for the superiority of men over animals. It is also important because this approach is markedly different (see Singer 1975; 48-9) from the perspective usually articulated by animal rights adherents.

The more usual rights approach is to argue not that the lives of animals, or man, possess inherent value, but that animal life is deserving of respect because of a fundamental principle of equality of interests among all species based on the shared consideration of each to extend its life and avoid pain. In Singer's words (ibid.: 48), 'similar interests must count equally regardless of the species being involved'. The economic benefit that a trapper will receive from a muskrat pelt, for instance, cannot outweigh the suffering and ending of life of the muskrat. This utilitarian approach forms the philosophical base of much of the contemporary animal rights movement.

Utilitarianism can lay claim to a historical legacy that extends back to the thoughts and writings of Jeremy Bentham (1789), Henry Salt (1894) and his Quaker contemporary in America, John Woolman (see Gilbert 1985), all of whom made explicit claim for the rights of animals. The critical question Bentham posed, 'can they suffer?', remains the driving force of the animal rights movement today.

Bentham's question was revived in the 1970s along two fronts. The first was through the philosophical explorations of Peter Singer (1975), John Harris (1971), and Rosalind and Stanley Godlovitch (1971), all of whom expressed moral opposition to the suffering which humans impose daily on animals. The second was the expanding efforts of a coalition of environmental and animal welfare activists to halt Canadian sealing. Each drew strength from the other. Philosophers, especially Singer, provided a moral rationale badly needed by the seal protest, while the hunt presented a clear-cut example of human economic self-interest overriding the moral considerations of animal suffering. As a result, seals and animal rights became entwined.

Another current in the seal controversy is the appeal seals, and marine mammals in general, have come to hold for proponents of the 'new' or 'deep' ecology movement. Deep ecology, as a distinct environmental perspective, appeared about 1970 (Naess 1973). It grew within a segment of the environmental community opposed to the anthropocentrism pervading the movement (Devall 1980). It received further impetus from the philosophical dissatisfaction many felt with scientific rationalism as an approach to the problems of global ecology (see Evernden 1985).

Regan has outlined the tenets of deep ecology as the following. Its core belief is that 'nature ... has value in its own right, apart from human interests' (Regan 1982: 212). The norm of deep ecology is that nature is always to be treated with respect for its inherent value. Attitudes of its adherents reflect 'a spirit of reverence and love ... appropriate to its independent value' (ibid.). It is here that deep ecology diverges from 'shallow environmentalism'. Nature does not exist for the benefit of *Homo sapiens* but in its own right.

Many proponents of deep ecology, especially in the movement's early stages, put emphasis on Western man's need to recapture environmental values best exemplified by Native Americans (see Udall 1962: 12; also Deloria 1970). The force of this depiction among deep ecologists is typified by the 'founding myth' of the Greenpeace environmental organization. As proclaimed in a pamphlet circulated by Greenpeace UK (c. 1984),

> An ancient North American Indian legend predicts that when the Earth has been ravaged and the animals killed, a tribe of people from all races, creeds and colours would put their faith in deeds, not words, to make the land green again. They would be called 'The Warriors of the Rainbow', protectors of the environment.

In fact, 'faith in deeds, not words' has been the credo of Greenpeace in their campaigns to disrupt commercial whaling and arrest the polluting of the marine environment.

In the 1970s, Greenpeace brought its action policy to bear on the Canadian sealing issue, and the organization remained thus involved until 1985. The prolonged involvement of this deep ecology organization in a protest which has been so damaging to Inuit ecology and culture seems to contradict the organic view of deep ecology regarding Native People.

Yet the seal has become a powerful symbol to deep ecologists as to the animal rights movement. Together, under the baby seal banner, this coalition took the same view of Inuit livelihood and lifestyle as it did of industrial sealing. The protest movement, while it cast aside speciesist attitudes, was unable to categorize Inuit seal hunting other than through its own ethnocentrically derived universalist perceptions of animal rights and values.

Canada's seal war

Part One: c. 1750–1950

Seal hunting, for both subsistence and profit, has a substantial history in all three of Canada's oceans. The details of aboriginal use of these resources is well beyond the scope of the present work. It is enough to recall that as early as 5000 BC , Maritime Archaic Indians were exploiting the harp seals found all along the Labrador and Newfoundland coast. By c. 3000 BC Palaeoeskimos were successfully winter-hunting ringed seals, and the first Europeans to enter British Columbia found Haida, Nootka, and Tsimshian Indians busily harvesting Pacific fur seals as part of a rich marine resource base. We will take a closer look at Euro-Canadian commerce in seals since it has direct relevance to the seal controversy.

Busch (1985) has aptly applied the phrase 'the war against the seals' to describe the world-wide activity that commercial sealing was for some 150 years. Not only the east and west coasts of Canada, but the White and Baltic Seas, the North Pacific, and the sub-Antarctic islands

41

were exploited by British, American, and other European sailors. By the beginning of this century, a dozen species of pinnipeds (see Bonner 1982) had been hunted to near extinction. Notable were the southern and northern fur seals (respectively, *Arctocephalus australis* and *gazella* and *Callorhinus ursinus*), the Northeast Atlantic and White Sea herds of harp seal (*Phoca groenlandica*), and the southern elephant seal (*Mirounga leonina*).

The earliest organized commercial operations in Canadian waters began in the mid- to late eighteenth century. Russian and British sea otter expeditions around Vancouver Island and in the Queen Charlotte Islands began to include fur seals. These skins, both otter and seal, were destined for trade into Imperial China (Busch 1985), with seal-skins becoming ever more important as sea otter stocks were over-harvested and depleted. By the end of the century, United States merchants, some of whom had first entered into sealing in the South Atlantic's rich elephant seal grounds, joined in the fur seal hunt, because of their desire to capture a part of the China trade (ibid.: 7). With the purchase of Alaska from Russia in 1867, American domin- ance of the North Pacific fur seal trade was complete. Elimination of Russian merchants from a North American base allowed US sealers to obtain hegemony over the most important fur seal grounds, the Pribilof Islands.

The importance of fur sealing along Canada's northwest coast was waning by the middle of the century because of overexploitation. After- wards, the Bering Strait and Pribilof Islands became the focus of *Callorhinus* hunting. In 1911 (Bonner 1982: 49) the principal fur seal- ing nations - America, Japan, Britain (for Canada) and Russia - signed the North Pacific Fur Seal Convention. The treaty ceding control of the Pribilof rookery and harvest to the United States remained in effect until 1985 and was important because it eliminated pelagic hunting, thus allowing northern fur seal populations to recover.

The other chief Canadian seal fishery was off the shores of New- foundland–south Labrador and in the Gulf of the St. Lawrence. Here the object was the 'hair' seal *Phoca groenlandica*, or harp seal.

The distinction between hair seals, like the harp and ringed seals (*Phoca hispida*), and fur seals is based on the way in which their pelage is constructed (Scheffer 1958; Bonner 1982). Hair seals have only sparse bundles of underfur (1–5 hairs) around long guard hairs; they rely on thick layers of subcutaneous fat, or blubber, for protection from cold arctic waters. Fur seals, like *Callorhinus*, have much thicker bundles of underfur surrounding each guard hair (50 or more) (Bonner 1982: 6). The density of a fur seal's pelage, on the order of $57,000/cm^2$, makes it an effective insulator and attractive fur for human use.

Jacques Cartier, the first European to visit and write about the Atlan- tic shore of Canada, noted that the Micmac and Beothuk Indians were well able to hunt harp seals. It is also likely that the Bretons, Basques, and Jerseymen who came to fish these waters long before Cartier, but who left no written accounts, used harp seals to enrich their diet. So abundant and obvious a resource were these herds, according to Busch (1985: 46), that in 1593 a British vessel arrived to open the seal fishery. Although some intensive harvesting of harps was carried out by inshore netting, it took two centuries before harp sealing became an important offshore industry in the waters around Newfoundland.

Northwest Atlantic harp seals became important as an industry at the start of the 1800s. Composite data (ibid.: 49; Colman 1937) indicate that the harvest rose sharply from somewhat less than 100,000 pelts to a peak of 500,000 plus by about 1840. From 1800 to 1915, the total take of harp seals, mainly whitecoats but also adults, is estimated (Busch 1985: 48-9) to have been roughly 35 million animals, or roughly 300,000 each year.

The harp seal fishery built financial empires and exacted a high cost from the men who entered it. On this, historians, from Busch to Chafe (1923) and England (1969), agree, although they often draw different conclusions about the social, ecological, and moral impact of 'The Great Hunt'. They share the view that it was the rigors of harp sealing, not the profit, that truly embedded it in the folk tradition of Atlantic Canada, and especially Newfoundland. Powerful evidence of this comes through data evaluated by Busch (1985: 49), who notes that the cost in ships and human lives between 1800 and 1865 in that fishery was close to 400 boats and about 1,000 men. The worst year, among many bad ones, for the whitecoat hunt was in 1912 when more than 300 men were frozen or drowned in one night.

The importance of the hunt's timing for rural Newfoundlanders (see Wright 1984; also Malouf 1986b), its dangers, potential profitability and folk meaning all carried over to the modern hunt. Even when harp sealing, especially the spring whitecoat hunt, changed from simply being a fisherman's supplemental activity to its modern industrial-commercial form, it continued to make a significant contribution to the economy of rural outports (see Malouf 1986c) by providing an economic bridge between social assistance and fishing.

Sealing by Inuit along Canada's Arctic coast has always been impor-tant. Evidence is strong (Maxwell 1974-5; Wenzel 1984a) that Inuit developed a sophisticated winter and open-water seal hunting tech-nology as early as 3,500 years ago. In these northern waters, the main species pursued have been ringed (*Phoca hispida*) and bearded seals (*Erignatus barbatus*) (see McLaren 1958a; Smith 1973a, 1987).

While subsistence use by Inuit of these species extends back for millenia, incorporation of arctic seal into the Western commercial system has a far shorter history than that of either Pacific or Atlantic seals. Although European explorers and whalers received seal meat and sealskin clothing from Inuit in barter for iron and tools, there is no record of any organized commercial activity involving arctic seals much before this century. It was only when the pods of great baleen whales began to disappear after 1870 that sealskins became more than a marginal item of exchange between Inuit and Whites.

Goldring (1986), in analysing records from Cumberland Sound, Baffin

43

Island, has provided some of the best documentation about the nature of this early trade (see also Damas 1988). He (ibid.: 163) states by the late nineteenth century: 'Just as the bowhead had been converted from a subsistence item to a commodity, surplus seal skins were sold to the stations . . .' According to Goldring's estimates, the volume of this annual trade in Cumberland Sound was 3,700 skins between 1883 and 1903.

As in the harp seal fishery (Busch 1985), the pelts of arctic seals were first desired by White traders as 'sculps', that is with their underlying layer of blubber intact. This suggests that, in the late whaling period, it was the need to make up shortfalls in rendered oil that led to European interest in arctic seals (Goldring 1986: 164) and that once a cheap substitute for marine mammal oil was available, this replacement interest quickly waned.

A commerce with Inuit based on sealskins therefore appears to have been short-lived (c. 1880-1920), as southern needs for the oil of sea mammals declined, and as traders discovered that the outside world was receptive to other arctic produce (Goldring 1986: 165). By 1900, items like walrus ivory, arctic fox pelts and polar bear skins had supplanted seal oil as an export commodity. Nonetheless, a vestigial trade in sealskins and sculps was instrumental in maintaining Inuit-White contact in the years between the end of bowhead whaling and the growth of world markets for white fox.

Part Two: 1950-1989
We have seen that the European commercial harvesting system of sealing grew rapidly and without effective regulation. As a result, numerous seal populations, here and world-wide, were brought to near extinction. Fortunes were amassed by traders from the harp and fur seal fisheries, even while phocid populations along Canada's east and west coasts were declining. It was the magnitude of these hunts that led Busch to write *The War Against The Seals*.

The only respite for these species occurred when environmental factors, such as prolonged storms or impassable ice, interrupted commercial hunting for a season or two. Through the 1800s, *Callorhinus* numbers dropped to such a low state that even the principal fur sealing interests saw fit to impose restrictions on their activities. There was no such action in the harp seal industry, but the data (Busch 1985; see also Malouf 1986a) show that the rich harvests of the eighteenth century were diminishing. Only in the Arctic did seal populations not experience serious erosion. Extensive European exploitation of ringed seals for trade was constrained by the remoteness of the stocks and the solitary nature of ringed seal behavior.

By 1900, only one species of southern seal remained commercially viable in Canada. With intensive hunting for fur seals removed from Canadian waters, all industrial activity concentrated on harp seals. In their pursuit, ships sailed from Newfoundland, the Magdalen Islands, and Nova Scotia each spring to one of the two major whelping patches in Atlantic waters. The most important was the mass of pack ice that drifted each winter into the northwest Atlantic. Often referred to as 'The Front', it was the most extensive and richest ground for harp sealers from Newfoundland. A second and smaller hunt area centered on the Gulf of St. Lawrence. Each spring, for up to two months, landsmen and pelagic hunters went to these two areas.

Unlike the Pacific fur seal situation, where British and Canadian hunters competed with Americans, Russians and aboriginal users, the Atlantic harp seal fishery was Canadian-dominated almost from its start. The other principal harp sealing nations, Norway and the Soviet Union, initially confined their activities to the populations of *Phoca groenlandica* found on the other side of the Atlantic. Norwegian and Russian hunters concentrated their efforts on the spring aggregations of whelping harp seals in the White Sea and on the 'West Ice' around Jan Mayen Island.

Bonner (1982: 38–41) has detailed the effects on those herds of wholesale industrial sealing methods: they were essentially depleted before 1940 and failed to recover in six years of near-zero hunting. Shortly after the Second World War, both countries were forced to abandon major operations in these areas. While the Soviet Union renewed its White Sea hunt later, results were so unpromising that only a much reduced hunt is still conducted. As for Norway, the depleted state of the Jan Mayen seal population and post-war exclusion from the White Sea fishery led its ships to shift attention to the Northwest Atlantic. This move undermined Canadian domination of 'The Front' and led to a new phase in the Northwest Atlantic seal fishery's history.

The appearance of Norwegian diesel-powered ships and superior techniques at the Front completed the demise of Newfoundland-controlled sealing there, an enterprise that was already suffering from the effects of two world wars, the Great Depression, and outdated technology. By the 1950s, the largest sealing companies in Canada were Norwegian-owned. Although Canadians continued to provide the bulk of the labor in the hunt, sealskin processing and the profits from the hunt were removed to Norway.

While the pelagic harp seal fishery was now foreign-dominated, landsmen, that is Canadian shore-based hunters, continued to operate in the Gulf of St. Lawrence and on the fringes of the Front. These landsmen, using longliner fishing boats of a few thousand tons, sailed from Newfoundland's outports, the north shore of Quebec, and the Magdalen Islands in pursuit of adult and young harps, whereas the deep-water hunt concentrated on whitecoat pups. Overall, however, the near-exclusive control that Norway obtained over the Canadian harp fishery only aggravated the declining condition of east coast sealing (see Busch 1985: Malouf 1986d).

If the first phase of the seal war was conducted by men against seals on a global scale, the second was initiated by activists who found 'The

Table 2.1 *Events in the anti-sealing campaign*

1955	Observers report on the inhumane killing of harp seals.
1964	The film 'Les Phoques' is aired in Europe.
1967	A 'Save the Seals' campaign is launched.
1971	Canada imposes harp seal quotas.
1972	The US passes the Marine Mammal Protection Act.
1977	Greenpeace's seal policy explicitly encompasses Inuit.
1983	The European Community agrees to a binding two-year ban on harp and hooded seal imports.
1984	Canada forms a Royal Commission to investigate the sealing controversy.
1985	The European Community renews its boycott. The Home Rule government of Greenland asks Greenpeace to differentiate publicly between Inuit and commercial sealing. Greenpeace declines.
1989	The EC votes for an indefinite boycott of sealskins.

Hunt' repellent. This phase was distinctly Canadian in focus. From the mid-1950s onward, through their efforts, the public's perception of the whitecoat hunt, and seal hunting in general, slowly changed. Where commercial sealing had once been accepted as an activity dictated by custom and necessity, it was now perceived as wanton slaughter.

The reasons for the emergence of this opposition are neither clear nor simple. Anti-sealing spokespersons have from time to time cited the cruelty of seal hunting, the past excesses of the industry, and the threat it poses of species extinction. They have pointed to sealing as the most blatant example of immoral killing of wildlife. In fact, these arguments arise only after critical turns in the seal controversy.

The beginning of the long war against sealing appears to have originated in genuine concerns for conservation and animal welfare, set in the atmosphere of the 1950s, when the horror of the Second World War and of nuclear weapons weighed on peoples' consciousness. The harp seal hunt provided a form of expression for this concern in much the same way as the Vietnam War and The Bomb have been interpreted as affecting environmental concerns in the 1960s. As an anti-sealing theme, animal rights was articulated quietly in the late, mainly European, stages (see Table 2.1) of the seal campaign.

The seal protest was born in 1955 when several independent observers expressed the view that the hunt was cruel and ecologically dangerous (see Davies 1970a, b; Coish 1979). These reports, which were soon followed by stunning depictions of mass slaughter (see Lust 1967), stimulated the first calls for extensive reform of the methods and scale of the harp seal hunt.

Two entrenched elements of the harp seal hunt served to conjure up a distinctly negative picture for outsiders. One was the use of clubs and hakapiks (spiked poles) as killing tools. The other was the sheer numbers of newly whelped seals that were taken annually. These factors led to lurid descriptions of 'baby whitecoats brutally beaten to death' (Davies 1970b: 362). The hunt was billed 'the greatest ... mass slaughter ever inflicted upon any wild mammal species' (Bruemmer 1977: 49). These elements gave life to the idea that any means was morally correct if it would put an end to man's war against seals. The words and imagery of Brian Davies, founder of the International Fund for Animal Welfare, implanted the idea that only a counterwar of equal ferocity could achieve the total abolition of seal hunting.

Many features of the Atlantic seal hunt, its apparent cruelty to seals and its brutalizing effects on men, had been criticized as long ago as the 1840s (Busch 1985: 60). By 1950 the larger ecological questions surrounding harp sealing were already being studied. The early protest, focussed on the issues of inhumane killing methods and the risk of extinction of Canada's harp seal population, prodded Canada into bringing the harp seal hunt under supervision. While anti-sealing campaigners and some marine scientists (see Lavigne 1976, 1978; Bonner 1982; Holt and Lavigne 1982) dispute the effectiveness of the steps that were taken, data (see ICES 1983; Roff and Bowen 1983; Malouf 1986e) suggest that by the late 1970s the survival of the Gulf and Front herds had been ensured.

Before 1976, the anti-sealing campaign centered on the need for sound conservation and humane killing practices. These arguments were not far from the thoughts of Canadian wildlife and marine mammal scientists. Therefore, between 1961 and 1971, a strong regulatory regime designed for species conservation (see Malouf 1986e) was created and successfully enforced on harp sealing. This structure included strict start and stop dates, catch limits, quota divisions among the various kinds of sealers, landsmen, pelagic or foreign entrepreneurs participating in the hunt, licencing procedures, and on-site supervision. In fact, after 1976, these issues ceased to form the protest's heart. From that year, an animal rights ethic concerning the morality of any use of seals became the key to the protest.

The implementation of conservation measures was a serious turn for the seal campaign. The dilemma is succinctly described in an observation by Jacques Cousteau, quoted in Allen (1979: 423):

> The harp seal question is entirely emotional. We have to be logical. We have to aim our activity first to the endangered species. Those who are moved by the plight of the harp seal could also be moved by the plight of the pig - the way they are slaughtered is horrible.

This was so much the case that a number of mainstream conservation and animal welfare organizations that had been sharply critical of Canadian sealing (World Wildlife Fund, Canada Audubon, the Ontario Humane Society) withdrew from the seal campaign when the ecological viability of the harp seal seemed assured.

This left some protest activists, to whom all sealing was inimical, in limbo. The decision of several large, well-funded groups to withdraw meant that continuation of an organized campaign would require a radical shift in protest strategy (see Allen 1979) if they were to maintain a constituency, funding and momentum. The International Fund for Animal Welfare (IFAW), whose *raison d'être* was to oppose all sealing, decided at this time to pursue a series of innovative confrontational tactics that allowed it to dominate the protest movement through the 1970s.

It is ironic that the seal protest found itself endangered by the implementation of the conservation measures it had originally called for. The IFAW, joined in 1976 by Greenpeace, therefore embarked on a strategy that continued to highlight cruelty and ecological threat of sealing, but presented these as endemic conditions which could only be corrected by the complete cessation of seal hunting.

The new protest strategy was marked by an escalation in campaign rhetoric and the appearance of what some have termed protest theater. Beginning in 1975, protesters from the IFAW, and then Greenpeace and other groups, began to appear each spring on the harp seal whelping patches in an attempt to disrupt hunt activities. Of more significance was the fact that the protest began to seek a forum outside Canada. Foreign political and cinema 'names' were invited to the ice. Brigitte Bardot drew wide acclaim during a brief visit to the Gulf in 1977 and the next year two US Congressmen from strong environmental constituencies, Representatives Leo Ryan (California) and James Jeffords (Vermont), accepted a Greenpeace invitation to observe the hunt. In an interview seven years later, Jeffords (1986, personal communication) could not remember the name of the group that had invited his participation, but recalled that he participated to call world attention to recently enacted American legislation on endangered species and marine mammals.

Such escalation had little impact on the harp seal hunt, but it did expose by degrees the inability of the Canadian government to rebut or adjust to the protest's tactical shifts. This was especially notable when the debate moved to Europe. Greenpeace and the IFAW seized the initiative by concentrating their rhetoric outside Canada.

To Europeans, with a long history of wildlife loss (see Thomas 1983; Geist 1988) and particular recent concern over seals (Lister-Kaye 1979), the matter of Canadian sealing was emotion-charged (see Coish 1979; Herscovici 1985; also, especially, Malouf 1986f). The architects of the protest's 'Euro-strategy' avoided confrontation on the intricacies of harp seal ecology and pursued the emotions of the European audience by declaring sealing immoral. While seal scientists presented population models of the seal herd and veterinarians declared clubbing as the most effective means of killing young seals, Greenpeace and the IFAW offered photographs of blood-stained seal pups. Careful science was made to appear to be on the side of the devil. Cousteau's plea for an ecological approach stood no chance against the glossy photographs of the IFAW.

In the late 1970s, it looked for a time as if Canadian counterattacks (see Lamson 1979; Busch 1985) were achieving some positive results. Although the protest theatrics of 1976 and 1977 had produced a sharp two-year reduction in world sealskin prices, the market returned in 1979 to even higher prices. This rally deluded industry, rural sealers, and government alike into believing that scientific appeals to reason had overcome emotion. Protests were noticably less fervent at the spring whitecoat hunt over the next few years. To the pro-hunt forces, it seemed that sealing had thus been saved.

In fact, both Greenpeace and the IFAW, because of the high costs and diminishing publicity returns of on-ice protest, had shifted their campaign focus from Canada to Europe and America. This was a relatively simple matter as both groups had become international. They were assisted by foreign-based organizations like Britain's Animal Welfare Trust and the Comité d'Action 'Sauvez Les Bébés Phoques'. Through newspaper advertisements and direct mail distributions, both organizations pounded home the depredations of sealing. Recipients of these direct mail packets also received pre-printed postcards so that they could register their revulsion by contacting Canadian government representatives, the environment ministers of their own countries, and their European parliamentarians (see Malouf 1986g).

The culmination of nearly three years of such activity, which Canada and the fur industry found themselves powerless to counter, was the decision of the European Parliament and Community to ban sealskin imports. In so doing, the EC nailed shut the coffin of industrial sealing as it had been practiced in Canadian waters for over 150 years. It also, unwittingly, struck a serious blow to the struggle of Canadian Inuit for control over their lives.

Two other points must be noted before concluding this overview of the Canadian seal war since 1950. First, when Canada refused to acquiesce to the protest's call for a government ban on sealing following the EC's 1983 resolution, the IFAW (see Herscovici 1985) set in motion a prepared campaign to encourage British consumers to boycott Canadian fish. While the fish boycott achieved no lasting effect, its audacity demonstrated the willingness of some activists to create 'social and economic hardship' (Steven Best as quoted in Herscovici 1985: 106).

The second point relates to the wording of the European Community ban (European Community 1983). Council Directive 83/129/EEC proscriptively identified only 'the skins of whitecoat pups of harp seals and the pups of hooded seals'. Because of Danish concern the directive explicitly tolerates Inuit sealing and other harvesting as a legitimate occupation. Anti-sealing activists, however, apparently convinced its authors to qualify this reference to Inuit activities to read 'as traditionally practised' and stipulated hunting which formed 'an important part of the traditional way of life and economy'. Since 1985, the International Wildlife Coalition has disputed whether present-day Inuit harvesting can be categorized as 'traditional'.

The protesters' view of Inuit sealing

The anti-sealing campaign was something new in man–animal relations. It was also a fresh chapter in the history of social activism. For three decades, a small group of committed animal rights activists have challenged powerful business, scientific and government interests. They came to influence popular and political opinion and decision-making about seals in the United States and Europe. The protest was at all times successful in controlling the terms of reference within which the sealing debate was conducted. Throughout the controversy, the protesters demonstrated a capacity for strategic and tactical mobility and they never lost sight of their stated goal: to put an end to all forms of commercial seal hunting.

Within this overall view, some aspects of the campaign against sealing require more careful analysis, especially the ethical and philosophical underpinnings of the movement. An understanding of these is critical if the least-known aspect of the seal protest – its impact on Inuit – is to be placed in perspective.

Two different, but not mutually exclusive, elements can be deduced in the philosophy of the anti-sealing movement. One is the 'deep ecology' orientation represented by Greenpeace and the Sea Shepherd Society. The other element is the utilitarianistic stance with respect to man–animal relations. Here the campaign seems to have drawn inspiration from the animal rights formulations of Peter Singer (1975, 1985; see also R. Godlovitch 1971). The seal activists had little difficulty in reconciling their abolitionist stance toward seal hunting with any harm their success might incur for Inuit.

When the seal protest first developed, about 1955, it was a call to arms against an inhumane and profligate commercial slaughter of wild-life. Inuit were not seen as offenders. Indeed, Inuit were themselves perceived as part of Canadian mythology, like polar bears and caribou, all living symbols of the country's northern heritage. Farley Mowat played an especially important role in developing this image in his books (see Mowat 1952, 1959), talks, and films.

The seal protest, in its early stages, did not involve Inuit. In the 1950s, when concern about the harp seal hunt first appeared, Inuit sealing was very much restricted to the pursuit of food. Commercial activity around seals, as has been described by Goldring (1986), had had a brief flutter of importance some fifty years before, but was then supplanted by a lucrative European trade in arctic fox pelts. Until the end of the Second World War, virtually all northern commercial activity was organized around fox.

The importance of arctic fox in that period is highlighted by the fur purchase pattern of the Hudson's Bay Company (HBC). At Clyde River, Baffin Island, in the years 1935–61, the total number of fox pelts shipped to London fur auctions was 9,414 (Wenzel n.d.a.), while only 4,402 sealskins were bought, a ratio of better than two fox skins to each seal. This bias is significant since after 1945, the main market for arctic fox, Western Europe, was no longer important because of the economic damage sustained from the Second World War.

A drastic reversal occurred in the HBC's northern fur buying after 1961, the year Norwegian processors developed a commercially successful process for tanning sealskins. In the next six-year period (1962–7), the Clyde HBC bought and shipped 8,219 sealskins and only 1,044 foxes, or nearly nine sealskins to one fox. In the interim between the end of the fox trade and the rise of seal, Canadian Inuit found themselves with no means to sustain their century-old trading relationship with *Qallunaat*.

The ramifications of the sudden lack of trade were serious (Graburn 1969). In some ways it bore a resemblance to the depression described by Goldring (1986) following the whaling era. Especially evident was the reliance on imported hunting equipment. As noted in Chapter 1, White-introduced diseases, together with the generally greater efficiency of firearms, stimulated a growing interest among Inuit for guns and ammunition. Without a market for fox, Inuit were finding in the 1950s that they could not obtain these tools in exchange for the produce of their hunting and trapping. It is, therefore, not surprising that Inuit sealing was ignored by the fledgling seal campaign. It was not only not commercial, but, in the eyes of many Euro-Canadians, it barely qualified as 'subsistence'. The perception of Inuit sealing as a marginalized activity persisted well into the 1970s.

In 1961, the Norwegian innovation in tanning created a market for ringed sealskins and provided an economic opening to both traders and Inuit. For the first time in more than a decade, Inuit had a commodity for which they could receive a reasonable value in return; southern supplies of equipment, dry goods, and foodstuffs became once again accessible. More importantly, this renewal of exchange added a badly needed new tool, the snowmobile, providing hunters with the necessary mobility to overcome the constraints imposed by the government's policy of population centralization.

While the prices Inuit received for ringed sealskins were initially modest, roughly $3.50 per pelt, this marked a drastic improvement from the days when sealskins fetched as little as $0.25 each. Ringed seal prices continued to rise and by 1966 reached $14.00 a sealskin. Among Inuit, the early and mid-1960s years are remembered as a time when hunters were again able to travel and harvest widely, when animals were again available in numbers.

While early concerns about Atlantic harp sealing passed over Inuit without effect, the outcry in Europe after the showing of 'Les Phoques' led to a tumble in the world price for sealskins. This protest-related faltering began in 1966 and hit a low in 1968 of approximately $4.00 per skin. Although the taking of whitecoat pelts was the cause of this first outbreak of popular revulsion against commercial sealing, the effects were felt not in the Atlantic Front and Gulf harp seal fishery, but by Inuit. Again, in the 1970s and 1980s, after the EC boycott, Inuit bore the brunt of economic losses.

The reasons for this are not completely clear. Because the finer-haired pelts of whitecoat harp pups are easily dyed, articles using dyed pelts were generally unrecognizable to all but the trained eye. Thus, the economy of the Atlantic harp seal hunt weathered the 1960s and 1970s protests and market recessions with reasonably little damage. Adult sealskins, on the other hand, whether harp or ringed, are coarser, do not dye well, and remained identifiable as sealskins. Inuit, whose ringed seal harvest is 99 per cent comprised of adult animals, were the suppliers of recognizable adult sealskins.

The impact of the 1966–8 protest on Inuit has generally gone unremarked, in all likelihood because the episode was so little felt by *Qallunaat* sealers. The exception was a brief note by D.C. Foote (1967a), titled 'Remarks on Eskimo Sealing and the Harp Seal Controversy', published in the journal *Arctic*.

Foote, who had just completed an economic survey (1967b) of eastern Baffin Island, noted the distinction between commercial harp sealing and Inuit ringed sealing. Inuit hunting was year-round and focussed on adult animals. It was relatively humane (since harpoons and rifles were used), and it was food-directed. The sale of sealskins, in the case of Inuit, amounted to little more than the commoditization of a by-product, the money from which was reinvested in equipment to facilitate food harvesting. Foote (1967a: 268) proceeded to show how important the cash income from sealskins was to Inuit families and communities. He ended his observations by pointing out that the protest was victimizing Inuit.

While Inuit were struck hard by the 'Save the Seals' campaign, whitecoat sales were virtually unaffected and the overall sealskin market rebounded. Northern sales began recovery in late 1968, and the world market for sealskins soon passed earlier records. By 1969, Inuit were receiving a top price of near $8 for adult ringed seals. In early 1972, the $10 level was reached and by the end of the 1972–3 fur year, Clyde River Inuit were receiving an average price of $13.83 per pelt (Wenzel 1983b: 84).

Through the early 1970s, ringed seal prices hit new highs each year, and by 1976 the twenty-nine Inuit villages of the Northwest Territories reported 45,928 sealskins sold (Davis *et al.* 1980: 65), with another 18,000 animals being taken by the Inuit of Quebec–Labrador. At $23.65, the average N.W.T. price per skin (Jelliss 1978), this hunt provided a cash infusion of $1.5 million into Inuit villages in 1976 alone. Even more important than the money income, the 1976 seal harvest offered more than 1.5 million kilos of food to Inuit.

The drama of protest from 1976 to 1978 came, therefore, at a time when ringed seal hunting had become the chief food-producing activity of Inuit and their prime local source of money income. The price drop that followed the widely publicized activities of Brigitte Bardot, Greenpeace and the IFAW hit Inuit hard. From an average price of $23.65, ringed sealskins fell below four dollars and remained there through 1979. Northern scientists (see Wenzel 1978; Williamson 1978) again pointed out, as had Foote ten years earlier, that the economic impact of the protest was being felt not by Atlantic whitecoat sealers, but by Inuit subsistence hunters.

The economic situation brought on by protest events from 1976 to 1978 was worse than what Inuit had experienced in 1966-7. By the late 1970s, imported equipment had become integral in all types of subsistence activities. Nylon cord was used for fishing nets, high-powered rifles in all kinds of hunting, and the snowmobile had become a universal form of hunter transport.

By the mid-1970s, Inuit hunting required money. The capital value of an outfit – snowmobile, guns, canoe and motor – could reach $10,000, although, by sharing within the village and kin group, harvesters kept these costs considerably lower. Of more immediate consequence was the everyday expense for maintenance and operations. Hidden items like gasoline, ammunition and spare snowmobile parts might reach $2,500 a year or more (see Wenzel 1983b: 86; Usher and Wenzel 1988: 33). Inuit were meeting one-third of these costs from sealskins (Wenzel 1989), while the remainder came from limited exports of polar bear hides, ivory from walrus and narwhal, and short-term wage work on summer construction in the villages.

Under the full weight of the new protest, Inuit cash income from sealing dropped by nearly 85 per cent (see Wenzel 1983b). The immediate effect was a decline in all types of Inuit harvesting because the same equipment used for seal hunting was important to almost all wildlife harvesting. As a result, the overall quantity of country food normally available to Inuit communities also declined.

The situation was exacerbated by two other factors. First, the arctic environment limited most other game to a short summer season. Second, while ringed seals could be readily found close to Inuit communities, most other species, especially in winter, required long, costly journeys in which success was far less predictable. What the 1976-8 protest demonstrated was that the ringed seal was still the single most important resource for Inuit, still able to play its traditional role in the food supply, and able to provide critical amounts of what modern Inuit hunters needed materially – money.

The protest of this period differed from that of the late 1960s in another significant way. In 1966, the target was the whitecoat hunt off Newfoundland and in the Gulf. In 1976, for the first time the goal became the cessation of all sealing in Canada, including Inuit harvesting. Robert Hunter, the first president of Greenpeace Canada, records (1979: 368) that his successor, Paul Watson, was instrumental in adding a 'Native' dimension to the seal campaign. The motive to include Inuit appears to have grown from two directions.

The first was a basic and incontrovertible belief within the protest movement that commercial exploitation of seals was an anathema. That attitude was strengthened by new writings on animal rights (see Godlovitch, R. and S., and Harris 1971; Singer 1975). The other source

53

came from the periphery of deep ecology, where a new perception emerged of the relationship between aboriginal peoples and the environment. Watson (personal communication 1985), for example, initially saw Inuit as historical victims of Europe's mercantilism in North America, but by actively abetting this commerce by continuing to supply the modern fur trade they are maintaining their own colonial victimization (see also Watson and Rogers 1982). Others, like Peters (1971) and Martin (1978), variously lent support to this view. The long-term implications of this new perception of Inuit sealing would not be fully realized until the 1983 EEC boycott.

As in the 1960s, the economic depression brought on by the 'Save the Seals' protest was relatively short-lived in the North. By 1980, prices Inuit received for seal pelts had fully rebounded to the $20 level, and this, coupled with no more than desultory protests in southern Canada during 1979 and 1980, led to a general belief that the seal campaign had faded away (Lamson 1979; Busch 1985).

The protest had, in fact, moved into the court of Euro-politics (see Herscovici 1985; Malouf 1986g), and for Canadian Inuit this change of venue spelled disaster. As debate became more distant from the North, the Canadian government, in its defense of sealing, lost sight of the unique attributes of the Inuit seal harvest, its meaning for Inuit autonomy, self-determination and cultural history.

In the European forum, sealing was treated as a problem of dollars and cents benefits and costs. By this measure, Inuit sales income appeared trivial next to the profits of processors and furriers.

The argument Canada offered missed the essential features of Inuit sealing: that the money income earned in 1976 from the sale of 3,000 sealskins at Clyde River covered half the operating costs of all hunting done by Clyde's full-time hunters; that seals supplied 100,000 kg of meat with a replacement value of one million dollars in imported foodstuffs to that community's 450 residents; that Inuit subsistence hunting is part of an ideology that provides each Inuk with social support, relatedness, and individual cultural identity.

The Canadian government defended the general notion of sealing as a 'tradition', but failed to set forth the link between seal hunting and Inuit culture. In the European political arena, emotion about the seal issue was already high, and any value attached to sealing as Qallunaat tradition had already been dismissed during Britain's own seal debate (see Burton 1978; Nelson-Smith 1978; also Lister-Kaye 1979).

Opponents of sealing played widely upon these feelings. Numerous articles and notes in periodicals like Nature (Beardsley and Becker 1982) and New Scientist (see Holt and Lavigne 1982; New Scientist 1982a, b, c, d, 1983a, b) condemned Canadian scientific evidence. Advertisements were placed by French and British seal action committees in the popular press. Even children's literature was used, and in the case of Brigitte Bardot's Noonoah: Le Petit Phoque Blanc (1978) the human tormentors of seals bore a disturbing likeness to Inuit.

Other arguments, like the links between Inuit hunting and Inuit jurisdiction over wildlife and local economic control, were never vociferously made. Those speaking in support of sealing were members of government agencies silenced by political negotiations between Inuit and Canada over Nunavut, the proposed Inuit homeland in the Northwest Territories.

In the end, Inuit simply became lost in the far corner of a White European and Canadian picture. Their stake in foreign seal markets was sacrificed to government policy on Native rights at home. As for the protest, having adopted an agenda of total abolition, it was unwilling and unable to recognize that Inuit subsistence was a matter of cultural right, as well as need.

3 THE CULTURE OF SUBSISTENCE

Stereotypes

Hunting peoples hold an intense attraction for the scientific and popular cultures of Europe and North America. In the sciences, no discipline has been more influenced by hunter studies than anthropology. While sometimes considered a quaint holdover from anthropology's early years, the study of hunters and gathers has experienced a resurgence since the first 'Man the Hunter' conference was held in 1968 (see Lee and DeVore 1968). Since then, symposia have been held and scores of books published (Bicchieri 1972; Jochim 1981; Winterholder and Smith 1981; Ellen 1982; Leacock and Lee 1982; Riches 1982), as well as hundreds of scholarly articles written. This influence has been far-reaching. Modern studies of hunters have affected our ideas about human response to environmental stress and about the development of social institutions. It has also led us to reconsider our conception of the role of hunting in human evolution.

Hunters fascinate the general public of Europe and North America, as much as they do scientists, because of the contrast they present to our own norms, behavior and style of life. Such fascination with 'primitive' cultures is apparent in Roman dispatches about contacts with the Gauls and Picts, in Chinese accounts of their encounters with Malay aborigines, and in the tales of Arab and Portuguese traders about the pygmies or 'monkey-men' of the Congo forest. Old World interest in the Native Peoples of the Americas was already present when Christopher Columbus, Jacques Cartier and James Cook returned from their travels.

Today, as in earlier times, there is a contrast of values, with the 'primitives' embodying what is noble and, thus, defining the decadence of our own 'civilized' culture. The idealizing of Native American environmentalism early in the deep ecology movement is one modern example of this. This image has also been expressed in art, in popular literature from James Fenimore Cooper to Jean Auel, and more recently in cinema with *The Gods Must Be Crazy*, although sixty years ago Flarety's *Nanook of the North* proved that a 'Native' film could be a commercial success.

These popular perceptions about hunters can be generally described as positive, ascribing as they do materially uncomplicated, egalitarian and environmentally harmonious patterns to Inuit, Bushman, or American Indian cultures, all the antithesis of modern life. In contrast, Western culture appears as a downward spiral to environmental degradation and personal alienation.

On the other hand, while the traditional life of an Inuk or Cree hunter is intellectually appealing, the specifics of aboriginal life and culture are often viewed negatively. We, for instance, admire Inuit the skills that allow them to survive in the Arctic, but the practice of eating raw meat, a necessity in the North, is looked on with latent hostility. The reader is appalled at the prospect of an arctic winter without secure shelter and warmth, or the prospect of life in Amazonia without medicine or insect repellant. Because modern technology makes northern life tolerable for us, we perceive things like snow-mobiles, television, and government-supplied houses as proof that Inuit traditional culture has been uprooted. We do not imagine that modern Inuit adaptation may include accommodation to these technical changes.

Upon comparing contemporary Inuit life with our own and discovering that Inuit hunters have adopted our tools, we often conclude that Inuit no longer retain their cultural traditions. Our perceptions that Inuit, because of our past interventions, are no longer a traditional people removes any onus from further cultural intrusion into their lives.

Today, southern understanding of Inuit is built on that kind of ethnocentric 'understanding'. Absent from it is the recognition that traditional Inuit culture is more than dogteams and harpoons. We recognize that our own cultural traditions are founded on philosophical values, not cars and skyscrapers, yet we fail to make that leap in our appreciation of Inuit culture. Confined to what we can touch, it is not surprising that snowmobiles and rifles diminish Inuit tradition in our eyes. We fail to comprehend the way Inuit represent their culture to themselves because our attention is distracted by the artefacts and tools that we recognize as our own. Cross-cultural interpretation goes astray because we view Inuit and other aboriginal traditional culture as being exotic, but also 'simple'. The first, as a term of distinctness, is accurate, but the second, connoting as it does the impossibility of misinterpretation of these cultures, is false.

No aspect of aboriginal hunting cultures is treated so simplistically as the notion of subsistence. The term subsistence is often applied by anthropologists and the public to mean the material state of hunters' lives. So used, it does not explain very much. What the term actually describes are the cultural values that socially integrate the economic relations of hunting peoples into their daily lives.

In everyday parlance, subsistence is used in one of two ways by us. One way is in a minimalist, often pejorative, sense, suggesting that human life is sustained at the barest possible margin. Newspapers daily describe the urban homeless as living 'at the edge of subsistence'. They survive, but thank God we are not they. Thus, the homeless are set apart from those more fortunate.

In the second, more sophisticated usage, subsistence describes a process by which an organism satisfies all its own needs and consumes all that it produces itself. Among anthropologists and economists, a subsistence economy is often characterized as a self-contained system. In popular culture, this model of self-sufficiency is understood as an ideal state. There is, of course, some contradiction between subsistence as an ideal and subsistence as bare survival. This perception, on the part of science and popular culture, emphasizes material production, especially the production of food, for the producer's own use.

Inuit are always characterized as subsistence hunters, they are said to have a subsistence economy, and are seen as living a subsistence mode of existence. They have been treated as the model of the successful subsistence culture. In such expression, Inuit subsistence is limited to material production and idealized as self-contained.

This Euro-North American notion of self-sufficiency, coupled with the idealization of what constituted the core of Inuit traditional culture, entangled Inuit in the seal controversy and now threatens their access to all northern wildlife. Among seal protesters, at least since 1975 onward, Inuit traditional culture was equated with just such an idealized view of subsistence. This view connotes life as being in an ideal state, whose disruption is symbolized by rifles, houses and airplanes. Western semantic conceptions of what traditional and subsistence mean for Inuit forged the trap of the seal controversy.

To follow this argument, it is useful to explore one anthropologist's critical analysis of the burden placed on Inuit by our conceptions of traditional culture. According to Norman Chance (1984: 647), our usage of tradition, 'telescopes a long historical past ... and poses the future as a never-ending present'. Among the things lost in such a timeless perspective are the dynamics of intercultural relations.

The seal protesters, using this wrong-way telescope, have concluded that 'modernization' of Inuit by an intrusion of southern economic and technological forces has ended any semblance of their traditional culture. Since the present cannot meet the measure of the past, they argue that the future can only move forward from a starting point of televisions and snowmobiles.

The seal controversy brought Inuit face to face with the popular notion in Europe and North America that a subsistence lifestyle can only exist as a closed system. Inuit statements about seal hunting as part of their traditional subsistence met a counterargument that such hunting is so dependent on imported technology and so tied to the southern economy that it no longer meets the protest's criteria of what constitutes real subsistence. Or, as Tony Smith (1988: 67) has expressed this idea:

> The ancestors of native Canadians undoubtedly killed animals for fur. Our view of what constitutes native tradition, however, must be based on an understanding of how natives lived as they were coming under the influence and domination of Europeans.

Inuit have found that their subsistence practices and cultural tradition are being judged in an ahistorical way – in such a way that they no longer 'qualify', so it seems, to be subsistence hunters by the very fact that Inuit and Europeans once met.

Beginning in 1976 (Hunter 1979; 368), the protest hardened its stance on Inuit sealing, subjecting it to two criteria: first, that it be traditional, essentially meaning that it be timeless as to its tools and methods; and, second, that it be part of a closed system of production and consumption. A satisfactory passing of these 'tests' turns not on the cultural context that Inuit provide, but on the definitions given by the animal rights and deep ecology coalition. To Inuit, tradition and subsistence are their present reality, while to those opposed to sealing, they refer to an idealized Inuit way of life of five hundred years ago.

Reconfiguring Inuit subsistence

Those who hold an animal rights perspective on Inuit hunting have developed an airtight argument that rejects the legitimacy of contemporary Inuit sealing and, as well, any need to understand another culture in its own terms. By focussing on the tools Inuit use and the degree to which their economy is self-contained, the movement has been able to reach its present abolitionist position without having to weigh the cultural meaning of subsistence for Inuit. Limited to terms of reference already established by the outsider's own cultural perspective, the rejectionist argument is parsimonious and comprehensive.

That approach to the sealing issue is not limited to the animal rights movement. Inuit themselves employ special terms of reference in identifying subsistence as part of their cultural tradition. Inuit argue that even at the height of the sealskin trade in the 1970s, the seals they caught provided them with a valued and necessary source of food. If money were the primary motivation for this activity, the success of the European boycott would have ended all their investment and effort in seal hunting. The fact that they continue to hunt ringed seals is proof not of the material importance of the species to them, but of the relevance of *natsiq* to their cultural traditions.

The end of the commercial sealskin market should have revealed the subsistence importance of seal hunting for Inuit. As Steven Best, one of the architects of the protest strategy in Europe (1984, personal communication), has explained, if seal hunting were truly part of Inuit subsistence tradition, then the EC sealskin ban should have had no effect on their lives. The boycott directive, stating as it does that 'whereas hunting as traditionally practised by the Inuit people leaves seal pups unharmed and it is therefore appropriate to see that the interests of the Inuit people are not affected' (European Community 1983), does not prevent Inuit from harvesting seals for food, fuel, or clothing; it merely prevents selling sealskins. Therefore, as Best (1984) sees it, if Inuit are harmed by a commercial boycott, it must mean that they are no longer self-sufficient and the traditional link between subsistence and sealing has been broken.

Best reaches the same endpoint as Tony Smith: that seal hunting no longer possesses cultural validity in the context of a modernized

Canadian North. Like Smith, Best relies on the same ethnocentric and ahistorical premises, adopting Western rather than Inuit criteria for determining subsistence.

How do we break this stalemate? Are Inuit subsistence sealers, or are they not? Let us look at Inuit seal hunting in its present cultural context. From an Inuit perspective, what is Inuit tradition today? What part do seals play in it? What do we 'know' about Inuit subsistence culture?

Inuit maintain themselves through the accumulation of knowledge about the environment that they share with the wildlife they hunt. Weapons, ancient and modern, provide hunters with very little direct control over the environment. The animals move over large areas on a seasonal and even daily basis. They are rarely concentrated and they are difficult to predict. To succeed at exploiting such a mobile resource base, Inuit necessarily developed a detailed understanding of the ecology of each species.

The Inuit hunter is responsive to the environment and the animals around him, but he must also understand the needs and abilities of his community. Because arctic hunting demands so much energy and information, and because Inuit live in small groups, hunting is necessarily cooperative. Young men and women contributed the energy necessary to wait long hours in intense cold at breathing holes or to cut, match and sew the heavy skins used for clothing, while the middle-aged and elderly contributed the specialized skills and knowledge not yet possessed by the young. The traditional unit of production was structured to maintain that blend of strength and experience. The membership of communities and work groups was shaped in terms of the social relations among its members. Rather than the best hunters joining together, as we might expect or do ourselves, Inuit hunters operate according to established patterns of interpersonal contact.

Inuit subsistence has, therefore, its own social institutions, principles, and rules. For Inuit, the basis of secure, successful subsistence is the social relatedness of one person to another, rather than individual prowess or special equipment. And the only means of establishing these extended, long-lasting relations is through kinship. Social relatedness through kinship becomes a means of redressing the unpredictability of the environment. As a result, subsistence is more than a means of survival. It is a set of culturally established responsibilities, rights and obligations that affect every man, woman and child each day.

Finally, Inuit subsistence has its own ideology. It comes in part from the belief that many animals were human in times past (see Hutchinson 1977), but it also arises from the social relatedness of its daily practice. Inuit do not segregate the qualities enjoyed by human beings from those enjoyed by animals. Animals share with humans a common state of being that includes kinship and family relations, sentience, and intelligence. The rights and obligations that pertain among people extend to other members of the natural world. People, seals, polar bear, birds, and caribou are joined in a single community in which animals give men food and receive acknowledgment and revival.

In all subsistence societies, it is these social and ideological considerations (see Brody 1987; Lee 1979; Testart 1988), and their meaning, that are primary. For Inuit, the non-material component of life is central. Harvesting involves the relating of society to the environment. This cultural adaptation is integrated in its pattern and goals. All living things are part of one system of reciprocal rights and responsibilities. In this cultural system, harvesting is the point of articulation between hunter and animal, society and environment.

Langdon (1984: 3), in addressing Alaskan Native subsistence, notes that it is

> through capturing, processing, distributing, celebrating, and consuming naturally occurring fish and animal populations that subsistence societies define the nutritional, physical health, economic, social, cultural, and religious components of their way of life.

We can certainly conclude that without harvesting, there is no Inuit subsistence. But the question remains, does Inuit harvesting constitute subsistence? Not all of these aspects of Inuit life are apparent to outsiders when we try to compare contemporary harvesting with our construction of the past. We must probe deeper.

Analysing Inuit sealing

Anthropologists have come to recognize that subsistence is a culturally embedded system of shared relations – the adaptation of society to the environment. This coherent systemic approach to a culture of sub-sistence differs markedly from the popular attitudes discussed earlier, where subsistence is relegated to being fringe, marginal, or 'simple'.

Such a systems picture of subsistence calls for a more demanding analysis of Inuit seal harvesting. This makes sense when we recognize that Inuit ecological and socio-cultural processes are as complex as our own industrial culture. Because daily activities are so closely bound to the local ecosystem, subsistence involves a much more complex set of relations between people and the environment. We must, therefore, identify the points at which seals and Inuit intersect. In this way we can isolate our analytical problem into subsets.

The first set pertains to Inuit environmental relations: how hunting is done, the tools and skills it requires, and, especially, the knowledge that is brought to bear for successful subsistence. To appreciate the natural ecology of ringed seals will help to correlate other ecological variables which affect the dynamic between Inuit and *natsiq*. The deci-sion of Inuit to hunt seals is made day by day in the context of physical and biological constraints on both seals and men. The ecology of subsistence sealing affects all the socioeconomic actions of Inuit.

A second set of relationships belongs to the socioeconomy, those activities that entail the 'processing, distributing, celebrating, and consuming', as Langdon (1984: 3) puts it, in which seals figure prominently for Inuit. This is because sealing is a socially interactive process in which economic value is derived through sharing. Subsistence consists for Inuit, at this level, of economic operations which are socially valued because they always reinforce the known 'rules of the game'. For Inuit, as with most subsistence societies, these economic 'rules' mirror the rules of kinship by which all interpersonal relations are regulated. Economic life is thus embedded in everyday social life.

The overall economic goals of Inuit subsistence differs from our own. Marshall Sahlins (1968; see also Lonner 1983: 44) has pointed out that the objective of subsistence is neither individual self-sufficiency nor capital accumulation, but a continuous flow of goods and services. Not the least, this flow of products includes security, respect, and leisure for all its participants. This difference lies in the way the system of kinship positions Inuit economically and socially to one another, thus providing each person with a mantle of personal security. Each person knows that well-defined rights and obligations are attached to these social relations and that they are shared by all the other people in the community.

The overlaying of kinship relations on economic operations has important effects. First, it eases the problems of production that confront individuals in a natural environment of risk because decisions are socially reached and carried out. Risks and decisions are shared. As a consequence, economic output is also shared. The social unit is continually reinforced, and production remains a social activity.

Social relations, established and regulated through kinship, are a most powerful means for linking individuals and these bonds are seen in all phases of Inuit subsistence. They function in small projects like the planning and execution of a day's seal hunt by three men and they operate in the cooperation of many families to process and prepare the hundreds of kilograms of fish that are taken every day during the autumn arctic char migration. In these activities, participants are socially joined to one another, these kinship ties structure the activity, and the activity reinforces interpersonal bonds.

Beyond practical value, kinship contributes to Inuit survival through the sense of solidarity it produces. The socially mandated responsibilities that touch Inuit as individuals in the ecological and economic processes of subsistence are reciprocated through rights of access. Mutuality, as much as the particulars of the hunt, make subsistence a part of Inuit culture.

Men and seals are connected in an obvious practical way, but the ideology of mutual interdependence also frames a 'conceptual environment' (Sabo and Sabo 1985: 77) for Inuit relations. Inuit relate to animals not as dominators, managers, or even stewards of wildlife (Wenzel 1986d), but as co-residents who share the same conceptual ideology.

Inuit say, for instance, that animals live in families and that these families are ordered like human families with the same social values that guide Inuit. Just as Inuit share the products they harvest among themselves, so seals or caribou share themselves with Inuit. Inuit hunters reciprocate this generosity by sharing with others as animals have with them. Thus, if a hunter fails to be generous, he contravenes human values and is culturally sanctioned through loss of social access to the subsistence system. Animals, too, react to the ungenerous hunter by withholding themselves from them.

The subtleties of the co-equality of animals and men into a unified conception of subsistence can be appreciated in the conceptual terms of the Sabos. While we see the hunting, killing and consuming of animals as the basis of subsistence, for Inuit subsistence is the result of a positive reciprocity that occurs when animals and men fulfil their obligations to one another.

The next few chapters will analyse the three main subsystems - the ecological, socioeconomic, and ideological - that are seen here as forming the traditional Inuit subsistence system. We shall see that the traditional dynamics of subsistence are alive in Inuit communities today. As an example of the intensive role of sealing, we shall take the Baffin Island community of Clyde River. The 530 Inuit residents of Clyde will be examined for several reasons.

The first is that there seals play a dominating role in the lives of Clyde Inuit, but are also just one resource in the overall Clyde ecologic–economic system. Second, historical data are available on the ecology and economy of the Clyde Inuit from a wide range of competent sources (Baffin Regional Inuit Association 1982, 1983; Borre and Wenzel 1988; Finley and Miller 1980; Foote 1967b; Kemp 1976; Wenzel 1989) since 1966. Reports on Clyde harvesting and economic activities are complemented by a number of ethnological analyses (Borre 1986, 1989; Wenzel 1973; 1981, 1984b, 1986a, c; Wenzel and Stairs in press, Worl 1986) of Clyde sealing within the wider framework of Inuit culture. Together, the thirty-five years of information on Clyde covered by these sources provide a comprehensive baseline available for few other Canadian arctic communities.

4 CLYDE INUIT AND SEALS: ECOLOGICAL RELATIONS

Ice and seals

The waters and ice along Baffin Island's northern and eastern coast form one of the world's ideal areas for ringed seals. From Cumberland Sound to Pond Inlet, the interface of land and sea is demarcated by steep-walled fiords that cut westward into the interior of the island (Figure 4.1). The heads of many of these fiords are 100 km from Baffin Bay. Almost exactly in the centre of this coast sits the village of Clyde River (70°27′N, 68°36′W).

While the region appears to be inhospitable and forbidding for mariners, its jumbled face of bays, fiords and islands is precisely why ringed seals, *Phoca hispida*, are present in such large numbers year-round. This seal, more than any other phocid species, is an ice-lover. In order to breed and survive, it requires the extensive and stable presence of land-anchored winter ice, called fast ice (see McLaren 1958a, b; Smith 1973a). The fact that such extensive ice cover is present makes *natsiq* the most sedentary of seals – an advantage for Inuit.

All along northeast Baffin Island, the glacier-carved fiords provide a multitude of protected points from which fast ice of the long winter can grow. Between late September and the middle of October, a skin of new ice begins to form in these fiords. It expands throughout the winter so that by March it covers not only the whole of Baffin Bay's littoral zone but also extends scores of kilometres into the open ocean. It only begins to deteriorate with the warming temperatures of May and often remains stable within the bays and fiords of the Clyde region until July and even August.

This platform of fast ice is a critical environment for ringed seals. It is central to their population density and distribution and to their reproductive ecology. Without landfast ice, *natsiq* could not survive year-round along Baffin's shores. From freeze-up in early autumn until break-up in late summer, the ice provides ringed seals with protection from cold, storm, and predators and, in the snow which accumulates on its surface, a place to rear their pups.

When sea ice first forms (a stage called *sikkuak*), it is thin (2–4 cm), greenish, and, because of its high salinity, slushy and elastic. At this time, ringed seals scratch the small openings that will be their lifelines to air when the ice grows a metre thick. These breathing holes

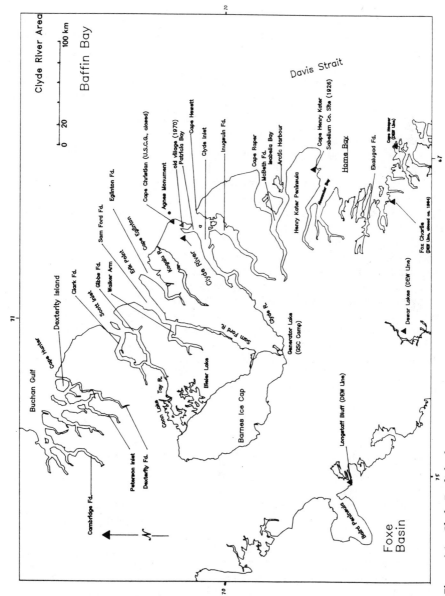

Figure 4.1 *Clyde English place names*

(Inuktitut: *aglu*, singular; *agluliit*, plural) will remain the only points of contact for the seal with the surface until the warmth of May. The *agluliit* are maintained by seals scratching at the ice from below and, by late winter are bell-shaped in cross-section, with a diameter of nearly one-half metre so that a seal may enter to breathe.

From atop the ice, *agluliit* look like small domes, perhaps 10–20 cm in height. The dome is caused by the seal's frozen exhalations and the sea water that each entry into the *aglu* forces out the opening. The ability of ringed seals to construct *agluliit* allows them to avoid the worst of the arctic winter and affords them a measure of protection from polar bears and Inuit, their two most important predators.

Like all pinnipeds, *natsiq* give birth to their young out of the sea. In spring, beginning in April and continuing into May, pregnant females haul out on to the ice in areas where snow has accumulated in the lee of upthrust ice. From *agluliit* that open under these snow banks, the females excavate *natsiarsiit* (see Smith and Stirling 1975), or birth lairs, where they pup. The dens provide pups with insulation from the still low temperatures of spring (−20°C) and, to a lesser degree, from polar bears, arctic fox, and, sometimes, Inuit. Landfast ice, with its pressure wedges and snow accumulations suitable for pupping dens, is critical for ringed seal survival.

The influence of a long, stable ice season on *natsiq* cannot be overestimated. Using McLaren's calculations of ice area to seal density formula (1958b: 28–9), we can estimate that the population found along the northeast Baffin coast is fully 130,000 animals. While the northeast coast measures only 800 km on a direct line, the actual shoreline, because of its many bays, islands and fiords, is four times this length. The stable fast ice found in fiords carries a density of seals as high as nine animals per km^2 and, as distance from land and ice instability increases, ringed seal density declines, until more than 16 km from land it is only one seal per km^2 (ibid.; Smith 1973a: 30).

The importance of seals at Clyde River

Clyde River, or *Kangirtuappik*, is situated in the middle of this rich seal habitat. Today, 535 Inuit, plus fifteen *Qallunaat*, live adjacent to Clyde's original Hudson's Bay Company site. Forty years ago (Wenzel 1984b), when the government began its relocation program, there were, perhaps, 175 Inuit living in five or six winter villages (Figure 4.2), between Buchan Gulf and Home Bay. Only a dozen Inuit, all HBC employees and their families, then lived at the Clyde post.

The Inuit of Clyde (Figure 4.3) are as intensively involved in seal hunting today as they were in 1821 when Europeans first recorded meeting the area's Natives. On 6 September 1820, a British navy party commanded by William Parry (1821: 276) contacted and traded with a small Inuit band living at the mouth of Patricia Bay, less than 20 km southeast of modern Clyde River. Parry noted the variety of uses these

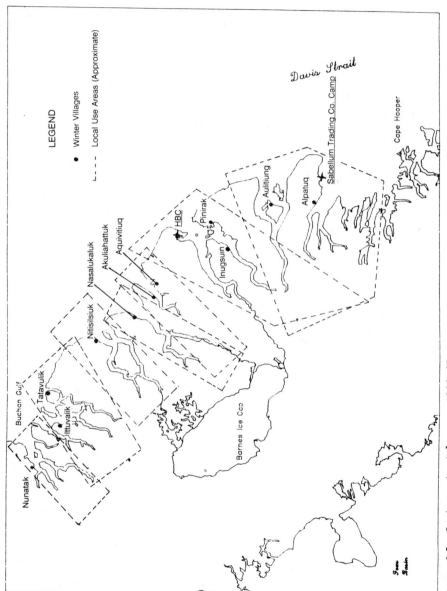

Figure 4.2 *Socio-territorial areas, 1920–45*

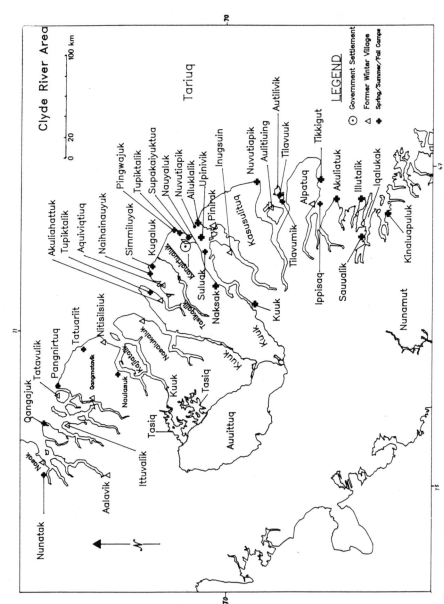

Figure 4.3 *Clyde Inuktitut place names*

Inuit made of seal products. Skins were manufactured into clothing and footwear, *qajaq* covers, tents, sled lashings, and dog whips and harnesses, while seal oil was used for cooking. Seal was presumably a main source of food as well.

During his one-day visit, Parry did not observe an actual seal hunt, but in 1888 Franz Boas entered the southern edge of the Clyde Inuit area and has left a detailed description of ringed seal hunting. Noting that the distribution and density of this phocid directly influenced the settlement pattern of Inuit north of Cumberland Sound, he (Boas 1888: 460-1) was the first to identify the ecological link between Inuit, ringed seals, and sea ice.

After Boas, further data about the early importance of seals are reported by the Hudson's Bay Company. Diary and account books from the post at Clyde and other Eastern Arctic communities make it clear that, while ringed seals were essential for Inuit survival, arctic fox pelts and walrus ivory were the objects of European commerce and that the HBC accepted sealskins only when fox was scarce. These same logs make it abundantly clear that Clyde Inuit concentrated first on seal hunting, rather than fox trapping.

While seals were critical for Inuit survival, they apparently did not figure in the area's early commerce. The trade record for the period 1935-45 (Clyde HBC Fur Purchase summaries (in possession of the author)) notes that only 6,004 fox pelts were received at Clyde and acerbic mention is made of the neglect by Inuit of trapping, reflecting a non-Inuit perspective found in Company diaries from other regions (see Goldring 1986; Damas 1988).

In this same period, the Royal Canadian Mounted Police, who annually patrolled the whole of the Clyde coast from stations at Pond Inlet and Pangnirtung, note the abundance of food, especially seal, in Clyde Inuit camps. Clyde Inuit were so wedded to sealing that, in order to improve trap returns, the HBC, between 1925 and the late 1930s, imported experienced fox trappers to the Clyde area from Cumberland Sound, Cape Dorset, and Lake Harbour.

After 1945, the market for fox fur collapsed. It might be expected that this event would also have affected sealing, since guns and ammunition could only be obtained by trading fox. Despite the loss of this trade item, however, both RCMP reports and personal Inuit accounts from the 1950s note that food remained plentiful, even though these trade goods were in very short supply.

Subsistence success, despite this scarcity of imported tools in the area can be traced to two factors. First, through the 1950s more than 60 per cent of the Clyde regional population (Wenzel 1984b) remained dispersed in indigenous villages centered on important seal hunting areas. Second, the main tools used in sealing – the breathing hole harpoon and dogteam – remained highly effective and efficient. It was not until resettlement was complete that the kinds of ecological, socio-cultural, and economic pressures associated with modern village life exerted pressure for technological replacement. Therefore, the people of

Clyde, like most others on northern Baffin Island, felt some, but by no means drastic, consequences from the loss of the fox market.

The development of a tanning process that made ringed sealskins acceptable to Europeans had the same economic impact at Clyde as Foote (1967a) notes for other parts of the Canadian Arctic. For the first time since 1945, Inuit had a commodity sought by outsiders. Moreover, unlike fox trapping, the hunting of ringed seal did not require effort in an activity separate from customary subsistence pursuits. From 1962 until the EC sealskin boycott, natsiq, for Inuit, meant not only the food security they had known for centuries, but also a new means of economic access to imported goods.

The new importance of sealskins (qlissik) for trade is evident from Clyde HBC customer records beginning in 1962. In 1961, the Company obtained furs valued at $8,276 from the purchase of 600 white fox pelts, 245 ringed sealskins, 39 ermine, plus some polar bear hides and walrus and narwhal tusks. From 1963 to 1967, however, Clyde fur receipts averaged $21,320 a year, with arctic fox contributing only 1,044 pelts over these five years versus sealskins numbering 8,219. Quite clearly, natsiq displaced fox in the Clyde Inuit economic transactions with Euro-Canadians after 1961-2.

The role of sealskins in the cash economy of the Clyde Inuit continued to increase through the 1960s and 1970s, despite four years (1966-7, 1977-8) of depressed prices brought about by a growing opposition to the hunting of harp seals, especially pups, along the east coast of Canada. Analysis suggests (see Figure 4.4) that the rising cash flow to Clyde Inuit at this time can be attributed to higher prices for sealskins rather than to an increase in the natsiq harvest. From 1966 to 1976, the price paid for qlissik at Clyde roughly trebled from about $6.00 per pelt to $18.00, while the volume of sealskin sales increased only 19 per cent. During this period, the Clyde harvest rose one-fifth, from 2,900 to 3,500 seals, roughly parallel with sealskin sales, but the village population also increased 20 per cent.

We can infer that Inuit at Clyde River were content to maintain a stable flow of skins, and that the increase price paid for sealskins did not stimulate a 'money hunt'. This conclusion is supported by overall community harvest data (the total number of seals known to have been killed and retrieved) which, until 1975, show that the volume of sealskins sold was fully 25 per cent less than the overall Inuit harvest.

After 1976, the harvest and sale of sealskins at Clyde River undergo dramatic change (Figures 4.5 and 4.6). For a brief time, Clyde harvests and sales run together, following a 1974-5 price upsurge. After 1978, sealskin sales drop in response to the 1976-8 seal protest and then the EC sealskin boycott. At the same time, the number of seals harvested fell back to the level of the early 1970s, or some 2,000 animals yearly.

A further factor contributing to the rise and fall of the sales and harvest of seals, and particularly the coincidence of the total Clyde seal harvest with skin sales in the mid-1970s, relates to Inuit access to polar bears and the price received for their hide. Polar bears during the

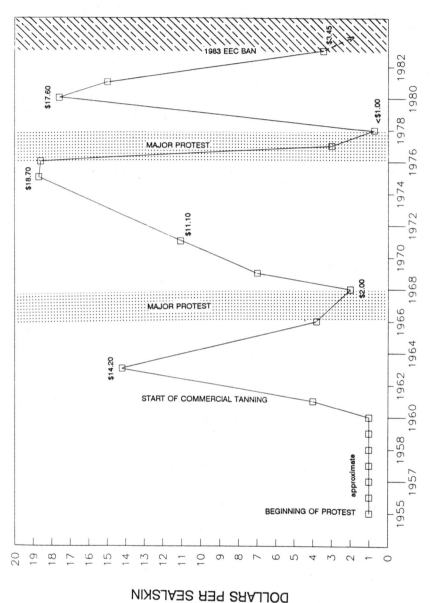

Figure 4.4 *Sealskin process, 1955–83 (Clyde River)*

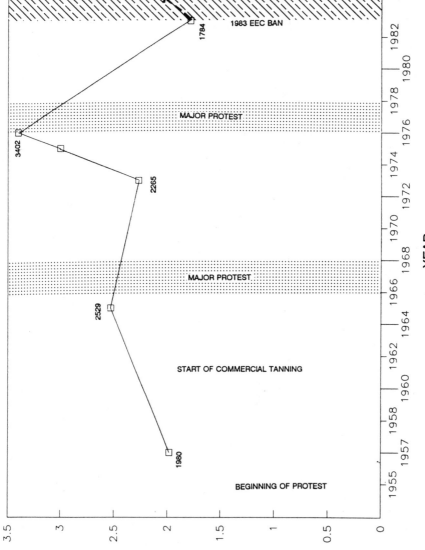

Figure 4.5 *Ringed seal harvest, 1955–83 (Clyde River)*

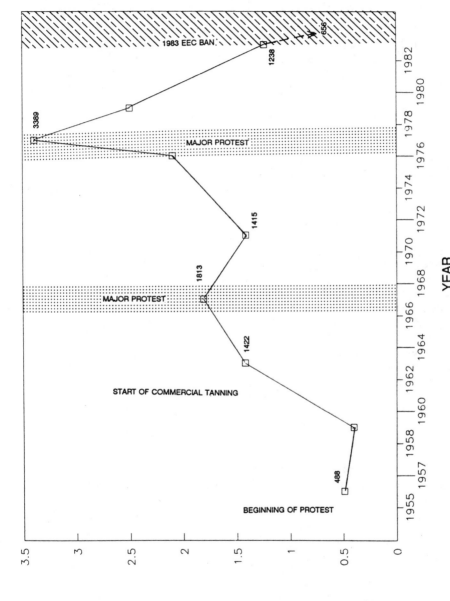

Figure 4.6 *Sealskin trade volume, 1955–83 (Clyde River)*

early 1970s provided an important cash supplement for meeting the cost of equipment needed for hunting.

When Canada signed the International Polar Bear Convention (see Lentfer 1969), a system of local quotas was established for Canadian Inuit. At Clyde, this quota was placed at forty-five bears. During the early part of the decade, the number of Clyde hunters coincided almost exactly with this quota (as important, prices for bear hides (see Wenzel 1983b: 84) were strong, averaging $987 in 1973–4). The mid-1970s, however, saw polar bear hunting at Clyde affected in two important ways.

The first was that the price for bear declined by half (see Smith and Jonkel 1975a,b; Smith and Stirling 1975; Smith 1977, 1978) to less than $500. Thus, Inuit turned heavily to ringed seal harvesting to make up the difference in cash resources previously provided by bears. Second, by 1975 the number of hunters eligible to harvest polar bears had swelled beyond the available quota. Thus, an increasing number of Inuit could no longer rely on a polar bear sale to provide extra cash and therefore increased their seal harvesting effort to make up this shortfall in income.

The decline in sealskin sales after 1978 correlates with the pressure exerted by the anti-sealing protest on the world sealskin market. As already noted, Clyde sealskin sales and revenues began to drop in the wake of the 1976–8 round of seal protests and, despite a brief rally in sealskin prices, revenues fell further with the Common Market decision to close its markets.

Sales of sealskins had halted, but what happened to Inuit harvesting. At Clyde the harvest fell by half from the high reached in 1979, then stabilized in 1984. From this we can draw two conclusions. First, the anti-sealing forces were mistaken in assuming that Inuit harvesting was entirely a response to outside demand. Second, the most substantial portion of the Clyde harvest was motivated solely by subsistence need.

This brief overview reflects the ways ringed seals have materially contributed to Clyde Inuit subsistence since the nineteenth century. We must now look at the specific manner in which *natsiq* and Inuit interact in the day-to-day ecological operations of the contemporary community.

The ecology of Clyde seal hunting

A. The ecosystem and harvesting

Of all the activities carried out by Inuit in the Clyde area, seal hunting is the most common. *Natsiq*, unlike other marine mammals, are present and active year-round and, unlike caribou, the major terrestrial resource and second most important food species at Clyde, are always close to the community.

The all-year cycle of sealing is critical because the region suffers severe constraints on most other resources. Clyde does not share the rich variety of summer migratory resources enjoyed by Inuit living elsewhere. Neither the large herds of caribou found in the Keewatin, the millions of geese and ducks that fly over James Bay, nor the pods of whales that concentrate around Pangnirtung and Pond Inlet are found in numbers at Clyde. For these reasons every day at Clyde River is a day for seal hunting.

Despite the routine of seal hunting at Clyde, each hunt still develops through a coincidence of unique ecological and cultural elements. Local conditions of ice and water, wind, temperature, and cloud cover affect seal hunting. Under such variable conditions, success depends on the availability of equipment, the composition of hunting groups, and, above all, the pool of knowledge that hunters have developed about the environment and seals. We can conjure up an image of Inuit patiently waiting for a daily 'allotment' of seals, but we can hardly imagine the rigors and complexity of this 'routine' task.

To be a good seal hunter at Clyde involves a commitment of human effort, endurance, and patience that seems excessive. *Natsiq* are always around, they seem to be everywhere, and tomorrow is another day, but the daily environmental uncertainties of the arctic force Clyde Inuit to hunt frequently and carefully. In winter, weeks may pass with men unable to hunt because of intense wind chill and blinding white-outs. In summer, fog or high seas often keep Inuit from the seals.

Boas recognized sealing as a patterning force in Inuit life. During his year's sojourn on Baffin Island, he correctly associated the distribution of Inuit winter settlements with their proximity to ice suitable for *natsiq* breathing holes.

> [The] sealing on rough ice during the winter is very difficult and unsuc-cessful, as it is hard to find the breathing holes and traveling is very laborious. It is only in the northern parts of Home Bay and in the large fjords that smooth ice is formed. The settlements of the natives are manifestly distributed in accordance with these facts ... Generally speaking, two condi-tions are required for winter settlements, viz, the existence of an extensive floe and smooth ice. (Boas 1888: 460-1)

Boas's century-old description of this relationship is still accurate. Because Inuit now live in government villages like Clyde River, they often find themselves in locations which were chosen not for their environmental and geographic proximity to game, but because a trading post, mission station, or deep anchorage provided *Qallunaat* with a link to the South. Clyde River is where it is because of the Hudson's Bay Company's need for a safe anchorage. From an Inuit perspective, however, the siting of modern Clyde means that, except for seals, hunters must travel long distances to find game that was once close to their homes.

To appreciate the ecological knowledge and skill required for successful hunting, we need to identify the variability of the 'normal' Clyde environment that hunters must recognize before they set out.

Table 4.1 Correlation of physical and biological conditions in the Clyde environment

	Jan	Feb	Mar	Apr	May	Jun	Jul	Aug	Sep	Oct	Nov	Dec
temperature	-23.3°C or less		-17.8°C or above			0.0°C or above			-17.8°C	-23.2°C or less		
daylight	no light	daylight increasing			total daylight			decreasing daylight				no light
snow		present					absent			present		
sea ice		uniform			melting	break-up		open water		freeze-up		uniform
lake ice		present					unsafe or absent			present		
caribou	winter range			spring migration			summer range		fall migration			inland
ringed seal		breathing holes		ice surface and dens				open water		breathing holes		
bearded seal						open water and ice surface						
polar bear	dens and sea ice			/ all bears on ice			coast and open water		dens and sea ice			
narwhal					north migration-leads			south migration-inshore				
fox		inland and sea ice					coast and inland			inland and sea ice		
arctic char		lakes and rivers			spring run		sea	fall run		lakes and rivers		
small game				ptarmigan and arctic hare								
migratory birds						geese, ducks, and sea birds						

The effects of weather on men and animals, the availability of daylight, and the translucence of the sea ice must be weighed. Any of these can alter the chance of a successful hunt and all must be included in the environmental 'cost–benefit' decisions that permeate Inuit hunting (see Table 4.1 for an environmental summary; also Tables 4.5 and 4.6).

From their accumulated knowledge of these environmental subsystems, Clyde hunters make primary decisions about when and where to harvest. At the most general level of consideration for hunters is the seasonal nature of the resources; many species are often too scattered or randomly distributed, if they are present at all, to be pursued intensively. At the next level are tactical considerations: how will the day's environmental peculiarities, like wind chill or snow compactness, influence hunting? Finally, factors like the distance that must be travelled to find a species and the return that can be expected relative to the effort that must be invested must be considered. Each hunt involves an elaborate calculation by hunters of yields and how alternately to deploy their time, energy, and material resources.

When we think of Inuit harvesting in this way, it is not surprising that ringed seals loom so large. They are present year-round in large numbers, they inhabit an ecotone that is generally readily accessible to Clyde hunters, and they provide a considerable return per unit of effort. For Inuit at Clyde, *natsiq* are a basal resource. The security of sealing allows the possibility of pursuing less reliable species when the opportunity arises.

B. Sealing in the Clyde harvesting system

This is, in fact, what Boas and other observers, including Inuit, note about sealing past and present. The all-seasons availability of ringed seals establishes ecological stability for pursuit of 'venture' resources that are more seasonal, less numerous, or less accessible than *natsiq*.

The importance of ringed seals becomes evident when we group resource choices by season (see Table 4.2). The seasonal patterns reflect Clyde subsistence decision-making and priorities under normal conditions of the physical environment, biological resources, and the ratio of human effort to return.

These groupings also reveal that despite the array of species, fifteen, used during a year, Clyde hunters concentrate their attention and effort on certain species. Within the breadth of the Clyde resource system, three distinct levels can be distinguished. We can identify prime species (*natsiq* in winter, char and narwhal in summer), secondary or venture species (caribou other than in autumn), and opportunity species, such as sea birds and hare. The spatial allocation of hunting effort toward a narrow set of target species reflects the constraints of the East Baffin Island environment at certain times of the year (Figures 4.7 and 4.8) and demonstrates the adaptive efficiency and flexibility of Inuit subsistence. Hunters recognize the ecological constraints, and

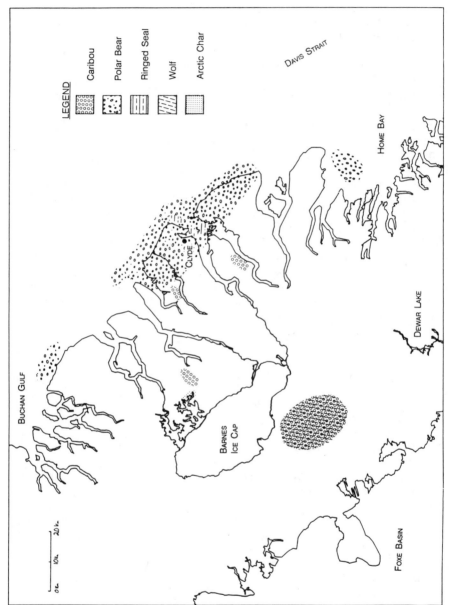

Figure 4.7 *Clyde winter activity areas, 1970-89*

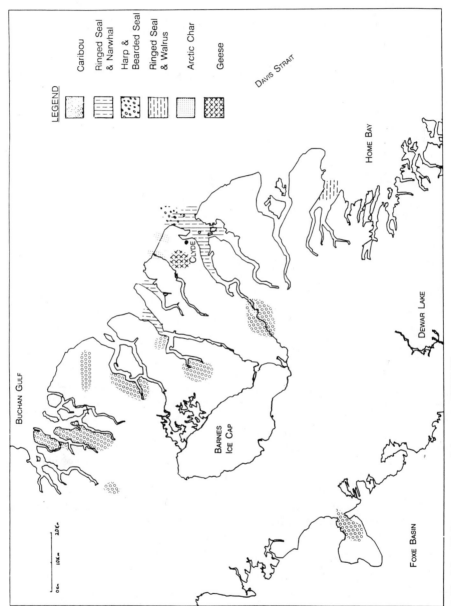

LEGEND

Caribou	
Ringed Seal & Narwhal	
Harp & Bearded Seal	
Ringed Seal & Walrus	
Arctic Char	
Geese	

BUCHAN GULF

BARNES ICE CAP

CLYDE

HOME BAY

DAVIS STRAIT

DEWAR LAKE

FOXE BASIN

0 10km 20km

Table 4.8 *Clyde summer activity areas, 1970-89*

Table 4.2 *Estimated Clyde River harvest, 1979**

	Winter	Spring	Summer	Autumn	Total
A. Sea mammals					
ringed seal	1,535	1,555	1,182	461	4,733
bearded seal	—	1	—	4	5
white whale	—	—	—	—	—
narwhal	—	1		4	5
harp seal	1	—	1	2	4
walrus	—	—	—	—	—
polar bear	18	—	—	3	21
B. Land mammals					
caribou	471	358	99	64	992
wolf	14	—	—	1	15
arctic fox	234	54		2	289
arctic hare	31	49	69	19	169
C. Fish					
arctic char	593	774	754	746	2,867
sculpin	n.d.	n.d.	n.d.	n.d.	n.d.
D. Birds					
ptarmigan	442	57	2	29	550
ducks	45	6	26	84	161
geese	—	14	5	4	23
guillemot	1	—	—	4	5

* estimated on 78% hunter reportage of actual harvesting.

Source: Finley and Miller 1980.

they take strategic decisions according to environmental conditions.

From our analysis of Clyde harvesting patterns, we can make three generalizations. First, we see that the potential spectrum of wildlife resources generally available in a given season is greater than would be apparent from the activities actually occurring. Second, Inuit, in their procurement practices, emphasize species that are geographically at hand, available in large numbers and that are in denser concentrations. Third, Inuit concentrate their subsistence efforts on those species that maximize biological return for hunting effort invested. On this basis, it may be said that not all harvestable species are equally attractive and no species is as attractive as ringed seal.

A more important measure of the significance of seals to Inuit living in the East Baffin environment is the amount of food they harvest and the proportion of this food that *natsiq* represents. We can calculate the average edible weight (EW) of the two species, ringed seal and caribou, most frequently captured by Clyde Inuit as being 23 kg and 45 kg, or one-half and two-thirds of each species respective live weight (LW) (Foote 1967b: 146). Examining harvest data collected by Finley and Miller (1980: 10) at Clyde in 1979, ringed seals provide 109,000 edible

Table 4.3 *Clyde Inuit diet by season, 1979[1]*

	Winter	Spring	Summer	Autumn	Total
A. *Marine mammal*					
a) ringed seal	35,305	35,765	27,686	10,603	109,359
b) all other A	2,533	145	49	1,063	7,012
c) total a + b	37,838	35,910	27,735	11,663	116,371
d) A as % of total E.W.					69.0
B. *Land mammals*					
a) caribou	21,195	16,110	4,455	2,880	44,640
b) all other B[2]	23	37	52	127	239
c) B as % of total E.W.					26.0
C. *Fish*					
a) all C species[3]	1,483	1,935	1,885	1,875	7,168
b) C as % of total E.W.					4.0
D. *Birds*					
a) all D species	332	122	37	115	606
b) D as a % of total E.W.					<1.0
E.					
a) ringed seal as % of sea mammal E.W.					94.0
b) ringed seal as % of total E.W. (A + B + C + D)					65.0
c) ringed seal as % of seasonal E.W. - winter					58.0
- spring					66.0
- summer					81.0
- autumn					64.0

[1] all weights in kg.
[2] only arctic hare; canids not eaten.
[3] includes only arctic char.

kilograms and caribou only 44,650 (see Table 4.3 for a complete breakdown of these data).

How much do *natsiq* contribute to the Clyde diet seasonally? This information can be derived by applying an average edible weight (as per Foote 1967b) to each species recorded in Finley and Miller's harvest census (see Table 4.3). In this manner, a more detailed perspective is obtained about the environmental importance of ringed seals for Clyde Inuit.

In this matter, the data in Tables 4.2 and 4.3 suggest several important things. The first is that ringed seal is clearly a dominant item in the Clyde food system, providing nearly two-thirds of the meat hunted annually. The other is that our model of Inuit hunting in which winter seal supplements summer windfalls of caribou and fish does not apply at Clyde River.

With the 1979 harvest survey providing a pre-seal boycott baseline, we can compare Clyde harvest information for the three years 1981-3 (see Table 4.4) that bracket the European decision on sealing. Ringed seals remain far and away the most important food species,

Table 4.4 *Clyde harvest by edible weight per species, 1981–1983*

	1981				1982				1983			
	Win	Sp	Su	Fall	Win	Sp	Su	Fall	Win	Sp	Su	Fall
Marine mammals												
Ringed seal	24,196	30,291	16,031	7,176	18,678	21,781	12,512	4,692	21,436	15,847	17,549	6,762
Bearded seal	272	340	2,108	1,020	204	408	340	136	136	204	884	680
Harp seal	74	222	407	222	111	—	37	148	—	—	444	37
Hooded seal	—	—	70	—	—	—	—	—	—	250	1,000	—
Walrus	—	—	500	—	—	—	—	—	—	77	—	—
Beluga	—	—	308	—	—	—	—	—	—	—	—	—
Narwhal	—	144	1,848	231	1,518	—	308	539	—	—	2,618	539
Polar bear	3,174	1,518	—	—	—	1,518	—	138	3,726	2,346	—	—
Land mammals												
Caribou	11,745	6,930	4,905	1,260	17,595	11,475	4,815	675	12,195	10,935	6,300	135
Arctic hare	30	107	14	30	28	211	19	22	30	84	9	104
Arctic fox**	—	—	—	—	—	—	—	—	—	—	—	—
Wolf**	—	—	—	—	—	—	—	—	—	—	—	—
Fish												
Arctic char	1,288	1,880	2,383	858	6,670	1,903	7,275	710	4,560	3,348	10,808	2,107
Sculpin	ND	ND	ND	ND	—	—	298	1,507	ND	ND	ND	ND
Birds												
Ducks	34	20	78	86	65	61	32	289	127	18	85	289
Geese	—	4	2	—	—	78	126	6	—	46	104	6
Sea birds	—	—	4	1	1	—	—	2	—	—	2	6
Ptarmigan	40	61	4	10	224	50	7	54	127	52	10	26

* Seasonal total harvest presented in kilograms of edible weight

** Wolf and fox are not used for food at Clyde River, but are harvested only for fur.

Source: 1981 – Wenzel Clyde River field data; 1982, 1983 – Baffin Regional Inuit Association unpublished reports.

consistently forming over 95 per cent of the winter harvest of sea mammals, and more than half (54 per cent) of the edible biomass entering Clyde River during these thirty-six months. The importance of *natsiq* increases during the spring and autumn (59 and 64.5 per cent respectively). Only in summer does seal's share in the diet fall to only half (49.3 per cent) the available edible harvest.

There is also some evidence that migratory resources are less reliable than is generally assumed. Finley and Miller show that fish and other marine mammals provided less than 6 per cent of the summer harvest, compared with 38 per cent in 1981 to 1983. Under these circumstances, ringed seal reasserts its presence in the harvest record. These data also point out that *natsiq* is a 'reserve' when other prey are scarce.

The summer–autumn harvest of caribou appears remarkably consistent, while winter caribou hunting at Clyde stands out as being much more important than is expected from general accounts of Inuit harvesting. Last, the contribution of birds and small mammals to the Clyde diet is negligible in all seasons.

In summary, in the procurement strategies of Inuit in the Clyde region, ringed seal figure prominently in all seasons. These strategies appear to reflect *natsiq*'s year-round presence in the hunting environment of East Baffin Island. Through their wide availability and large numbers, *P. hispida* provides a stable base that underpins the whole of the Clyde subsistence system.

The ecological security of *natsiq* allows hunters to expend effort and resources in 'venture' harvesting which is qualitatively valued, but far less predictable than seal hunting. Winter caribou hunting, for example, requires substantial investment by hunters and leaves families exposed if unsuccessful. It can be undertaken only because of seal hunting. Overall, we see that Clyde Inuit hunting remains closely linked to objective of food security.

A seasonal ethnography of sealing

The interaction between hunters and seals in the natural environment is what determines the material success or failure of Inuit subsistence as an individual and societal adaptation. The problems and constraints that surround hunting are the texture that animates much of Clyde Inuit life.

Environmental circumstances change from one trip to another and this unpredictability defines the nature of arctic hunting. In many cases, these changes, like the shifting of a hunter's shadow over an *aglu* as the sun moves, are nothing but small details that are adjusted to in the course of a day. However, to non-Inuit, such details often pass completely unnoticed. Of more consequence is the seasonal variability hunters experience. The patience, endurance, and knowledge *Qallunaat* associate with Inuit winter *agluliit* sealing are no less necessary in spring, summer, or autumn sealing.

A. Winter seal hunting

The *aglu*, or breathing hole, method of hunting seals in winter used at Clyde River today confirms to Boas's (1888: 475–7) classic description of 100 years ago in *The Central Eskimo* of breathing-hole hunting. Termed *mauluktuk* hunting by Clyde Inuit, it is also accurately referred to as 'the waiting method' because of the many hours hunters spend at an *aglu*. This is still the technique used in 99 per cent of all Clyde sealing that takes place between freeze-up and May. Until the long warm days of May and while, as will be described, Inuit sealing technology has undergone some change, this basic method of hunting is constant.

Mauluktuk sealing commences once the new ice of autumn has stabilized and seals have begun to excavate the *agluliit* that will be their lifelines to the surface through the winter. When this young ice (*sikkuak*) is 10 cm thick – enough to support a snowmobile – Clyde hunters travel out on to the ice in search of tell-take signs of new *agluliit*. Because the ice is fresh, it is fairly flat, so the hunters watch for the slush that is deposited on the surface as seals open these holes. For the first few weeks after freeze-up, these holes are usually unhuntable because the ice is swept clear of snow by the wind and its translucence allows rising seals to see hunters from below. Instead, each newly identified *aglu* is marked just after freeze-up with snow blocks so that they can be located later (see Wenzel 1973).

From the middle of November through February, the period when daylight is briefest, seal hunting activities at Clyde most resemble Boas's description. Men rise long before the appearance of day at 11 a.m. to prepare for the day. Their first action is to check the velocity and direction of the wind. Wind velocity is the factor that makes conditions 'too cold' for Clyde hunters. It also causes loose surface snow to begin moving, making it difficult to locate *agluliit*. Direction is important because if it comes from the west and the land, there is a high probability of a white-out or *piksuktuk* developing, a situation that is always uncomfortable and often life-threatening.

With good weather, the hunter checks and fuels his snowmobile, loads his *qamutiik* (sled), and heads for the ice before it is light. Here we note the greatest contrast with Boas's (1888: 475) sealing narrative. The disappearance of the dogteam deprives us of one of our most romantic conceptions of Inuit hunting.

Dogteams were, in fact, efficient, but distinctly unromantic. From 1971 through 1973, I observed the use of dogteams in seal hunting at Aqviqtiuq, then a small village of twenty-four people and 140 dogs on Eglinton Fiord, 75 km north of Clyde River. Dogs were allowed to run free so they could protect themselves from polar bear attack. Preparatory to travel or hunting, the women of the village had first to capture the dogs that belonged to each team, then place them in harness and secure them to the sled, all the time preventing surly dogs from fighting. The preparation of four dogteams totalling sixty animals, the average number used by the Aqviqtiumiut in seal hunting, took six women roughly one hour of moderately difficult work. The women then helped the men load and secure their equipment on each *qamutiik* before beginning their domestic activities.

Preparations for a seal hunt now take between fifteen and thirty minutes. The spark plugs on a snowmobile may have to be replaced or the carburetor thawed. The sled used at Clyde today is essentially identical to that used with dogteams, about 6.5 m in length, weighing approximately 50 kg, and able to easily a load of 500 kg with ease.

The other equipment for sealing is little changed. A sealskin laid over the sled rungs to prevent snow from soaking the load from below, a wooden box containing a pressure stove, matches, tea kettle, cups, sugar and bannock, a snowknife, spare spark plugs and extra ammunition, and, finally, a caribou parka stuffed with extra caribou socks, sealskin mittens and boots and a sleeping bag in case the hunter gets wet or is overtaken by weather form the rest of the load. Tents are not carried because snowhouses are regarded as safer winter shelter for sea ice camping.

Five to ten gallons of gasoline and a few litres of stove fuel make up the last of a hunter's essentials. With these items in place, a man positions his rifle, harpoon, and retrieval hook along the sides of the sled. The sealskins or canvas is then folded up and overlaid with one or two caribou skins, useful for sitting or sleeping on or as emergency boot and mitten repair material. The whole bundle is then lashed to the sled with a 15 m length of rope made from bearded seal hide.

A hunter follows one of two main paths from Clyde to the ice. The first leads overland and directly east to an area of small islands and grounded icebergs along the outer coast known as Pikaluit (literally, the icebergs), 40-50 km from the settlement. Most, roughly 80 per cent, of all the local *mauluktuk* sealing by Clyde Inuit is done here. On any one day, as many as thirty men may be concentrated in this 900 km² area. The other area, called *Piniraq*, lies 50 km southeast of the village at the mouth of Inugsuin Fiord where islands and points of land cause open pressure cracks in the ice. Hunters sometimes go alone to Pikaluit because they know other hunters will be present if weather or mechanical problems arise, but it is more common for two or four men to hunt as a group, and such groups often form before leaving the settlement.

Hunters travel at moderate speed, stopping only to make adjustments to their loads. As they near the sealing area, they slow their pace to scan the nearby ice for *agluliit*. When a party of two travels, the men move in file examining the same area for the ice domes that may mean a seal; larger groups of four or more machines disperse into a line so that a wider area of ice can be scanned by at least two pairs of eyes. Hunting alone through a day is unusual, in part because of the potential danger presented by mechanical breakdown, changes in the weather or accidents, but more so because collective hunting tactically increases the probability of at least one hunter in a group successfully capturing a seal which all can then share.

Table 4.5 *Time allocation in three winter hunt samples* [1]

| Hunt type | Locale | Time (hr:min) | | | |
		Travel	Search	Hunting	Seals
1972					
dogteam	Aqviqtiuq	1:30	1:30	2:00	nil
dogteam	Aqviqtiuq	1:15	2:40	1:45	nil
dogteam	Aqviqtiuq	1:30	1:35	4:00	1
dogteam	Aqviqtiuq	1:20	0:50	3:50	1
dogteam	Aqviqtiuq	1:30	1:05	4:45	3
dogteam	Aqviqtiuq	1:25	1:55	3:10	1
1974					
dogteam	Pikaluit	3:45	1:55	2:05	1
dogteam	Pikaluit	3:40	2:20	2:45	2
dogteam	Pikaluit	3:05	3:00	2:40	1
1985					
snowmobile	Pikaluit	2:00	2:35	1:20	1
snowmobile	Pikaluit	2:40	1:40	2:35	nil
snowmobile	Pikaluit	2:05	3:00	2:55	2
snowmobile	Pikaluit	1:35	1:30	2:05	2
snowmobile	Pikaluit	2.20	3:10	3:05	1

[1] all data are from the author's field notes.
[2] Umijuak is a small island that marks the start of the Pikaluit sealing area.

When hunters arrive at Pikaluit or other likely ice, they immediately begin to criss-cross the area in search of *agluliit*. This apparent randomness is caused by the difficulty of identifying the holes. Searching (see Table 4.5) consumes considerable time.

Although the pattern of searching seems random, Clyde hunters use features of sea ice topography to assist them. They look for the identifying bumps that signify possible *agluliit* and also direct their search to areas where sea currents and ice pressure cause ice fracturing. When such a crack is located, hunters concentrate on them because they are areas where seals may recently have opened breathing holes.

While *agluliit* are no more than 2–3 cm openings in the ice at freeze-up, by January domes up to 20 cm in height have developed – round shapes in an icescape where the surface is either a flat plane or sharp-angled pressure ridges. Snow accumulation still makes locating *agluliit* a difficult task, and hunters look first for newly frozen areas, like pressure cracks near icebergs and islands or recently closed polynia. They then follow a crack or search a new ice area until either it disappears or an *aglu* is spotted.

Snowmobile searches differ markedly from those carried out with dogs. As Boas (1888: 475) notes, hunters formerly used one or more dogs from their team to locate breathing holes by smell. At Aqviqtiuq, before hunting there was mechanized in 1974, a hunter, once in an expected sealing area, simply allowed his team to pick its own trail.

The dogs quickly located and moved on to an *aglu*.

To determine whether a breathing hole is still active, hunters examine the small 3–6 cm opening that admits air into the dome. At Clyde, hunters never touch an *aglu*, but listen for the sound of water or, if there is sufficient daylight or moonshine, look to see if ice has formed in the hole. A hunter may stop at four or five holes before locating an active one. Clyde Inuit will not hunt an *aglu* if there are signs that a polar bear has recently visited it, since they feel that the bear's scent will keep seals away from using the hole.

Once an active breathing hole has been identified, the hunter will leave his sled and ski-doo several metres away, and make his approach on foot. Dogteam hunters are always careful to place their dogs several tens of metres downwind and to overturn their sleds so that the dogs cannot approach the hole during the wait. Once a member of a hunting group stops to hunt a particular hole, others in the group disperse and seek holes nearby, usually positioning themselves about 50 metres from the first man so as not to disturb the hunt already in progress.

The equipment used today includes either a rifle of at least .303 caliber or a harpoon, and often both. If no harpoon is used, the hunter carries a *nitsik*, or short-handled gaff with which to hook the seal once it has been shot and prevent it from sinking. If a harpoon is used as the primary weapon, then no gaff is needed since, as Boas (1888: 476; see also Nelson 1969) notes, its toggling-head remains attached to the hunter via a sealskin line. Many men who use harpoons keep a rifle at hand in case a polar bear appears. Also, since the main shaft of the modern Clyde harpoon is made from a metal rod (often the steering shaft from a snowmobile), it serves as a chopper for opening the *aglu* once a seal has been struck.

A hunter stands next to the *aglu*, always making sure that he is downwind and casting no shadow across it. Hunters stand straight-legged, but bent at the waist so that they may hear the seal blow when it enters the hole. They watch closely because seals often force water from the hole when entering it.

Men rarely make any other preparations for their wait, such as placing a caribou hide underfoot or building a windscreen of snow blocks, than removing and standing on their mittens. Clyde hunters say that this keeps a man alert, so hands are warmed by pulling them inside the sleeves of the parka. The harpoon or cocked rifle is placed across the top of the hunter's boots so that when he goes to strike there is minimal rustling of clothing. No method other than listening is now used at Clyde in *agluliit* sealing (for other methods see Balikci 1970; Boas 1888; Mathiassen 1928).

The sound of a seal breaching and blowing is distinctive. Since an animal spends ten to thirty seconds in the hole, hunters, on first hearing a seal rise, reach and position their rifle or harpoon directly over the dome's small surface opening where the ice is thinnest. With the next breath, the hunter strikes. Almost any shot directly down into the hole will hit the seal in the head, neck, or shoulder. If a harpoon is

Table 4.6 *Strike-retrieval ratios in Clyde seal hunting* *

Hunt type	Atts./hits	Kills	Retrievals	S:R Ratio
1. *Mauluktuk*				
a) harpoon (53 obs.)	41/36	36	35	1:0.97
b) rifle (65 obs.)	52/44	44	38	1:0.86
2. *Uuttuq*				
a) walking (24 obs.)	19/13	12	12	1:0.92
b) ski-doo (44 obs.)	49/30	24	23	1:0.76
3. Open *Aglu*				
a) harpoon (1 obs.)	2/2	2	2	1:1
b) rifle (28 obs.)	20/19	18	16	1:0.84
c) gaff (9 obs.)	6/3	2	2	1:0.66
4. Canoe				
a) all rifle (128 obs.)	157/61	59	39	1:0.63
5. Open lead				
all rifle (36 obs.)	55/42	40	31	1:0.73
6. Float ice				
all rifle (2 obs.)	3/2	2	2	1:1

* composite data collected at Clyde River from 1971-4, 1980, 1982, 1984-8 and at Aqviqtiuq in 1971-3, 1978 and 1985.

used and a clean strike made without the ice deflecting the moveable harpoon blade, the capture of the seal is ensured (Table 4.6).

If a rifle is used, the hunter must move quickly even if the seal has been immediately killed, since a dead or wounded animal will sink or dive before a harpoon or gaff can reach it. After shooting, the hunter drops his rifle and thrusts the harpoon or hook into the *aglu*, breaking it partially open. With the seal secured, the hunter goes about chopping the ice from around the hole and hauls the carcass on to the ice.

Nine times out of ten a seal is cleanly killed. If not, the hunter must break its neck. He then moves the carcass a few metres from the *aglu* so as not to offend other seals and begins the skinning, with his first cut extending from the top of the anus to the chin. The knife is slipped between skin and blubber and the animal essentially rolled from its skin, the only major cuts now needed being to remove the hind and fore flippers. Ideally, when the sealskin comes free, only a thin layer of fat remains attached to it.

Nearby hunters, on hearing a shot or observing another man haul a *natsiq* from its hole, converge on the kill site. The first man to arrive brews tea. Once the skinning is complete, the successful hunter opens the seal's abdominal cavity and places the animal's liver and a small slab of blubber on the ice. Except for the man who captured the seal, everyone is free to eat as much as he wishes, although full butchering almost never takes place before returning to the settlement. The hunter finally washes the sealskin in the *aglu*, places the meat under the sled cover, and ties the skin to sled so it can drag over the ice to remove more of the fat. All the hunters, if there is still good light, then resume their search for active breathing holes.

Most hunts conclude when waning daylight makes *aglu* location impossible. Hunts may be interrupted also by weather changes, the appearance of a polar bear, or an accident. Snowmachine breakdowns, however, almost never mean the end of hunting; the unfortunate man usually catches a ride on the sled of another hunter.

Only a few hunters deliberately remain on the ice overnight, generally because the first day's hunting has been unsuccessful. Waiting time (shown in Table 4.5) is considerable and hunters, despite excellent clothing and equipment, are often uncomfortable.

A typical day of mid-winter sealing divides into two to four hours of travel to and from the ice, two to three hours searching, perhaps one hour making tea and refueling, and two to five hours waiting beside *agluliit*. When a man returns to the village, he will spend several hours delivering meat to his father or oldest brother's house. With this done, a hunter will begin preparations, mostly minor repairs to equipment, for the next hunt, while his mother or wife takes responsibility for the meat and sealskins brought back to the household.

B. Spring sealing

If winter at Clyde has a certain constancy, spring can only be characterized as a series of fast-paced biological and physical shifts. Around mid-April, Clyde hunters adjust to numerous changes in the natural rhythm of the sea ice environment. Daylight extends to eighteen hours, reaching twenty-four in late May, and daytime temperatures rise to a mean − 16°C, or some 10° above the March average. *Natsiq*, over the next three months, cease depending on their winter *agluliit* and begin to haul out on to the spring ice and are soon swimming in open water leads.

A subtle but important event occurs early in the season, when pregnant females (*nattiaminikiq*) excavate pupping dens in the snowbanks that have accumulated around upthrust ice. These dens, insulated by one-half metre or more of snow, provide shelter for the females and young from the cold, as well as from hunting polar bears and arctic foxes. Fed on a fat-rich milk diet, a normal pup within three weeks increases its body weight from 2 kg to about 20 kg and leaves the lair for the sea.

The second sign of spring is the new use seals make of *agluliit*. When warm temperatures cause the ice domes to collapse, the widened holes are used by the seals to haul out on to the open ice. On warm days when winds are moderate and solar radiation is trapped by low clouds, each exposed breathing hole has at least one basking seal (*uuttuq*) lying on the ice next to it. This is the one time of year that it is possible to appreciate the large numbers of *natsiq* found near Clyde.

Before break-up, meltwater atop the ice prevents the seals from hauling out to bask. Instead, as *agluliit* enlarge into pools and pressure cracks open into wide leads, *natsiq* move into open water. Clyde hunters are forced to adapt their sealing tactics to this succession of shifts in *natsiq* behavior. Special techniques span the spring gap between *mauluktuk* and open-water boat hunting.

So long as *agluliit* are still firm, men continue to use the waiting method, although a hunter must be alert that his shadow does not betray his presence. Hunters begin to journey further, taking advantage of the long days, and they search for areas of rough ice and deep snow – sites that are generally avoided during winter – because these locales may hold active *natsiarsiit*. Pups are a highly desired food and Clyde hunters spend considerable time searching for dens during the three – or four – week period (roughly mid-April to mid-May) when denning occurs.

The annual harvest of *natsiaq* at Clyde amounts to fewer than 100 animals, and rarely will a hunter account for more than two or three pups the whole season. It is surprising, therefore, how much hunting effort is spent, approximately five hours per pup with five attempts per successful capture (Wenzel n.d.a.).

There is only one method for *natsiaq* hunting. Hunters, in their search for breathing holes, keep watch also for deep snowbanks. When a hunter sees a considerable accumulation of snow around a tilted slab of ice, he dismounts from his snowmobile and investigates on foot. The sign that a birth lair is concealed in the bank is the hollow return sound the hunter's footsteps make on the snow. When a hunter hears this echo, he immediately probes the snow with thrusts of a harpoon. When the harpoon breaks through into the den below, he throws his full weight on to the den roof in an attempt to collapse it before the seal(s) can escape via the *aglu*. With the collapse of the roof, the hunter peers in, and if the pup is still inside he pulls it clear and kills it. A fortunate hunter may occasionally manage to take an adult in a lair, but this is even rarer that the capture of a pup.

Natsiaq hunting is a highly specialized and short-lived aspect of spring sealing along the Clyde coast. By the end of May, hunters turn to stalking *uuttuq*, or seals basking atop the ice. The object is to approach a seal dozing beside its *aglu* and strike before it is alarmed and flees into the hole.

In the 1950s, Clyde hunters stalked sleeping seals by walking or crawling behind a white screen (*tiluaaq*) across several hundred metres of open ice. When about 10 m from the seal, they would slide a harpoon along the ice or leap up and strike the *uuttuq* with a thrust. A few hunters even remember their fathers approaching *uuttuq* by imitating its behavior (see Balikci 1970).

By the 1960s, rifles had replaced harpoons as the primary weapon for *uuttuq* hunting, but the long, concealed approach using a white screen continued until the mid-1970s. The rifle had the advantage of allowing a man to shoot from a slightly greater distance, 30–50 m, and thus to expend less time stalking. Data on Aqviqtiuq *uuttuq* hunting in 1972 (Wenzel n.d.a.) shows that the average stalk time in such hunts was twenty-seven minutes and that only half the attempts resulted in a shot, still fewer a kill (see Table 4.6). The only spot for sure kill of a seal is its head, a target about the size of a grapefruit. Either a miss or a wounding shot invariably meant the escape of the animal.

When dogteams were used for spring hunting, men necessarily hunted in pairs so that one could control the dogs while the other stalked. Because dogs had to be left a considerable distance, up to one-half a kilometre, from the target seal, hunters often faced a long, halting approach. Once within 200 m, a man could only move crouched behind a white shield and only when a seal lowered its head to rest. Detailed observation of spring hunts showed that seals are extremely wary while on the ice surface, dozing sometimes for only a few seconds at a time. Clyde *uuttuq* hunting by dogteam was barely successful one of every two attempts, much less than the rate of success of breathing hole sealing.

The wide availability of snowmobiles after 1970 radically changed spring hunting. Clyde hunters soon adopted a more direct approach, driving their snowmobiles from downwind toward a seal. Although the noise alerts the target seal, it often remains on the ice, confused by the sound and by the camouflage, a white *tiluaaq* stretched across the snowmobile's front, used by hunters. Surprisingly, using this method, a man can approach to within 50 m of a seal. Snowmobile *uuttuq* hunting is about as successful as the walking method, so hunters use less time – about five minutes – in stalking and can pursue more seals. *Uuttuq* hunting continues only as long as the ice is free of meltwater. Once extensive melting occurs, about early June, open *aglu* hunting begins in Clyde.

Open *aglu* hunting resembles winter *mauluktuk* sealing in that hunters wait at breathing holes, but because the hole is now exposed extreme caution must be taken not to alarm an approaching seal. The method here is for several hunters to locate contiguous *agluliit* and then conceal themselves about 2 m from each opening until a seal surfaces. Sometimes sleds, kettles, and even parkas are placed over unmanned openings to frighten seals away from them.

When a seal appears, the hunter immediately shoots, harpoons, or hooks it with a long-handled gaff. Most hunters prefer to use a harpoon or gaff, rather than just a rifle, because a wounded seal immediately disappears. As data indicate (refer to Table 4.6), despite its apparent difficulties, open *aglu* hunting is reasonably productive.

One last technique is often employed in late spring when there are numerous wide leads through the ice. The end of spring at Clyde is often characterized by an incomplete breaking of the landfast sea ice. Cracks begin to appear at points of land or by islands and soon expand into channels of open water as much as 20 m across. Such conditions impede travel, but also offer the opportunity for another form of seal hunting.

Nelson's (1969: 271–97) description of North Alaskan floe edge sealing corresponds to what Clyde hunters do. Hunters conceal themselves behind rough ice overlooking a channel and watch for swimming seals. They wait for a *natsiq* to surface within 10 or 20 m and try for a head shot. As with *uuttuq*, anything else and the seal will sink.

Even a killing shot does not guarantee success because the floating seal is still far from reach. Throwing gaffs and small lead boats are used in Alaska and the Western Canadian Arctic to assist retrieval, but these refinements are not found at Clyde. Instead, Clyde hunters try to position themselves so that the current will sweep the dead seal within reach.

To avoid losses and to set a better shot, hunters try to lure swimming seals as close to their position as possible by imitating the scratching sound of a seal basking on the ice. A seal claw or piece of wood is rubbed along the ice surface, and curious seals sometimes approach to within 6 m of a hunter.

It is difficult to estimate the time and effort expended in the various types of spring sealing, as hunts may last up to twenty-four hours and are often combined with wider travel. Also, the activities of one hunter affect those of men nearby, especially when stalking *uuttuq*. In general, *uuttuq* and open *aglu* hunts are highly successful, while lead hunting is much less so.

C. Open-water hunting

Although sea ice may persist at Clyde as late as August, by this time it is no longer possible to travel by snowmobile. When broken, wind-driven ice is still present, sealing, except for hunts on foot over the broken ice, comes to a halt. In most years, however, it is possible to hunt by boat even when some ice remains, either by transporting canoes on sleds to the floe edge or by travelling along open leads. Once there is enough open water to launch boats, nearly all summer sealing is conducted from them, or from drifting pans of ice.

The boats used by the Clyde Inuit for open-water sealing were all, until recently, cedar and canvas canoes ranging in length from 4.8 to 7.3 m, with 25–40 hp outboard engines, and able to haul up one and one-half tons. Sealskin boats, either *qajaq* or *umiak*, disappeared from the region sometime in the 1930s, replaced by wooden whaleboats from the HBC. These large craft, up to 12 m, were used by entire extended families. Today, boats are manned by two to four hunters. Besides fuel, oil and spare parts, and all the equipment usual in winter hunting, boat hunters often include a tent or canvas tarpaulin in case unexpected camping is necessary.

Open-water hunting takes two forms. In the first, when men, or whole households, are travelling to summer hunting or fishing camps, seal hunting is opportunistic. Seals are fired upon when encountered and success is only occasional. The second type is planned. Hunters almost never shoot while the canoe is under power. When a seal is sighted close enough to hunt, the engine is shut down and each man scans a quadrant of nearby water. One man usually does the same kind of scratching along the boat's side as was described for lead sealing. All other human movement is kept to a minimum in order not to frighten the seal.

Open water sealing is most difficult and has the lowest success rate. Seals rarely approach even a drifting boat closer than 10 or 15 m and motion from the sea disturbs the hunter's aim. The seal, too, is in motion. Foote (1967b: 114) evaluated the likelihood of a hit in this kind of hunt as being only 15 per cent. My observations at Clyde show a higher rate of hits (47 per cent), but also that retrieval of shot seals was only 30 per cent of those hit.

Retrieval is the most difficult aspect of open water sealing. Currents, ice, and wind all make recovery difficult. Worse, during August, ringed seals undergo molting and a reduction in the proportion of their live weight from blubber. Thus, they lose much of their buoyancy and may sink within five or six seconds of being shot.

Although gaffs and harpoons are carried, animals are usually hauled by hand into the boat. A gaff or harpoon is used only when a sinking seal is still visible below the surface. Once a dead animal is retrieved, it is placed across braces so that its head hangs over the side of the canoe. This prevents accumulation of blood in the bottom of the boat. Butchering is always done on stable ice or on land.

Open-water hunting often seems chaotic with seals popping up anywhere. Some hunters concentrate their efforts in the vicinity of small islands, such as those at the mouth of Clyde Inlet and Inugsuin Fiord, often landing to scan the sea and have a steady shooting platform if seals are near. Searches also occur near floating ice, which provides the same advantages as islands.

Even in summer, open water hunting can be physically uncomfortable, since conditions are always 5–10°C cooler than on the land. What are breezes on land feel like gales when in a small boat. Inuit are always conscious of the dangers of storms, drifting ice, and unintended dunkings. The presence of other predators, walrus or killer whales, may also cause Inuit to abandon the water.

Natsiq hunting, for all its difficulties and the intensive effort it requires, is the primary marine subsistence activity in summer and autumn. Clyde hunters do turn aside from it when the opportunity arises to capture narwhal (*tugaluk, qillilungaaq*), bearded sea (*ujjuk*), or walrus (*ivvik*). Walrus today are very rare as a result of HBC commercial hunting in the Clyde area (Wenzel 1983b) during the 1930s and 1940s.

Narwhal, which may appear any time from mid-August through September are doubly valued at Clyde. The *muktaaq*, or skin, is considered a premier food, the more so because narwhal harvests vary greatly from year to year, with an average harvest of twenty-two animals. The male's ivory tusk also is valued at $35.00 per pound, although a partial boycott in the United Kingdom (Harper 1984) has recently depressed the market.

Bearded seals and walrus are the two largest pinnipeds found in summer in Clyde waters. *Ujjuk* skin is used at Clyde to make sealskin rope for dog traces, harpoon lines, and sled lashings. As noted above, walrus are scarce near Clyde today. Since 1978, the two or three that are harvested annually are used to make a specialty food known as *igunaaq*. When the opportunity arises to hunt narwhal or larger pinnipeds, ringed seal hunting is put aside.

Modern technology and traditional sealing

Questions about the impact of modern technology on northern ecology and Inuit culture have, as we have seen, deeply affected attitudes toward Inuit seal hunting. Certainly Boas's rich descriptions of Inuit hitching up dogteams preparatory to hunting is an image at variance with the engine noise and gas fumes that mark the start of a modern hunt.

Animal rights critics argue that Inuit hunting can no longer be considered 'traditional'. High-powered rifles, snowmobiles, and outboard engines are artefacts of southern culture which demonstrate the dilution of Inuit society and an increasing ecological imbalance between Inuit and their environment (see Best 1986: 207; see also Regan 1982 and Mowatt 1984).

In these arguments, the 'sub-text' claims that Inuit have paid for their modern technology with their culture. The old natural equilibrium between man and animal, between a society and its ecosystem has been disrupted and the integrity of Inuit, as a self-sustaining subsistence culture, has been smashed, leaving a pale reflection of Western consumer society. Because of that perception of a 'shattered' culture and ecology, we must come to grips with the issue of what is culturally and ecologically fundamental to Inuit subsistence.

The ecology of hunting peoples has been a key area of research since Sahlins described hunters as the 'original affluent society'. The equilibrium view so prevalent at that time has evolved without discarding the initial notion of balance. However, anthropology today tends to see hunting as an active system of environmental relations dependent on harvester decision-making rather than technology itself. Consistent with that, we have already seen that the key dynamic in Inuit sealing is the choice that hunters make about where, when, what, and how much to harvest.

Demonstration of disequilibrium hinges on evidence for the decimation of local animal populations by Inuit in recent times. In the past, Inuit have been blamed for the overexploitation and decline of the Arctic mainland caribou herds of Quebec, Labrador and the Northwest Territories, various arctic and Subarctic furbearer populations, and various marine mammals, especially cetaceans. Close study of these cases has produced equivocal or negative evidence as to Native responsibility. In the often cited case of caribou, biologists now believe that caribou numbers fluctuate naturally, and that the caribou famine experienced by Keewatin and Nouveau Quebec Inuit (and described vividly for western Hudson Bay by Farley Mowat in his 1959 work, *The People of the Deer*) was rooted in natural ecology rather than overhunting.

In other examples, overexploitation can be firmly linked to the entry of large numbers of non-Native users. The decline in numbers of beaver in Subarctic Quebec in the 1930s has been linked to the participation of Whites who entered trapping during the Depression. In Northwest Alaska, the decline of caribou in the late nineteenth century coincides with the appearance of substantial numbers of Euro-American whalers. Overharvesting of these herds occurred in order to supply *Qallunaat* with food. Depredations of the commercial whaling industry on bowhead whales, off Alaska and in Arctic Canada are well known, but Inuit have never stood accused of overexploitation of these large whales.

Closer to our own time, other questions about the impact of Inuit hunting on the environment can also be found. In the early 1950s, Canadian government agents questioned the effect of large concentrations of hunters resulting from resettlement on wildlife (Kemp *et al.* 1977). This concern led to the transfer of nearly a score of Inuit families from the Quebec coast of Hudson Bay to the Northwest Territories (see Kemp *et al.* 1977; Hammond 1984). These twice-relocated Inuit are still attempting to return to Nouveau Quebec. Likewise, according to Quebec and Baffin Island Inuit, government agents halted protective distemper inoculations of dogteams in the 1960s because the cost in wildlife to feed such large numbers of animals was deemed ecologically harmful. For all these assumptions, there is little evidence of negative impact on wildlife because Inuit adopted new technologies.

Conversely, these technologies have provided Inuit with the means of offsetting some of the disadvantages of contemporary northern life. The snowmobile relieves some of the worst ecological pressure on seal and other wildlife close to the centralized settlements created by government policy. Resettlement schemes created the problem of too many hunters using the wildlife in too small an area, a situation which the snowmobile has helped relieve.

Snowmobiles have also been adapted to lessen the necessity for large group hunting. In *mauluktuk* sealing, as was explained earlier, optimal efficiency (see also Smith 1981) requires the participation of several hunters. In Clyde River today, the need for cash calls for participation in wage employment; hence the number of men free to hunt at will has declined. This shortage of manpower is overcome by the use of snowmobiles by just a pair of hunters. One man can station himself at an *aglu* while the second drives a ski-doo in a wide circle. In this way, seals are prevented from using some *agluliit*, while the watched hole is quiet.

Artefacts like the rifle, by opening up new areas of hunting, have relieved other potential ecological problems. In the past, the open water of summer meant the virtual cessation of ringed seal use, because *qajaq* and harpoon-equipped hunters could not get close enough to be effective. In Northwest Greenland, where the use of motorized boats in seal hunting is forbidden, rifles are an essential tool of open-water *qajaq* hunting. Rather, summer was the time when Inuit moved inland for caribou. One hesitates to speculate what the situation would be today if villages like Clyde River, Pond Inlet, and Arctic Bay, all of which have doubled in the last seventeen years, relied solely for their summer food supply on the limited numbers of the North Baffin caribou herd.

There are some new tools that have had negative effects on the wildlife economy. Before twine and nylon nets were introduced, most fishing was done by jigging through the ice or by building stone weirs on streams to intercept migrating fish, especially arctic char. During these runs, everyone who could hold a fishing spear manned the weir, but the size of the harvest was limited by available time and energy and by awareness of what size harvest was sufficient.

The use of nets changed both aspects of fishing. Time and energy ceased to be a strong constraint since netting is a passive activity. Once set, nets need only to be checked periodically and at the user's leisure and they can capture large numbers in a brief setting. The user has little control, except to remove the net altogether. Over-fishing is even more likely when mesh size is small and many users are active at just a few localities.

This is, in fact, the story at a number of formerly very productive arctic char rivers in the Northwest Territories, including some in the Clyde area. While local populations of arctic char have not be exterminated, injudicious use of nets has severely reduced the availability of fish.

In evaluating the ecological impact of these new technologies, we must ascertain whether they drastically lessen the physical and perceptual control Inuit traditionally exerted over their harvesting. Certainly the use of rifles, snowmobiles, and motorized boats has presented Inuit with complicated tools and a restructured set of costs, but there is little evidence that new artefacts have had a more serious impact on *natsiq* than did dogteams, harpoons, and the *qajaq*.

Ringed sealskins stretched and drying at Clyde River

Beach clutter at Broughton Island, NWT, 1974

Moving a snowmobile through the summer ice

Young girl snacking on dried fish, Clyde River

Polar bear warning notice, Churchill, Manitoba

Airing Caribou skin mattresses, Kuganiuk, Somerset Island

Winter inland fishing using a Leister, Clyde, 1971

Drift ice seal hunting near Clyde River

Partially butchered ringed seal

Young girl eating fresh seal

Skinning a Peary Caribou on Somerset Island

Clyde midnight sun

5 THE CLYDE INUIT ECONOMY

Subsistence as economy

By common definition, peoples whose livelihood is derived mainly from the capture of wild resources, both animals and plants, are generally referred to as practitioners of a subsistence economy. Their survival in a little modified natural habitat is the basis for the intellectual and romantic allure that such societies hold for scientists and the general public. Inuit hold a place in the front ranks of this category. While the Kalahari bushmen or Australian aborigines might be mentioned by most anthropologists as typical hunters and gatherers, Inuit remain for the public something of an archetype because they operate in an environment that has repeatedly defeated all but the most intrepid Westerners.

There is reason for this perception. Lee (1968: 48), in surveying the economic base of thirty-four North American aboriginal cultures, identified just five groups for whom hunting supplied at least half of their food. So identified were three Eskimo societies in the survey and two Subarctic Indian bands. Of that select small group, only the Copper Eskimo and the Chipewyan Dene are listed as having had no traditional dependence on plants. What Lee fails to note is that the Chipewyan and the Copper Eskimo both made extensive use of plant products gathered in the course of their boreal forest or treeline activities (see Jenness 1922; Smith 1981). In fact, it is the Inuit groups of the Arctic archipelago and Baffin Island who most accurately portray the hunting lifestyle generally imagined for Inuit.

Such certainly appears to have been the case in the Clyde area at the time of the first European contact. William Parry, in describing (1821: 283–7) the tools, clothing, and food he saw or bartered for, leaves the distinct impression that wildlife products were central to Clyde Inuit life. Only his mention of stone cooking lamps and pots, the heather (*Andromeda tetragona*) bedding, and driftwood harpoon shafts and boat parts suggest that wildlife did not supply all of the wants of the Inuit he met.

The brevity of Parry's visit provides only the scantiest of cultural snapshots. From subsequent ethnographic information about Clyde (see Boas 1888; Foote 1967b, Kemp 1976, 1984; Wenzel 1973, 1981) we can state confidently that the modern ecological cycle (summarized in Table 4.1) differed little from Parry's time. In all likelihood, the main differences are to be found in the year-to-year timing of subsistence activities and, to some degree, their geographic range.

A remarkable degree of stability has characterized man–land relations on eastern Baffin over one and one-half centuries and, most likely, since before the arrival of Europeans. Certainly hunting - for seals, caribou, polar bear and lesser species - formed the core of the aboriginal Inuit economic system. Left in this light, Parry's 1819 account of the bartering he did with Clyde Inuit suggests that he introduced a new dimension to the local economy of these hunters.

If this were the case, then it differs from what most of us consider a normal understanding of the concept of economy. As Lonner (1980: 2) explains, economy is 'the structured arrangements and rules which assure that material goods and specialist services are provided in a repetitive fashion'. Or, to paraphrase Karl Polanyi (in Dalton 1971), economy is the institutionalized orderly movement of things to persons.

This definition presents us with an apparent contradiction when we link the terms subsistence and economy. The notion of subsistence carries with it the simple, and simplistic, implication of 'living off the land' - a situation which only can be ordered by nature. In this framework, subsistence becomes a synonym for ecology. Yet the basic idea behind the term economy is human-directed order and structure. Matters are even further complicated when an understanding of what constitutes economic behavior is constrained by what we consider normative - exchanging money for specific goods or services, contracts and rents, and so forth.

In fact, most of us distinguish between 'formal' and 'informal' types of economic activity every day. The first is based on money, using it as its medium and as the yardstick for establishing absolute value of transactions. The idea of a formal economy also incorporates within it legal and institutionalized means of imposing sanctions for bad behavior. On the other hand, notions of informal economy, like the lending of a tool between neighbors, rests solely on the reciprocal expectations and understanding of cooperation that exists between the participants.

The arrangements of the indigenous Inuit economy are to us informal, rooted as they are in social custom and obviously quite distinct from the framework that has attended economic interactions between Inuit and *Qallunaat*. While we generally conceive of our own informal economic arrangements as situational, aboriginal Inuit material transactions were structured through fundamental rules of kinship and age relations that regulated virtually all aspects of interpersonal contact. Because these relations of social production were, and remain, part of the economic system, it is necessary to examine Inuit subsistence as a material and social whole.

The socioeconomic 'closure' that defines Inuit subsistence requires that we reconsider our ideas about formal and informal economic behavior as forming two distinct and exclusive functional categories. Because Inuit material transactions with *Qallunaat* almost always involve the exchange of labor or local products for money, or, as in the fur trade, a system of barter in which Europeans determined the worth of Inuit products, non-Inuit 'understand' these activities to represent all that the modern Inuit economy is. To many southerners, it is the use of money that brings order and 'sense' to these exchanges.

In the Clyde subsistence system, there is no doubt that money has become an element of economic relations. Contrary to *Qallunaat* perception, however, it has not become the 'bottomline' of Inuit economic behavior. While money often passes between Inuit and certainly is used for the purchase of the imported hunting equipment, ammunition and fuel, the day-to-day tenor of economic life at Clyde is structured not by money's presence or absence, but by a system of social rules – kinship and intergenerational respect (*nalartuk*) – that are understood by every Inuk in the village.

To us, the 'sharing' that Inuit do appears to be *ad hoc*, admirable but informal – at most a minor procedure to supplement the cash problems that plague the North's 'formal' economy. What this view overlooks is that *ningiqtuq* is as highly organized a system of resource distribution as any of the means we use. Its invisibility relates to the fact that Inuit sharing frequently includes non-monetary items, notably food, and neither involves mediated estimations of worth nor an expectation of the immediate return. Instead, *ningiqtuq* is premised on the knowledge that a person may expect to receive reciprocal treatment from others because of the responsibilities that kinship, village co-residence, and cultural solidarity confer on each person.

Ningiqtuq: *the economy of sharing*

Stefansson, during one of his stays in a Copper Eskimo village, mentions (1913: 176) that

> a girl of seven or eight had not begun to eat with the rest of us, for it was her task to take a small wooden platter and carry the four pieces of boiled meat to the four families who had none of their own to cook.

While information about the food, tools and techniques of aboriginal Inuit is voluminous, information on the social behavior integral to the management of economic relations is much more limited. Weyer (1932: 176), for instance, states only that 'The apportioning of the products of the hunt is sometimes so wide as to include the entire settlement, sometimes so narrow as to be limited to a family or even the individual'. While the classic ethnographic literature (see, for instance, Boas 1888; Jenness 1922; Rasmussen 1929, 1931; Spencer 1959; Balikci 1964) does supply some specifics about sharing – such as hunters immediately eating the liver of a freshly killed seal – little attention has been given to the more encompassing economic practices of Inuit.

Sharing, at the time of a kill and in the village, is an important feature of past and present Inuit economic behavior. If any rationale for this is needed, it is that it compensates for the highly unpredictable nature of hunting. Inuit recognize the risk by hunting cooperatively, but even then every hunter is not always successful. A second advantage of sharing is that Inuit villages and camps included non-hunting dependants, such as widows and the infirmed. It was important, therefore, not only to produce food but also to ensure that it reached those who could not provide for themselves. Sharing, as much as harvesting, was essential to community well-being.

The customary basis for sharing among Inuit is rooted in kinship (Damas (1972b: 222) refers to the efficacy of kinship relations). Kinship is the main mechanism for socially organizing and regulating the flow of material goods, especially food, among Inuit, although Damas (ibid.) qualifies this by noting that some aspects of sharing are 'exclusive of kinship, and in others overlap kinship'. I argue that even in the case of modern communities, where resources are frequently shared outside the extended family, there is a structuring which operates co-relative to kinship.

The organizing role of kinship in Inuit society was recognized by Boas (1888: 578) even in his earliest work: 'The social order of the Eskimo is entirely founded on the family and on ties of consanguinity and affinity.' He observed that the regulation of hunting includes '. . . the obligations of the successful hunter towards the inhabitants of the village . . .' (ibid.). Later work by Damas (1963) and Heinrich (1963) established an even firmer association between social relations and economy, especially regarding the focal role of the consanguinal extended family, or *ilagiit*, in traditional Eastern Arctic Inuit community organization.

Heinrich (1963: 68) especially argued that kinship was the most important non-technological adaptive element in Inuit culture because of its inclusive role in regulating all aspects of Inuit behavior. For instance, unlike the economic situation in our own society, in which legal and financial institutions order relations, among Inuit only the rules of social organization offer a stable framework for economic cooperation.

Damas (1963), through his research among the Iglulingmiut, a group closely related by dialect and ecology to Clyde Inuit, provides a substantive example of how this framework functions. He identified kinship as a behavioral system operating between pairs of socially referenced individuals. Within the *ilagiit*, cross and intra-generational ties are founded on blood, but he (1963: 39–45) also describes non-blood affiliative behavioral patterns (such as those dominant in modern settlements) as closely mirroring primary kin relations.

In later work (1969a, b, 1972a, b), Damas elaborated on the effect of social relations in Inuit ecological and economic patterning. In particular, he shows (1972a: 40–1, 46–7) how denotation of economic pairings are linguistically modeled on family relationships. The Inuktitut term, for example, for the relationship between a father (*ataata*) and son (*ilniq*) is *ilniriit*, with the suffix *-iit* combining with the word for son. In such a pairing, the use of *ilniq* as the term's root marks the subordinant position of the son to his father. This same suffix also is used to reference economic associations, like that of boat crewmen, *umiaqqatigiit*, and, among some Inuit (Damas 1972b: 224-5, 227-30), food sharing partnerships. In essence, the suffix *-iit*, generally denotes cooperative association.

A second important feature of the *ningiqtuq* system is the unbalanced nature of its operations. As Birket-Smith (1959: 146) described it, 'division is not equal . . . [and] proceeds according to very defined rules'. In anthropology, such an unbalanced pattern of exchange, in which expectation of material return is deferred until there is need, is referred to as generalized reciprocity and has come to be regarded as a signal attribute of subsistence systems (see Sahlins 1972; Lonner 1980; Langdon 1981). In the few analyses that have been done on eastern Inuit economic relations (Damas 1972b; Nooter 1976; Borre and Wenzel 1988; Wenzel 1981, 1986c, 1989), such a 'skewed' means of transfering resources is a key feature of *ningiqtuq* sharing.

A. Sharing within the extended family

In the Clyde region, sharing game is referred to as *ningiqtuq* (Wenzel 1986a). Properly, the term refers to the unrestricted distribution of the meat from large animals – walrus, polar bear, whales – to anyone who wants some; in practice, however, it covers nearly all the customary sharing practiced at Clyde.

The centerpiece of the system, called *tuqagaujuq*, is the sharing carried out within the extended family, itself the core of the economy. In *tuqagaujuq*, meat is 'shared up' from hunters to their oldest blood-related male kinsman, who serves as the leader (variously, the *isumataq* or *angajuqqaaq*) of the *ilagiit* (see Damas 1969a: 49). Boas (1888: 581) described the *issumautung* as the titular head of a village, a view consistent with the *ilagiit*-based nature of traditional Clyde area settlements (Wenzel 1981, 1984b).

An important responsibility of the *isumataq* was to order the distribution of this general store among the nuclear households of the *ilagiit*. Piungnituq, then head of the last *ilagiit*-based village in the Clyde region, often noted that it was his 'job' to see that 'everyone always has food' (Wenzel 1973). So central was this responsibility that this part of the *isumataq* role was described by other camp residents by the term *niqiliriiq*, from the root *niqi-* for meat, loosely meaning the caretaker of food resources. The *tugaqaujuq* resource pool was accessible to all members of the *ilagiit* through a process called *tigu-tuinaaq*, literally to take without asking.

Despite its ubiquitous nature, the extensiveness and complexity of intra-*ilagiit* sharing at Clyde is more difficult to describe than the preceding analysis suggests. This is especially true when it is overlaid by more generalized, or non-kin restrictive, *ningiqtuq* practices. Figure 5.1 provides a basic graphical representation of the internal sharing

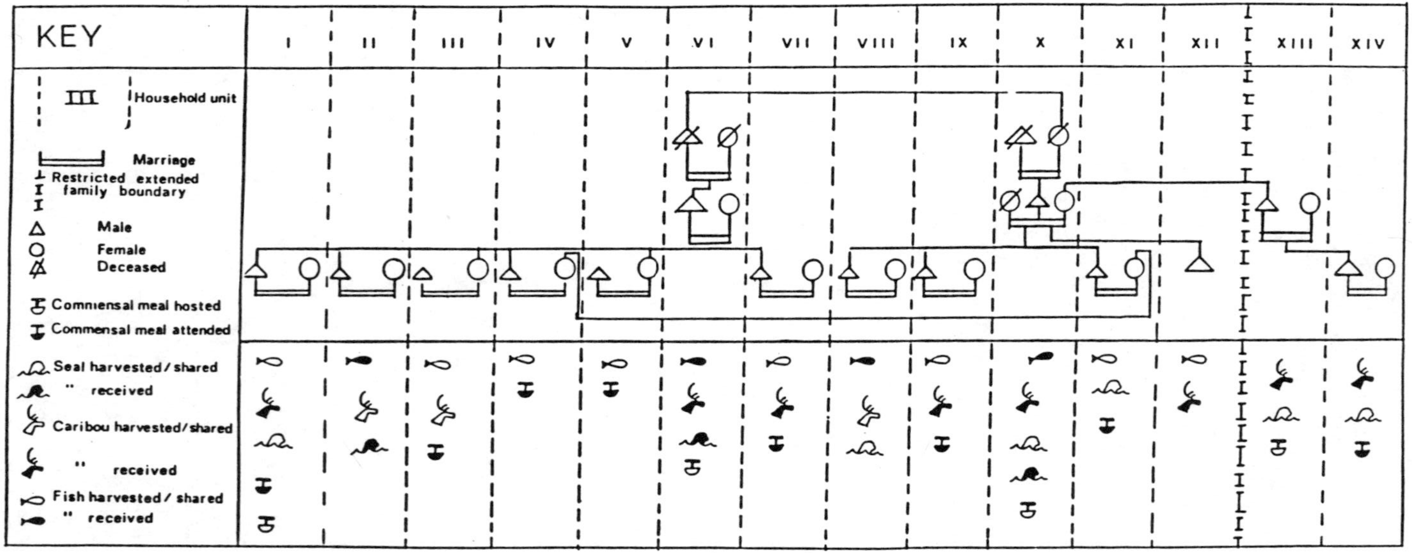

Figure 5.1 *Extended family food allocation, 1984 (Clyde River)*

activity of one prominent Clyde *ilagiit* for a few weeks in 1985. As the figure shows, several times during this brief period a number of commensal, or communal, meals were held by senior members of this family. While only the participation of *ilagiit* members is shown, the scope of these *nirriyaktuqtuq* meals forms the next tier of the Clyde sharing economy.

B. Commensal sharing in Clyde

Besides the *taqagaujuk-tigutuinaaq* distributional system basic to Clyde *ilagiit*, several other mechanisms facilitate resource allocation on a wider community scale. The most inclusive means was the communal meal, known generally as *nirriyaktuqtuq* and at Clyde as *kaiyukquiyuk*. *Nirriyaktuqtuq* commensalism, described by Damas (1972b) as active in the three Inuit societies he has analysed, consisted of an extended family head or the senior member of a camp group calling together all those present locally to share in a meal.

Damas's reconstruction of *nirriyaktuqtuq* commensalism closely resembles the practice as described by Boas (1888: 577) nearly a century earlier at Cumberland Sound:

> When the meal is ready the master of the house stands beside it, crying Ujo! Ujo! (boiled meat) and everybody comes out of the hut provided with a knife. The dish is carried to a level place and the men sit down around it in one circle, while the women form another. Then large lumps of meat are passed around, everybody cutting off a piece and taking a swallow of the soup.

One advantage of Boas's observations is that they add texture to theoretical treatments, like that of Damas, of Inuit commensalism. Not to be overlooked, however, is that such 'deep' description provides a behavioral baseline for judging whether open sharing still is a part of the Inuit economy.

In both theoretical and practical terms, *nirriyaktuqtuq* sharing continues at Clyde today. Moreover, communal meals are far from a rarity. On just one day in 1989, four different village-wide meals took place and, even in the depths of winter, a week rarely passes without one or two *nirriyaktuqtuq* gatherings.

Clyde *nirriyaktuqtuq* organization today is remarkably like Boas's account of the meal he witnessed. What long-term research at Clyde also revealed (Wenzel 1989) is that far more variety as to the form and type of *nirriyaktuqtuq* commensalism exists than was noted either in Boas's treatise or the work of Damas.

Nirriyaktuqtuq gatherings in Clyde are always announced by the children of the host going door to door (or tent to tent). Information about the kind of meal that is to be eaten – boiled or raw seal, caribou, young or old seal, arctic char or *muktaaq* – is given by the particular cry shouted by the children. Boas, for instance, notes that the host of the meal he describes repeatedly shouted *Ujo* (*uuyuk*), meaning that boiled meat was being prepared. At Clyde, if a meal involved frozen, rather than cooked, meat, then the children would run to each house crying *quaktuq*. Likewise, a cry of *mungii* indicates raw fish, while other cries tell prospective participants other foods that are to be served.

While the particulars of how commensal meals were conducted in Boas's time may differ slightly from those now held in Clyde, with regard to key socioeconomic features they are exactly alike. The first such feature, as Damas (1972b) clearly points out, is that membership in the host's *ilagiit* is not a requirement of *nirriyaktuqtuq* participation. The object of this practice remains the same, to provide food for all those that one shares residence with. The other important structural feature is that extended family leaders remain the organizational focus of *nirriyaktuqtuq* food distribution.

Three other forms of sharing completed the aboriginal Clyde food sharing system. These were *akpaallugiit*, the inviting-in of a special guest, *niqisutaiyuq* or *qauktuaktuq* (*payuktalik* in Damas 1972b), the giving of meat to non-kinsmen, and *minatuq*, the opening of food caches for anyone's use. The first two exclude *ilagiit* members as the recipients of the food shared. Until very recently, *akpaallugiit* sharing in Clyde was limited to elders, and *payuktalik* carrying focussed on the households of widows or women whose spouses were absent. As for *minatuq*, it appears to be a variation on *tigutuinnaaq* practice in which the food access usually afforded to members of *ilagiit* is extended to non-kinsmen. It should be noted that decisions regarding *minatuq* and *payuktalik* distribution is still seen as the prerogative of *ilagiit* leaders.

C. Summarizing Clyde Inuit economy

The stuff of Inuit subsistence, at Clyde and across the arctic, was meat. Wildlife harvesting supplied clothing, fuel, even rope and bedding, but most of all food. A singularly focussed mode of production, economics appear quite simple. Inuit hunted animals as food for themselves and their families in order to have the energy to produce food in the future.

Kemp (1971), in one of the few detailed studies of Inuit natural economy that has been done, demonstrates that harvesting, while costly in human effort and time, also provides ample benefit to sustain itself. These (ibid.: 108-9) data show, first, a recurring, if small, net annual bioenergetic balance for the population of twenty land-based Inuit he studied and, second, that ringed seal were the key component in this small group system. These conclusions are also borne out in other Inuit community studies (see Riewe 1977; Finley and Miller 1980; Wenzel 1981) where *natsiq* may account for as much as two-thirds of the food energy entering even larger villages. Kemp's data, on the seasonal nature and bioenergetic importance of ringed seals among Inuit living on the land, are, therefore, also robust with respect to larger Inuit community living situations.

Table 5.1 *Material-sharing parameters of the Clyde economy*

Resource state	Access	Primary mechanisms	Social focus
Surplus	—— Open ——	1) *nirriyaktuqtuq* —— 2) *minaqtuq* 3) *akpaallugiit*	Community
Normal	—— Open ——	1) *tuqagaujuk/* —— *tigutuinnaaq* 2) *nirriyaktuqtuq* 3) *quaktuaktuq*	a) *ilagiit* b) *nunariit* c) community
Contracted ——	Open	—— 1) *nirriyaktuqtuq* —— 2) *quaktuaktuq*	Community
Depleted	—— Closed	—— *tigutuinaaq*	—— *ilagiit*

Kemp also shows that even in his 'micro-study' *ningiqtuq* exchange played a prominent role in the maintenance of economic relations, with several millions of calories of food being exchanged between households. In fact, the amount of food redistributed through customary sharing was equivalent to all the calories brought into the study community by its hunters in one month of intensive harvesting. Imbalances in the relative availability of food between households was corrected by 'social controls ... directing and mediating the flow of energy in the community' (ibid.).

We can summarize the relationship of Clyde Inuit economic-ecologic activity to community dynamics (see Table 5.1) as follows: 1) the generation of a material resource pool through cooperative harvesting; and 2) the allocation of resources through social regulation. That resources are harvested, stored, consumed, and replenished is all a part of Clyde Inuit natural ecology. That these resources are shared within and between Clyde *ilagiit* in a way that is inclusive of all members of the community, is, however, the result of social structural processes of which kinship is the main element.

To outsiders, this organized system of resource allocation, because it is 'informal', is simplistically treated as if it were nothing but the product of some 'natural economy' phenomenon. The reality is that Inuit sharing is an adaptation that, through social means (see again Figure 5.1), provides wide scope for individuals to obtain access to all the material resources available in the community. *Ningiqtuq*, if it is nothing else, is a system of economic relations that is consistent with Inuit socio-cultural conceptions of the relationship between individuals and society.

6 SEALS AND SNOWMOBILES: THE MODERN CLYDE ECONOMY

For the Native peoples the fur fashion industry destroyed their way of life and replaced it with what was essentially a culture of indentured labour. (Best 1986: 203)

Fur trade relations (1923–45)

Our data base suggests that the pattern of aboriginal Inuit subsistence in the Clyde region was very stable until massive intervention by the Canadian government after the Second World War. That stability may come as a surprise, since the popular image that has been developed regarding the period of Inuit-*Qallunaat* contact through the fur trade is widely regarded as a time when subsistence was disrupted and even ruptured (Best 1986; Smith 1988; Miller n.d.). Comparison with the fur trade dynamic we find among Native groups farther to the south (see Feit 1973; Tanner 1979; Morantz 1980) suggests some need for explanation.

Unlike Dene and Algonkian hunters, Inuit could treat fox trapping as part of their normal harvesting regime. Fox trapping could be most intensively practiced where there were concentrations of winter *agluliit* (see Freeman 1976 Vol. III: 125–8) hence pursuit of arctic fox complemented hunting of ringed seals. Clyde hunters, like most Inuit, did not have to choose between food and fur production. We can go so far as to argue that successful trapping depended on continued seal hunting.

The actual shape of the harvesting economy practiced in the Clyde region during this period is difficult to determine accurately because quantitative information about non-market production is spotty. Arctic fox was the main commodity sought by Whites (see Table 6.1), and sealskins were, at best, secondary in any trade. As Damas (1988: 108) points out, the HBC paid (in goods) up to $15.00 for a fox pelt, but only $1.00 for a sealskin.

Walrus ivory, polar bear hides, and caribou skins rounded out the local Clyde River trade economy, but figures on the extent of their relative importance are absent from the sources (like post diaries) available. In the case of walrus tusks, the local HBC organized its own hunt, using a Peterhead vessel based at the post. (This may explain why such products are not included in the store's export

Table 6.1 *Clyde HBC fur purchases, 1935-45*[1]

Year	Bear	White fox	Blue fox	Seal[2]	Ermine	Other[3]
1935	—	741	21	—	62	—
1936	—	204	7	—	21	—
1937	—	332	9	420	19	—
1938	—	631	16	—	45	—
1939	—	748	38	—	93	—
1940	—	296	6	237	7	—
1941	—	569	22	491	16	—
1942	—	969	37	193	49	5
1943	36	767	32	212	120	6
1944	18	362	1	351	21	9
1945	6	192	4	319	6	1

[1] source: Clyde HBC (U.23) Customer Records (N.B. original copied by the author at Clyde River, June 1973).
[2] may include other species besides *P. hispida*.
[3] 'other' species are recorded as follows: 1942-5 wolf, 1943-6 arctic hare, 1944 - 2 wolf and 7 hare, 1945 - 1 wolf.

Table 6.2 *Clyde HBC Operations Record, 1935-44*

Year	Furs ($)	Sales ($)	Net profit ($)
1935	9,637	8,040	1,043
1936	2,061	1,755	3,384
1937	3,294	3,039	3,191
1938	6,613	5,082	962
1939	7,570	7,013	1,710
1940	2,131	2,512	3,377
1941	5,043	4,096	4,263
1942	16,129	14,166	n.d.
1943	14,166	12,257	n.d.
1944	7,374	11,322	n.d.

Source: Clyde HBC Operations Record, copied by the author at Clyde River, June 1973.

records.) For the last ten years of the fox trade boom (see Table 6.2), the Clyde store consistently produced a profit for the HBC.

Records about Inuit domestic wildlife use are even more limited, and the best source is Inuit memory. According to Inuit who remember that era, neither trapping activity nor shortages of imported goods seriously interfered with Inuit subsistence activities. As one Inuk (Piungnituq 1974, personal communication) described those years, 'Inuit just did not pay very much attention to foxes'. The Clyde post log reinforces this idea. Traders' comments make it seem that Clyde

Inuit invested far less effort in trapping than the Qallunaat felt they should, with more than one Inuk referred to as 'lazy' because his fox tally did not meet HBC expectations.

There is very little evidence of long-term scarcity of food species. While caribou and walrus harvests sometimes were below expectations due to ecological circumstances, there are no data to suggest episodes of deep starvation. The Royal Canadian Mounted Police, who filed annual summaries of conditions prevailing among the Inuit of each district, generally noted that seal harvesting adequately met Clyde food needs.

Interview data on settlement and community patterning during the fur trade years (Wenzel 1984b, 1986a) show that Clyde Inuit suffered no serious dislocations due to resource depletion. While geographic mobility appears to have been high, Inuit information suggests that the principal reason was the establishment of new social alliances between *ilagiit* through marriage. Of the seven *ilagiit*-based winter village sites in the region (see Figure 4.1) occupied during the fur trade, only one, in the McBeth Fiord–Isabella Bay area, was abandoned by its core group (Wenzel 1984b) in a case attributable to endemic illness.

The main problem with the fur trade at Clyde, so far as we can infer from Inuit memory, was that traders were unable to maintain their end of the relationship. Inuit ably integrated trapping and exchange into their adaptation, but the supplying of remote posts was often interrupted by arctic conditions, fluctuations in the fur market, and war.

How Clyde Inuit were affected is hard to determine. Inuit certainly experienced shortages of ammunition, cloth or tobacco, and many Clyde elders recall from 1939 to 1944 short supplies of bullets and flour. Piungnituq remembers how he and his father used and reloaded four cartridge casings for almost two years because no new supplies had arrived.

Inuit seem not to have been heavily dependent on the fur trade. This is illustrated in the experience of the Inuit of Somerset Island, who saw the HBC withdraw from both Port Leopold and Fort Ross during the 1930s and 1940s. According to Kemp *et al.* (1977), these Inuit were not reduced to starvation conditions that early observers like Low (1906) and Hantzsch (1977) feared would prove to be the outcome of intensive contact with southern culture. According to Illaut (1976, personal communication), who moved to Somerset in about 1925 and still lives there, 'People still had seals and bear in winter and caribou and fish in summer, no one was hungry'.

Such information from Clyde and Somerset Inuit presents an adaptive picture of Inuit–White economic relations that adds substance to Goldring's depiction of situation in Cumberland Sound, the most intensive trapping area of the Eastern Arctic: 'The Inuit lived comfortably on seals until they wanted coffee or biscuits, then trapped a few foxes to warrant a trip into Pangnirtung'. (1986: 171) In 1939, Stewart, writing in the HBC's Ungava district annual report (HBCA, quoted in

Goldring 1986: 171), noted that the local Inuk was a 'sealer and whaler but a very poor trapper'. So, even at this late stage of the fox trade, the HBC still hoped that Inuit would become 'Hudson's Bay men.'

The data at hand do not indicate that many Inuit experienced the kinds of cultural consequences that are often attributed by some scholars (Duffy 1988; Zaslow 1988) and by animal rights critics (Best 1986; 1989a) to the fur trade relationship. True, where Inuit, as in the Keewatin, were ecologically dependent on terrestrial resources like caribou, declines in herd strength caused hardship.

Scientists and government officers, at the time, attributed this depletion to overhunting by Inuit using rifles introduced by the fur trade and the diverting of Inuit from food harvesting. Thus was born the idea that the arctic fur trade was pernicious. Further experience of caribou crashes and re-analysis of the 1940s experiences by Keewatin and Quebec Inuit suggest that fluctuation is a natural phenomenon.

At Clyde, where subsistence depended on ringed seals, no such hardship was experienced. Certainly contact with *Qallunaat* created problems, notably the periodic recurrence of endemic illnesses (Clyde HBC Diary 1941-4), but the fox trade seems to have been no deterrent to food production. As Goldring (1986) points out, Inuit adapted whale boats and firearms to increase their subsistence efficiency.

The early government era (1945-60)

The Second World War ushered in a new stage which can be conveniently termed the government era. While the social, economic, and political policies that were to reshape Inuit life began after the war, the wartime years saw an unprecedented influx of *Qallunaat* into the Arctic, and their experience contributed to the post-war push to 'modernize' the North and Inuit (see Hughes 1963).

In terms of the cultural adaptation required, the government era can be considered a drastic environmental shift, the most powerful in its effects on Canadian Inuit since the Little Ice Age (c. AD 1450-1850). While this was a wholly natural phenomenon, there are some similarities. Both episodes changed the effective environment in which Inuit lived and have, therefore, induced new Inuit ecological and economic adaptations.

The cold of the Little Ice Age (see McGhee 1978) brought an end to the reliance of Canadian Thule Culture on bowhead whales. All along the arctic coast, from the Alaska-Yukon boundary to Greenland, the pattern of Inuit adaptation underwent evolution. A significant change was the abandonment of large multi-family winter villages of twenty or more houses and their replacement by a more dispersed pattern of *ilagiit* settlement, convenient for the exploitation of smaller game, the foremost of which was the ringed seal. Food resources were now available in smaller, mobile packets and ecological success meant that the Inuit unit of production had to be mobile. The new settlements were smaller, supported by a localized selection of resources.

The extended family was the ideal socioeconomic unit, complete and cohesive enough to meet socioeconomic needs, but small enough to exploit efficiently dispersed and varied resources. The ringed seal, because of its year-round presence and dense distribution, became a central component of this 'small game' system. *Natsiq* was the base resource in most areas, secure from the risks that attended other species. This ecological pattern remained in place not only through early contacts with Europeans, but also to the end of the war.

The massive post-war incursion of government, and the southern world in general into the arctic imposed changes on Canadian Inuit comparable to those of the Little Ice Age. The onset of the government era also brought with it massive change in the pattern of Inuit ecology and settlement demography. The *ilagiit*, as the core of residence and community, was in the span of a decade undermined by Canadian northern policy. Throughout the Northwest Territories and Arctic Quebec, the result of this policy was a closing of Inuit villages and the relocating their residents into large 'central settlements'. The objective of this concentration was to make health, social and educational services on a par with those found in southern Canada available to Inuit. The effect(s) of this centralization can be illustrated by the Clyde experience.

For 1951, Foote (1967b: 64) records a total Clyde area population of 128, a figure which roughly corresponds to my own count of 120–40 Inuit (Wenzel 1984b: 52). Only five or six nuclear households, perhaps twenty-five to thirty-six people, lived at the Clyde River HBC post. Most still maintained fixed winter residence in six villages spread between Buchan Gulf and Henry Kater Peninsula.

The pace of relocation at Clyde is evident by 1961, when at least 111 of the 162 Inuit present in the region wintered in the new settlement (Foote 1967b). My own figures (1984b: 52) suggest that as many as 130 people were established in the central village by this time and that just fifty Inuit remained in just three indigenous *ilagiit*-based communities. Within fifteen months, one of these also closed and its members joined the swelling population of Clyde River village.

We must now examine the impact of government rearrangement imposed on the Clyde River Inuit economy and ecology. With a more concentrated population, ringed seal took on an even more important ecological role, since it was the only species numerous and fecund enough to tolerate the kind of harvesting pressure that followed such a movement. Under these circumstances, no other species had the stamina of ringed seals.

The government era also imposed money as an all-purpose medium of exchange. Since Parry's 1819 encounter, barter had been the mode of exchange between Inuit and Whites. Barter was advantageous to Inuit. Traders supplied them with tools and goods in return for fox pelts, but the settlement and land use regimes under which Inuit lived did not require excessive reliance on these commodities. The imports enhanced harvesting efficiency and supplemented diets, but seal harvesting remained the basis of subsistence. Trapping could be carried on without interfering in food production by traditional means. Inuit, therefore, retained substantial control over the economic choices they made since food production bore little relation to exchange decisions.

Government centralization changed this situation. Environmentally, Inuit suddenly were handicapped, and imported technologies took on new importance to harvesting. Rifles and powered boats allowed Inuit to operate with less risk than they could afford before resettlement.

However, this new dependence came at a substantially increased cost. This was because centralization made money the cornerstone of the exchange economy. Money took on a role held by none of the 'staples' of the fur era. Furthermore, in contrast to the overall *Qallunaat* presence found in the fur trade (see Damas 1988: 121), Whites were increasingly present in the new settlements as nurses, teachers, and administrators, all of whom, unlike their fur era predecessors, were well supported from the South.

Inuit found themselves relying on *Qallunaat* for access to the North's new money economy. Inuit at this time were easily attracted to military and civilian construction sites, since they had little to exchange for money but their direct labour. By the 1920s, when government consolidated its influence in the North, Inuit lost substantial control over the exchange economy.

For sales data from Clyde (Table 6.3) confirm this. From 1925 to 1944, Inuit received an annual average of $7,436 for the furs they traded. Between 1951 and 1960, the average annual receipt from fur sales at Clyde was barely half of that ($3,931), and in fewer years. Damas (1988: 122) paints a similar picture of overall decline, with an Inuit fur economy valued at $840,115 in the mid-1940s falling to about one-tenth of that ($85,343) in 1949-50.

Since Clyde had no DEW line or air base, the local wage economy provided entry for only three or four full-time Inuit employees and social assistance became the chief source of cash. Just when money prevailed as the medium of exchange with *Qallunaat* and was perceived as an important resource for harvesting, Inuit had no access to it.

We have no quantitative information on the food harvest in the Clyde area at this time. The numbers of sealskins traded to the HBC in many years (see Table 6.3) fall well below the needs of even a modest Inuit camp, but starvation is not reported. In the fifteen years after the war, Clyde people, like Canadian Inuit in general, were economically marginalized. Conditions truly resembled those that are negatively appended to the idea of subsistence. As an unintentional consequence of government resettlement policy, Inuit were separated from their resource base. Because harvesters were crowded into relatively small areas, many of the resources that were within easy reach were reduced. This situation was exacerbated even further

Table 6.3 *Clyde fur sales, 1947-60**

Year	Fox	Seal	Bear	Ermine	Fur value ($)
1947	502	190	15	90	n.d.
1948	187	285	13	2	n.d.
1949	251	396	17	—	n.d.
1950	327	28	17	6	n.d.
1951	465	—	10	58	5,205
1952	350	—	0/17	—	2,352
1953	116	172	21/25	—	1,504
1954	304	—	0/31	33	2,501
1955	182	173/488	0/30	7	1,947
1956	173	169/351	0/52	—	2,156
1957	50	292/356	0/16	—	1,473
1958	229	229/436	0/27	12	3,704
1959	480	0/279	0/40	16	9,630
1960	n.d.	n.d./169	n.d./60	n.d.	8,845

* after 1951, polar bear data from both the Clyde HBC Fur Records and Foote (1967a: 44) are presented (HBC/Foote); after 1954, seal data from both the HBC and Haller *et al.* (1967) are presented (HBC/Haller).

Source: Clyde HBC Fur Purchase and Operations Reports (copied by the author in Clyde River, June 1973).

because fox, formerly so attractive to Whites, was no longer of value. This market change deprived Inuit of a local cash source that was consistent with subsistence pursuits.

Duffy (1988), in a chapter appropriately titled 'Providing a Living', describes the concerns expressed in government circles during this period about the economic state of Inuit. These analysts generally attributed Inuit economic problems to the failure of the subsistence system. What many have failed to recognize (Weick, personal communication) is that it was the exchange component of the North's economic structure that had failed. The 'Inuit economy' was still providing Inuit with the essential item – food – as it always had.

The misinterpretation stemmed from the emphasis *Qallunaat* placed on money as a measure of cultural well-being and productivity (see Dalton 1968). They assumed that if hunting did not produce enough cash return to balance the investment Inuit made in harvesting, Inuit hunting must be uneconomic.

Inuit, however, took a different view of money. Like arctic fox during the fur trade, money had, to use Polanyi's term (in ibid.: 178-80), a 'special-purpose value' for them: to facilitate, not replace, customary subsistence operations. In this frame of reference, money becomes another scarce, but necessary, resource for hunting.

Inuit harvesting continued to provide the material and social capital that was the goal of subsistence. What Inuit lacked was any effective means of diverting some portion of harvesting production to the acquisition of cash. Southerners had made money a resource needed by hunters, but had not monetized any of hunting's outputs. To acquire the cash which *Qallunaat* controlled, Inuit had to divert time and energy away from subsistence.

Government policy of the 1950s was built on the assumption that 'the basic economy of hunting and trapping would no longer be able to '"provide a suitable livelihood"'' (Duffy 1988: 153). Planners relocated Inuit without providing support for harvesting, but Inuit did what they had always done; they adapted available resources and opportunities into the scheme of subsistence. They undertook a process of adaptive *bricolage* in which money was treated as a resource and its use value appreciated. But food, which was only available through hunting, remained the thing that gave subsistence activities their objective and security.

More important, the social practice of sharing and reciprocity, based largely on kinship, remained intact. Planners had expected wage employment to supplant harvesting, but too few jobs were created and most were shortlived (Duffy 1988: ibid.). The southern planning model was founded on a conception of household behavior, whereas Inuit relied on cooperative (*ilagiit*-based) production and consumption.

In the course of the 1950s, Inuit became subsistence *bricoleurs*, jacks-of-all-trades in putting together the resources necessary for harvesting. While *Qallunaat* were redefining the northern economy and the place of Inuit in it, Inuit were maintaining the one option that was materially and socially productive for them, using all the resources and opportunities that were available. How this *bricolage*, or mixed economy, subsistence adaptation was achieved is revealed in anecdotes and memories from both Inuit and Whites. As one DEW Line contractor complained, 'A guy would come and work for two, sometimes only one, week. I'd give him his pay and he'd be gone. I'd hear he went hunting . . . Then I'd train another', (Anonymous 1971, per. comm.)

Clyde Inuit remember casual jobs as the only way to get the money they needed to buy ammunition. One man, who worked for the HBC during the period, recalls that by earning $10 a week he was able to purchase enough ammunition and kerosene for his camp stove so that he and his two brothers-in-law could usually supply seal meat for half the households, some forty people, in Clyde River. It meant that he, like other full-time wage workers in Clyde, could not hunt as much as he might want, but their pay helped other hunters in their respective *ilagiit*.

Money became at least partially incorporated into the *ningiqtuq* economy. Although its redistribution was limited to *tugaqaujuq* sharing, moving from subordinate kinsmen to *ilagiit* heads, *isumataq* used these funds to purchase supplies – flour, ammunition, sugar – for use by the entire extended family. Unlike wild food, the money itself was not subject to *tigutuinaaq*. Rather, the *isumataq* used the money to purchase store goods, beginning with harvesting and daily households needs, and these were then shared 'downwards'.

Ilagiit allocation was supplemented by the *ad hoc* distribution of such things as ammunition and fuel between cooperating hunters (*nunariit*). Also, a new form of *ningiqtuq* sharing arose, called *niqitatitanaq*: the distribution of game directly between unrelated hunters. According to Clyde Inuit, this ensured continued cooperation between hunters and also compensated for the greater access to cash and/or imported goods held by a few men.

One other 'sharing' practice that arose in the 1960s needs to be discussed. This was the sharing of jobs. While the 'practice' was never systematized, the few casual-seasonal wage opportunities available informally circulated among a large labour pool, ensuring a wider distribution of money.

The here-and-gone work pattern that so irritated foremen and planners was a factor in maintaining an effective subsistence system. Under government resettlement and the failure of the fur economy, hunting could no longer provide all the material resources needed by Inuit. But by maximizing the limited cash resources available, Inuit were able to reassert their customary socioeconomic structure. The *bricolage* of money and harvesting allowed subsistence operations and goals to dominate the Clyde economy for the next twenty years.

The *bricolage* era, 1961–83

In 1961, a strategically important event took place. An advance in the commercial preparation of hair-seal pelts (Foote 1967a: 267) opened a place for ringed and harp sealskins in the markets of Western Europe. Sealskins took on cash value.

In the Canadian North, sealskins had had only minimal exchange value and were mainly used by Inuit for the domestic manufacture of clothing and *qamiik* (boots). After the post-war collapse of the fox market, the HBC did offer prices in the range of $1 for *natsiq*, but this was never intended as anything but a token. European interest in *qlissiq* (sealskins), therefore, had substantial economic significance in the North. For the first time since the collapse of the fox trade, Inuit were afforded a cash resource that fitted into normal subsistence practice. Walrus, polar bear and narwhal also had trade value, but sustained exploitation was restricted by seasonal constraints, low biological productivity, and small populations.

Within two years (1963), hunters (Foote 1967a: 267) were receiving as much as $12 for adult *natsiq* skins and $17.50 for *natsiavinnik* (yearlings or 'silver jars'). The prices cited by Foote represent a N.W.T.-wide average. At Clyde, hunters only recall that the early 1960s saw the local cash situation improve markedly. Judging from Foote (ibid.) and Jelliss (1978), the years 1962–4 mark a watershed with respect to the Inuit money economy.

This new income was funnelled directly into harvesting. Duffy (1988: 166) reports that in 1953 there were only two unpowered whaleboats and one motorized 5.4 metre, freighter-type canoe at Clyde. Broughton Island (ibid.), the next village south of Clyde, as late as 1961, had only two canoes and three whaleboats. Neither community possessed a snowmobile until 1962. By 1966, Clyde's inventory of boats had increased to twenty-five canoes and two powered whaleboats (ibid.), along with twenty-seven outboard engines. The first Inuit-owned snowmobile arrived in the fall of 1962 and by the mid-1960s ten were in use.

The importance of this new equipment, especially snowmobiles, was that it widened the range at which hunters could function, thus escaping the limited zones of exploitation imposed upon them by resettlement. But a second reason entered into consideration, too. This was a massive die-off of dogs from two major episodes of canine distemper between 1964 and 1966. Clyde Inuit estimate that at least 500 dogs died locally. By 1971, only 185 dogs were available in the area for work and breeding.

The demand for skins was important to the 200 Inuit at Clyde because there were few steady wage opportunities. The three full-time jobs in Clyde provided less than $5,000 of income to the community, and other opportunities were of short duration: besides some specialty work, there was only stevedoring during the HBC and government resupply and one or two housemaid positions in the homes of Whites. Such jobs paid as little as $0.50–1.00 a day.

Social transfer payments into the mid-1960s often provided between one-third to one half of Inuit income, but a considerable portion of these transfers were arranged in the form of coupons redeemable for specific purchases, like children's clothing, infant formula and housing rental. To obtain cash for reinvestment in subsistence, sales from seal harvesting were primary.

Duffy (1988: 166) suggests that the ecological advantages of modern equipment were offset by higher operating costs. Inuit did confront upward-spiralling prices on these imported tools, but managed to cope by spreading capitalization costs over two to three years. According to Duffy, the combined costs of fuel, motor oil, and ammunition amounted to $4.46 per sealskin sold at Clyde during the 1960s. He seems to argue that these costs drained *natsiq* harvesting of profit, but the price received by Inuit for sealskins substantially exceeded $4.50 from the mid-1960s to 1983, except in 1967–8 and 1976–8 when seal protest activity was intense. Additionally, this cost estimate does not include the tenfold food value that each seal represents after operational costs.

The money-flow cycle associated with mechanized harvesting after 1962 was a three-year treadmill (see Table 6.4). In the first year a hunter was pressed to pay off much of the cost of his machine, in the second the main expenses accrued from the costs of daily operations and periodic maintenance, and in the third year maintenance costs rose sharply from excessive wear and tear. When expenses became prohibitive for the results achieved, the hunter bought a new machine

Table 6.4 *Equipment depreciation, Clyde River, 1985**

Item	Number in sample	In use <3 years	In use >3 years	Mean use years
snowmobile	53	40	13	2.7
canoe/boat	35	8	27	6.9
boat motor	26	10	16	4.7
rifle	149	89	60	4.3

* sample size: 44 of 110 adult males.

Source: Usher and Wenzel (1988: 35).

and the cycle began again. Access to cash through sealskin sales greatly increased the degree to which Inuit could exercise choice with respect to where they invested their efforts. During the early stages of the government era, money was scarce and no cash opportunity could be eschewed.

Sealskins gave hunters the option to forego wage participation, and to invest time and energy in customary subsistence activities. A strong external market definitely helped: from 1962 to 1982, income from sealing in the N.W.T. generally went up (see Jelliss 1978: 4), except during two episodes, 1966-8 and 1977-8, of particularly intense anti-sealing campaigning. Interestingly, the proportion of biomass contributed by ringed seals stays between 42 and 50 per cent in seal-dependent communities like Clyde (Wenzel 1990). In other words, harvesting activity, when it increased, did so in all spheres, not just in sealing. The animal rights movement, we should recall (Best 1984), has contended that modern Inuit seal hunting has been stimulated solely by cash profit. These data contradict that contention.

In fact, Inuit were responding to other factors beside the price of sealskins. Of great importance was the rapid growth of their population as a result of improved health care. Clyde's population, between 1960 and 1980, grew from approximately 200 Inuit to about 450. Under such circumstances the only species Clyde people could rely on for food was *natsiq*. The other factor was the steady upward price spiral of imported equipment. These two combined pressures intensified the need for an easily accessible local commodity that could provide food and money.

We must now return to the question of the true significance of modern harvesting equipment. Smith (1988: 67-8) believes Inuit hunters had become dependent on guns, power boats, and snowmobiles because of the erosion of traditional skills or because these tools made life 'easier'. In fact, Inuit reliance on imported equipment relates mainly to southern-influenced changes in their ecological situation.

The first, as we have seen, was that, in the new settlement scheme, hunters had to operate under increasingly less efficient circumstances. Second, in an improved health care environment, the *raison d'etre* for centralization, the Inuit population of the Eastern Arctic expanded.

Table 6.5 *Clyde harvesting costs, 1971-2, 1975-6*

	Cost ($)		
	Period 1 *1971-2*	*Period 2* *1975-6*	*% Change*
A. Capital items			
snowmobile	1,400	2,300	40
canoe (6.7 m)	1,200	1,800	33
outboard motor	1,300	1,800	28
.222 cal rifle	145	250	42
.303 cal rifle	99	150	33
canvas tent	n.d.	n.d.	n.d.
sleeping bag	65	99	35
camp stove	28	45	38
Subtotal A:	4,237	6,444	35
B. Replacement items			
track assembly	n.d.	200	n.d.
ski and frame	20	n.d.	n.d.
slider	n.d.	n.d.	n.d.
piston	30	42	29
crankshaft	n.d.	n.d.	n.d.
spark plug	1	2	50
Subtotal B:		insufficient data	
C. Expendables			
gasoline (190l)	113	125	10
av. yearly use = 2839l	1,695	1,875	10
box .222 ammunition (20 bullets)	5	8.5	42
av. yearly use = 50 boxes	250	425	42
Subtotal C:	1,945	2,300	16
Combined total:	6,182	8,744	30

Source: Usher and Wenzel (1988: 33); Wenzel (1983b: 86).

Third, children, especially boys in their adolescence, no longer became physically involved in harvesting because of southern educational requirements. This last meant not only that young men were less prepared to function as hunters, but also that in villages like Clyde the overall population was adding ten members per year while the number of active harvesters was increasing by only two or three.

When the external demand for sealskins was strong, the rising cost of harvest operations posed little problem, but when the market weakened and prices plunged, as they did in 1966-8 and 1977-8 and import costs continued to climb, subsistence for food and money at Clyde was placed in a precarious position (see Foote 1967a; Wenzel 1978). Changes in capital and operations/maintenance costs (Table 6.5) in just a five year period were considerable.

If the sole object of economy was the production of cash income,

Table 6.6   *Clyde wild products cash income, 1979-80*

Species	Pelts sold	Income received	Price per skin	Income per hunter
ringed seal	2,504	45,688	18.24	550.45
other seals*	57	884	15.50	10.65
polar bear	42	43,717	1,040.88	526.71
fox/wolf	109	3,641	33.40	43.86

* bearded and harp seals only.

harvesting would have been unsustainable. Even in strong market years, like 1979-80 when sealskins fetched $20, Clyde hunters sold wildlife products commercially valued at only $94,000 (Table 6.6), or $1,133.79 per hunter. This income figure, when compared to the basic annual gasoline costs of a harvester in 1975-6, indicates that in strict monetary terms harvesters operated at a deficit.

Inuit hunting, however, is not oriented to monetary profit, but to food. In this regard, wildlife harvesting remained at least as successful an adaptation during the 1960s and 1970s as it was for earlier generations of Inuit. In general terms, it may be said that, while the government era was a time during which imported harvesting equipment became a necessary part of Inuit ecological activities, 'country food' remained the dominant element in Inuit diet and nutrition.

There are several reasons why wildlife continued in this critical food role. The first is ideological and will be discussed in a later chapter. The other relates to the economics of modern northern life and the relative costs of imported versus country food.

Although the growth of southern influence in Inuit communities during these decades included an explosion in the variety and amount of imported foods, Inuit recognized very quickly that the monetary cost of these goods was prohibitive. Initially, the tenuousness of South-to-North transportation, mainly by ship during the short summer, meant that the only foods that could be imported were of the canned or dried variety and thus bulky. This meant that food supplies were shipped in volume and this cost was passed along to the village-level consumer. Prices were often so high that many northern *Qallunaat* received their food through special sealift orders that were heavily subsidized by the government. As for Inuit, they found many of these preserved goods less than palatable. The one exception was carbohydrates – white sugar, soft drinks, and candy – which now inundated Inuit villages.

Fresh vegetables, fruits, and meat only became available in settlements like Clyde in the mid-1970s when improved air transport made it feasible to import these items in a reasonable condition. For the first time, whole milk, apples, and lettuce appeared on the shelves of northern stores. What did not change (see Table 6.7) was the high cost of imported food, for a while regular air service meant fresh

Table 6.7 *Clyde one-day sample menu, 1984**

Meal	Item/quantity	Cost ($)
Breakfast:	8 large eggs	2.85
	4 whole oranges	3.28
	175 g canned ham	3.51
	1 l whole milk	3.40
	8 slices white bread	0.81
	4 tea bags	0.20
	sugar, margarine, jam	0.40
subtotal		14.45
Lunch:	processed cheese, 227 g	2.75
	8 slices white bread	0.81
	canned soup, 1,183 ml	1.25
	canned peaches, 539 g	2.08
	4 sodas, 280 ml each	3.40
subtotal		10.29
Supper:	330 g T-bone beef steaks	21.88
	500 g frozen vegetables	4.30
	dehydrated mashed potatoes	0.61
	1 l whole milk	3.40
	8 slices white bread	0.81
	apple-raisin cake mix, 400 g	2.29
	4 tea bags	0.20
	sugar, margarine, spices	0.40
subtotal		33.88
Snacks:	8 sodas, 280 ml each	6.80
	potato chips, 200 g	2.69
	4 candy bars	2.40
subtotal		11.89
Total one-day cost		70.51

* estimated for a four-person family.

stocks could be brought in at least weekly, now travel time, in-transit storage, weight and handling added to the cost. Inuit certainly took advantage of these new foods, especially of things like fruit and milk, but overall use of fresh foods remained limited because of the amounts in which they were available and their price tag.

On the other hand, wildlife, and especially *natsiq*, harvesting allows Inuit to avoid the prohibitively high cost of imported food reliance. Essentially, while dependence on store food can run in excess of $25,000 per year, harvesting, even with the costs of periodic capitalization and annual operations and maintenance, proves to be a monetarily more economical alternative. Independent data by Finley and Miller (1980: 10) from Clyde River for 1979 (Table 6.8) illustrate this point.

These data show that Clyde hunters produced 1,651 kg of wild meat

Table 6.8 *Clyde edible harvest levels and frequency, 1979*

Species	Total harvest	EW (kg) harvested[1]	Number per hunter[2]	EW produced per harvester
ringed seal	4,733	94,660	54.4	1,088
other seals[3]	9	1,260	0.2	14
narwhal[4]	5	385	0.1	4
polar bear	21	2,898	0.2	33
caribou	992	36,704	11.4	421
fish	2,867	7,167	33.0	82
wolf/fox[5]	304	—	3.4	—
small game	169	84	1.9	1
birds	719	719	8.3	8
EW subtotals		143,877		1,651

[1] average edible weight per species from Foote 1967b and the author's field notes, Clyde River 1971-4.
[2] estimated on a monthly harvester reporting mean of 87 men.
[3] includes only bearded seal and harp seal.
[4] edible weight calculated for *muktaaq* only.
[5] furbearers are not eaten in the community.

Source: Finley and Miller (1980: 10, 21).

each, or 334 kg of fresh food for each person in the village. This 1,650 kg of country food is important for two reasons. The first is that wild foods are more nourishing than even many fresh items found in the HBC store (see Table 6.9 for a nutrient comparison between *natsiq* and beef). The other is that, unlike store foods, wild meat, and especially seal, is very accessible to village residents, both because of the relative geographic proximity of these resources and because of *ningiqtug*. These last two points are apparent in data from Broughton Island, another Baffin community closely comparable to Clyde (see Table 6.10)

Having seen the available store alternatives, we are able to appreciate the attraction of harvesting as the most efficient way for Inuit to produce food. We are also better able to appreciate the role of subsistence not only as a buffer between Inuit and the natural environment, but also with the *Qallunaat* sector of the modern northern economy.

It should come as no surprise that harvested foods offer Inuit the most economical and efficient investment of their scarce monetary resources. Numerous studies over the past fifteen years (Usher 1976; Berger 1977; Wolfe 1979; Ames *et al* 1988; Borre 1989) have reported that the net dietary return for each dollar invested in harvesting is far greater than for imported foods. Harvesting consistently provides a higher yield of food per dollar spent than can be got from wage labour.

This can be demonstrated in a more elaborate benefit – cost examination. It is evident when harvesting activities are subjected to benefit–cost-type examination. In July and August of 1984, I monitored

Table 6.9 *Nutrient comparison of seal meat and beef*

	gm.			mg.		
Food	Protein	Fat	Calcium	Iron	Thiamine	Riboflavin
Seal	30	1	50	3	0.3	0.8
Beef	17	23	10	1	0.1	0.2

Source: Royal Commission on Seals and the Sealing Industry in Canada (Malouf, 1986h: 243).

Table 6.10 *Inuit seasonal wild food consumption, Broughton Island, N.W.T (sample size – 18 households)*

	percent consumption frequency			
Food type	Autumn	Winter	Spring	Summer
whale/*muktaaq*	55.6	38.9	33.3	77.8
ringed seal	100.0	100.0	100.0	100.0
caribou	72.0	94.4	77.8	77.8
arctic char	77.8	83.3	100.0	88.9
all other foods*	0.0	5.6	6.0	30.0

* other foods include harp seal, birds, and small game.

Source: Indian and Northern Affairs Canada (1986: 62).

the hunting activities of five full-time Clyde harvesters over a six-week period (Wenzel 1985b). These men were mainly involved in the pursuit of free-swimming marine mammals (ringed seal, narwhal) using motor-powered canoes, seeking caribou inland on foot, and fishing for arctic char with nylon nets and by rod and reel. Except for char fishing, the men had to invest large amounts of money and energy in their search for animals.

Detailed records were kept on each man's cash operational costs, the hours each spent away from the community in hunting, any sales of wild products, and the game captured. The total edible weight produced relative to operating costs, including time, was then compared to the cost of purchasing the same amount of food at the HBC.

As the data demonstrate, both the time (508 hours) and monetary ($5,419.34) investment required by harvesting is prodigious. However, the bio-energetic rewards are quite substantial. The cash cost of a comparable amount of food (3,500 kg) by store purchase would have been $24,458. By any calculation, therefore, harvesting proves itself economical.

Even more interesting are the results achieved by hunters when we

Table 6.11 *Net rate of profit from harvesting as compared to store food purchases at Clyde River, 1984*

Parameter	No imputed ($) value added	Imputed ($) value added
1. Edible Weight Harvested (kg)[1]	3,494	3,494
2. Harvester Costs	$5,419.34	$5,419.34
3. Food sales ($)	none	none
4. Fur sales ($)	none	none
5. Imputed values[2] ($/kg) factor	none	$7.00
5a. Added $ value (5)	none	$24,458.00
7. Gross $ yield (−2)	$5,419.34	$19,038.66
8. Time invested	508	508
8a. Time cost[3] ($8.00/hr × n hrs)	−$3,556.00	+$1,776.00
9. Net yield ($/hr) (2+8a/8)	−$17.66	+$78.45
10. Cost per kg (2+8a/1)	$2.56	$1.04

[1] sample harvest included 4 adult narwhal, 27 ringed seal, 234 arctic char, 3 snow geese, 4 ptarmigan, 9 caribou.
[2] imputed value of food is based on the average price of fresh meats in the HBC.
[3] productive hunting time was assigned a monetary value based on the minimum hourly wage in Clyde ($8); non-productive time (sleeping, repairs) was either assigned a value of $0 or a negative value. Thus, search, travel, production, and processing were calculated at $8/hr (268 hours (53%) = $2,144); sleeping and eating $0/hr (194 hrs (38%) = $0); and field repair of equipment −$8/hr (46 hrs (9%) = −$368).

Source: Wenzel (1985b: 16).

take into account their time. When monetary value is assigned to both the country food produced and the time spent in its production, hunters are earning more than $75 per hour.

The cost-effectiveness of harvesting in 1984 is also comparable to dogteam hunting. In 1971, I (Wenzel n.d.a.) gathered data on four *Aqvi-qtiummiut* hunters during four weeks of winter sealing. During that period, hunting was done on twenty-one days (452 hunting hours) and a total of thirty-four *natsiq* were captured. Harvesters used 204 hours in actual hunting, another 160 hours in the repair and manufacture of equipment, and eighty-eight hours in travel to and from the ice. They spent more time in travel, but were rarely absent from the community overnight and carried out all their equipment repair and fabrication activities at Aqviqtiuq.

Table 6.11 shows that modern harvesting calls for significant inputs of labour and money, but also that these investments greatly reduce the much higher monetary cost of settlement life. In 1984, sealskins were without exchange value, yet harvesting was demonstrably important to the Clyde economy; before the EEC boycott, harvesting produced as much food and even more money and was a particularly efficient way for Inuit to use their resources.

Hunter data from the early 1970s demonstrate how much wild products monetarily contribute to Inuit (Wenzel 1990). In 1973, three-quarters of the $4,045 that a Clyde Inuk needed for capital harvesting equipment (snowmobile, outboard engine, canvas canoe) was met by cash receipts from sealskin, polar bear, ivory, and fox. Of that cash income aggregate, ringed seals provided between one-half and two-thirds of the edible harvested biomass entering the community.

While money cannot substitute for the 'natural capital' which harvesters bring to hunting, in the post-war northern environment it has complemented Inuit skills and provided a means of overcoming the ecological and economic disadvantages of government policies. Non-Inuit imagine that the wage employment that came to the modern North yields a more consistent cash income, but they forget that 'gainful' work has been a rare commodity in Inuit settlements and when present often diverted time and energy from hunting. Harvesting not only continued to meet the food needs of active hunter households and the *ningiqtuq* economy in the 1960s and 1970s it also provided the only sure means for Inuit to acquire the money that government policy made a fact of Inuit life. Simply put, sealskins contributed to Inuit re-establishing balanced access to the spectrum of established and new resources needed to maintain their subsistence culture.

Since 1982: the seal boycott era

Directive 83/229/EEC had immediate consequence for subsistence in the Canadian North. Inuit *bricolage* developed in small, strongly tradition-based communities like Clyde River as a means of sustaining customary social goals. The success Inuit had in integrating money into the subsistence scheme eased problems generated by the 'Southernization' of the post-war arctic.

The immediate effect of the European boycott was economic. Inuit very quickly lost control over their local village economies. Seals, because they provided at once food and money, had given Inuit access to both traditional and modern resources. 83/229/EEC unravelled the *bricolage* that formed the modern subsistence adaptation by reducing access to money and thus complicating the circumstances of the traditional food economy.

This presented Inuit with a conflict as to how to invest their time and energy. To choose harvesting would lead to the loss of needed cash resources, while other options meant losing time – the most important traditional resource in effective harvesting.

Table 6.12 *Clyde ringed sealskin sales, 1979-80 to 1984-85*

Year	No. of hunters	Sealskins sold	Total value ($)	Av. price per skin ($)
1979-80	83	2,504	57,824	23.09
1980-81	90	3,377	58,516	17.32
1981-82	88	1,172	16,263	13.87
1982-83	63	1,238	12,577	10.15
1983-84	56	656	4,682	7.13
1984-85	62	532	3,719	6.99

Year	Harvest per hunter ($)	Sealing per hunter ($)	Hunter income from sealskin ($)
1979-80	1,272	697	54
1980-81	918	650	70
1981-82	612	185	30
1982-83	890	199	22
1983-84	353	84	23
1984-85	569	60	10

* harvest income from all species.

Source: Clyde HBC Fur Purchase Records.

A. The new economics of harvesting

European boycott activity placed Inuit in a double bind. They were trapped between plunging monetary returns (Table 6.12) for the one resource that reliably brought in food and money, and the need to raise ever more to sustain food production.

The result, beginning within a year of the EC decision, was the loss of local control over their means of subsistence. The only avenues that remained for money were wage employment or transfer payments. Wage work had a high cost in time and energy, while welfare threatened to leave Inuit economically marginalized.

One way to understand the impact of falling sealskin prices on harvesting is to think of the value of the harvesting outfit in terms of its cost in *natsiq* skins, the commodity which Inuit could supply to Whites (this novel method was developed by Muller-Wille 1978). By translating dollar values into sealskin units (SSU), as in the following table (Table 6.13), we can begin to appreciate the meaning of the EC's decision to a Clyde hunter.

As Table 6.13 shows, by 1985 the average price of a sealskin in small communities like Clyde had dropped to that of the mid-1960s (see Jelliss 1978: 4), but Inuit were no longer able to sustain the volume of everyday harvesting operations that subsistence required. This decline was so steep that by 1985 the combined SSU cost of just one Clyde hunter for a year would have required the sale of 2,906 sealskins, more

Table 6.13 *Clyde harvesting cost comparison in dollars ($) and sealskin units (SSU), 1975–76 and 1984–85*

	1975–76 (SSU = $16.40)	1984–85 (SSU = $4.50)
1. Capital items		
snowmobile	2,300/140	2,800/621
canoe	1,800/110	3,000/667
outboard motor	1,800/110	3,300/733
.222 cal rifle	250/15	660/147
.303 cal rifle	150/9	350/78
sleeping bag	99/6	290/65
camp stove	45/3	70/16
subtotal	6,444/393	10,470/2327
2. Snowmobile parts		
track assembly	200/13	390/87
piston	42/3	80/18
spark plug	2/1	4/1
subtotal	244/17	474/106
3. Operational items		
gasoline (227.3 l)	125/8	128/29
av. annual use = 3409.5 l	1,875/120	1,920/435
ammunition/box: .222 cal × 20	8.5/1	11.5/3
av. annual use = 50 boxes (1,000)	425/26	575/128
annual use subtotal	2,300/146	2,495/563
Combined costs	7,113/393	13,439/2906

than all the skins sold by all Clyde hunters in 1979–80, the year when the per skin price was highest.

As a consequence, harvesting at pre-boycott levels was not sustainable. Inuit were alienated from the biological resource that allowed them to manage their economy and fit southern economic demands into the customary subsistence pattern. For the first time since the 1950s, control over the economics of subsistence returned to the hands of non-Inuit.

Many of the technological needs of post-centralized subsistence harvesting, from snowmobiles to spark plugs, began to rise beyond the reach of hunters. In 1980, one sealskin ($23) paid for the gasoline and ammunition needed for a day of hunting by snowmobile or boat. In 1985, a pelt ($7) barely brought in enough money to pay for bullets.

This affected even the most stable element of food subsistence – ringed seal hunting (see Table 6.14). In 1981, *natsiq* had provided nearly two-thirds (77,694 kg) of the edible biomass that entered Clyde River. In 1982 and 1983, seal was barely one-half this total. The same trend affects the months from autumn through spring, when·seal meat

Table 6.14 *Clyde seasonal seal harvest, 1981–83*

Year/Season	No. of seals harvested	Edible weight (kg)	Edible biomass all sources (kg)
1981:			
winter	1,052	24,196	40,856
spring	1,317	30,291	41,517
summer	697	16,031	28,662
autumn	312	7,176	10,894
1982:			
winter	812	18,676	45,092
spring	947	21,781	37,485
summer	544	12,512	25,769
autumn	204	4,692	7,195
1983:			
winter	932	21,436	42,337
spring	689	15,847	33,197
summer	763	17,549	39,813
autumn	294	6,762	10,681

is the most important item in the Clyde diet.

These data by no means suggest that the people at Clyde are in imminent danger. Nor even that Clyde Inuit face the remote possibility of starvation from lack of wildlife. What they do raise is the possibility that Inuit who depend heavily on *natsiq* as a major seasonal resource may conceivably meet times when this abundant species may not be as readily available within the community as it has been in recent years. This scenario is not so far-fetched, in the summer of 1988, Clyde Inuit (Palituq, personal communication) in fact commented that seal meat was becoming one of the most difficult foods to obtain through inter-*ilagiit* sharing.

Clyde Inuit have made up for the as yet only occasional shortfalls of seals by shifting emphasis to food species which entail lower costs in time and money. Harvest data for 1981–3 collected by the Baffin Regional Inuit Association (1982, 1983, 1984; also Donaldson 1988) indicate that the arctic char seem to be the species that has been turned to. The local catch has increased markedly, from 6,400 kg (EW) in 1981 to 20,800 in 1983. A similar shift also appears to be occurring with regard to caribou, although the numbers are too preliminary to be conclusive.

In other words, in the Clyde area, Inuit are adapting to the cost dilemma of sealing by focussing greater attention on species that can be harvested from fixed sites (arctic char) or whose capture relies primarily on the investment of human energy (caribou). It remains to be seen whether these low cash-cost species can ecologically sustain this increased harvesting pressure.

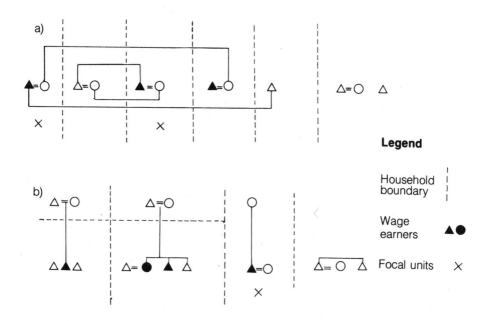

Figure 6.1 *a) Suluak camp composition, 31 May–5 June 1985 and b) Nuvuktiapik camp composition, 19 June–26 July 1985*

There is other evidence that Inuit in the Clyde area are attempting to offset the effects of the seal ban on the exchange sector of their economy by limiting the money they spend on other activities. This can be seen in the change (Figure 6.1) that has taken place recently in the distribution and composition of summer camp groups.

Before centralization, an *ilagiit* would leave the winter village in May and occupy several temporary living sites convenient for intercepting caribou, migrating marine mammals, and arctic char. After resettlement, most Clyde Inuit continued to maintain the customary *ilagiit* pattern of social organization (see Figure 6.2) in summer camp.

After the 1983 disruption of the local money economy, the Clyde summer camping pattern underwent a process of contraction and mixing. Summer villages, which once were established as soon as children were free of school at sites as much as 200 km from Clyde, began to be placed nearer to Clyde River, with most located in the Clyde Inlet – Inugsuin Fiord area and where the *ilagiit* no longer necessarily form the social core of such groups. Many recent Clyde summer camps seem to be composite constructs, with one or two well-equipped nuclear families providing their co-residents with access to equipment and fuel in return for cooperation in harvesting. In 1985, one site, Suluak, became something of a 'commuter' camp. Several wage workers moved their families there for parts of the summer,

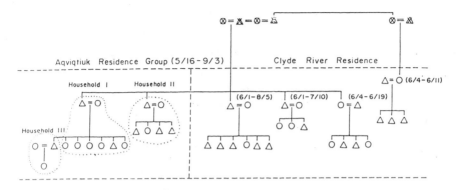

Figure 6.2 *Eglinton Fjord summer camp grouping, May–September 1972*

while they travelled back and forth each day to Clyde. Longer-distance camping, as was found before the early 1980s, now is restricted mainly to mobile male hunter groups pursuing large game like caribou and narwhal.

Contraction of the summer camping zone is an indicator of the impact of EEC action on Inuit control over subsistence resources. Loss of sealskins as an exchange resource has had its most severe effect on hunters 25–50 year old, a group that customarily contributes the most time and energy to the subsistence system. They are also the age group which have depended heavily on cash from sealskin sales and with the most limited access to wage employment because they lack Euro-Canadian linguistic and job skills.

The other group hard hit by the ban's effects is composed of young men under 25. Many of them have only marginal or beginner hunting skills because their younger years have been spent in school. They cannot, even with prodigious investment of time and energy in harvesting, produce the cash necessary to becoming independent hunters. They are further frustrated by the preference given in the contemporary employment environment to older men with large families to support.

B. The social impact of the ban

In the years since 1982 the European Community ban on commercial seal imports tore a huge hole in the modern ecological and economic adaptation of Canadian Inuit. In an attempt to repair conditions, the Federal and Northwest Territories governments have rushed to shore up the northern economy with the same fervor and insight as in the 1950s. As a result, government programs once again pervade much of Inuit life because Europeans have unknowingly altered the resource configuration of modern Inuit subsistence. The architects of 83/129/EEC attempted to acknowledge aboriginal sealing, but their

128

conception of Inuit subsistence was out of date. They did not grasp the reality of Inuit life after a century of economic contact and thirty-five years of intensive *Qallunaat* colonization.

A hasty look at Clyde River suggests that enormous improvement has occurred in the cash ledger of the village. Full-time wage employment has grown nearly 30 per cent since 1975, and Inuit wages now account for 58 per cent of the money entering the local economy. Clyde boasts a hotel partially owned and operated by a local Inuk, a 100 per cent Inuit municipal administration, a Hudson's Bay Company store five times larger than a decade ago, satellite telecommunications with telephone and television in nearly every home, a half-dozen individually owned fibreglass speed boats for hunting, and a 15-metre 'mother' ship for communal hunts. Present-day Clyde is a far cry in appearance and apparent wealth from what was fifteen years ago and to a stranger the local economy looks healthier than ever.

But what if we stay a little longer, and probe a bit deeper. We would see that, although the permanent job rate in Clyde has grown steadily for almost ten years, less than 15 per cent of the Clyde adults are employed full-time (Borre and Wenzel 1988). While more money (4 per cent) is now spent on food at the HBC, it bought 8 per cent less than in 1978. The ratio of snowmobiles to hunters has decreased (from 0.55 machines to 0.44). Larger and more expensive boats are beached around the village, but few leave the community during the work week. Instead, on week days, no more than two or three canoes with three and four hunters depart for a day of seal hunting. The two most noticeable groups of men in Clyde are the knots of teenagers who gather on the steps of the HBC, and the middle-aged hunters who, alone or in twos, work to repair a broken snowmobile or outboard engine.

As much as the money from wages now dominates Clyde's economy, only thirty-five to forty half-or full-time jobs are available to an adult population of 265. This tells us something about the way the ban, and the government's rushed response to it, have distorted the economy of the village. Rather than nearly all adult men having regular access to cash from their hunting, they now compete with women and post-school adolescents for the few secure jobs found in the village.

What some access to the wage economy can mean to harvesting is illustrated through an examination of the hunting activities of sixteen Clyde men (Table 6.15), aged 25–60, from 1981 to 1984. While all are considered active hunters, half the group held at least half-time work. These data, while limited, suggest that access to wage income, an important factor at Clyde before the EC ban in certain harvest activities, is becoming increasingly so.

With regard to the four-year aggregate harvest of the Clyde area's four major food species, the activities of part-time hunters in the sample group came to weigh, year by year, more heavily. In 1981, they

Table 6.15 *Clyde harvester survey, 1981-84*[1]

Year/ species	Harvest by wage workers	Harvest by non-wage hunters	Harvest (%) wage/non-wage
1981			
natsiq	286	313	48/52
whale[2]	3	4	43/57
caribou	105	47	69/31
fish	143	488	23/77
1982			
natsiq	216	225	49/51
whale	1	0	100/0
caribou	175	47	79/21
fish	578	658	47/58
1983			
natsiq	191	326	37/63
whale	5	1	83/17
caribou	138	44	76/24
fish	1,498	572	62/38
1984			
ringed seal	327	316	51/49
whale	14	6	70/30
caribou	144	70	64/36
fish	930	655	59/41

[1] data base: 509 (66%) of a possible 768 harvester months over the four years
of the survey.
[2] includes beluga whale (4) and narwhal (30).

took 45 per cent of the entire harvest; by 1984 (one year after the seal boycott), the contribution of part-time harvesters rose to 61 per cent. This growth occurred despite the fact that these men had no additional time available for hunting.

This means that money for the purchase and operation of harvesting equipment is still the critical resource. Men with access to wage work have access to money and can therefore bring home animals. Non-wage hunters basically find that they cannot hunt either as much or as productively because of their lack of cash. Indeed, many of the full-time hunter sub-sample stated that they had experienced times during the sample years when they could not afford to repair or operate their equipment. Seven of the eight employed hunters possessed outfits (boats, motors and snowmobiles) with a purchase value of $15,000–$28,000; no full-time hunter had an outfit with a purchase value exceeding $11,000 and only two men possessed snowmobiles less than two years old.

The part-time harvesters explained that they needed expensive equipment, such as fibreglass boats with speedy 90 hp engines, because they had so little time for hunting. While their equipment was far more expensive to operate, they were willing to meet the extra cost in order to hunt.

The data also suggest that high cost types of harvesting, such as caribou and narwhal, are becoming the province of wage supported hunters. The part-time hunters noted that they planned their vacations to coincide with the expected arrival of narwhal or to take advantage of caribou and, with their cash and more powerful vehicles, hunted beyond the range of non-wage supported men.

Members of this sub-group also perceive sealing as a minimal activity. While seal hunting still has some value for food production, very few of the wage earners felt that a day of seal hunting justified the expense of their large boats and gas-consuming engines and a few of them felt that bigger game contributed more to the community.

From the data, two distinct strategies of harvesting can be discerned. Non-wage hunters have scaled back their activities because of prohibitive monetary expense. Their activities are concentrated in areas close to village since more distant activities depend on the cooperation of wage-employed kinsmen.

One middle-aged man, who for the last fifteen years has proved to be among the most productive of Clyde seal hunter, annually averaging about 250 animals, noted that in 1985 for most weeks he could only afford five gallons (22 l) of gasoline ($13.50), roughly what Clyde men before the 1983 ban used in a single day of winter sealing. He was therefore concentrating his efforts solely on *natsiq* within 20 km of Clyde, 'because they give people food'. This man is still widely regarded in the community as a full-time hunter; he has never worked for wages nor, until 1985, accepted social assistance, but his inability to afford fuel costs, which he formerly covered from sealskin sales, now restricts him to no more than two days of hunting a week. He remains a productive seal harvester, but regrets that he cannot hunt more because it is now more difficult for him to give seal meat to elders.

The problems encountered by this much respected older hunter also affect younger men. One experienced hunter commented that he himself could only go caribou hunting with one of his employed kinsmen because he could rarely afford gasoline to travel to the distant areas where caribou concentrate. When the same man goes winter seal hunting, however, he often takes two or three younger men, unable to buy fuel for themselves, along on his *kamutik* so that they can hunt for the day.

Interviews with sample hunters who held jobs showed a distinct pattern to their participation in sealing, with most men leaving the village only one evening a week or on a free Saturday during the winter. They explained that fatigue, the difficulty of *mauluktuk* hunting in darkness, and a desire to spend time with their children all affect their efforts.

131

The same group did, however, spend more concentrated time in long-distance harvesting for 'big game' and are increasingly becoming the prime contributors of caribou and narwhal. Their access to the most expensive and advanced equipment allows them to substitute money and technology for time. Members of this group compress the time they spend on the land into discrete segments, planning and splitting their three or four weeks of annual vacation to coincide with the expected appearance of 'prestige' species. Meat from caribou and other high-cost species therefore is usually abundant in the village only after their forays, in something akin to a 'feast and then famine' pattern.

The post-seal boycott period at Clyde has several characteristics that clearly set it apart from earlier phases of Inuit–*Qallunaat* relations. The first is that non-wage-supported hunters suffer severe constraint in the overall scope of harvesting. This is because, at the very least, the operational expenses of all types of hunting, which in the past were recouped from sealskin sales, are no longer available. Further, success as a harvester has become increasingly dependent on wage labor, since only wage-supported hunters can afford present-day equipment and operations costs. Successful harvesters now appear to rely more heavily than ever on 'state-of-the-art' technologies.

Also, the ability of Inuit to harvest for food subsistence has become as closely linked to non-traditional skills as to ecological experience and acumen. For example, English has become an important qualifier in the present economic environment. This is placing a larger burden on a few harvesters to meet growing village food needs.

As a result, certain aspects of the *ningiqtuq* sharing system are being eroded. Whereas a decade earlier equipment and cash were pooled within *ilagiit*, at present sharing is constrained by the high monetary cost of equipment, the time required to replace lost, damaged or borrowed personal equipment, and an awakening among job holders to the personal price exacted by wage labor.

Even with respect to traditional resources, *ilagiit* reciprocity has been reduced at various times of the year in response to the unavailability of certain foods. When wage-time constraints on harvesting are coupled with episodes of bad weather or poor ice, the *ningiqtuq* situation becomes extremely circumscribed and sharing between extended families suffers.

Several new institutional forms of sharing have recently arisen in Clyde that help in coping with this situation. The most important centers on the church, which, at the direction of the elders, periodically hosts village-wide feasts of caribou, *muktaaq*, and seal. These are planned, and congregants contribute the necessary food. *Muktaaq* and pots of boiled meat, accompanied by bannock prepared by the women, are served. In this new form of *ningiqtuq*, the church elders assume the role of extended family leaders, the *ilagiit angiukaaq* or *isumataq*.

A second form of sharing which has increased in recent times involves individual gifts of large items of equipment, such as a rifle or second-hand snowmobile, at Christmas or birthdays. Clyde Inuit do not consider this part of 'real' *ningiqtuq* practice because such celebrations are derived from *Qallunat* practices, but they nonetheless serve as a means of distributing difficult-to-obtain goods.

While more money has entered the local economy of communities like Clyde River through the expansion of the exchange economy (via government job creation), data presented here suggest that this approach to the cash shortage problems confronting Inuit harvesting is creating a new problem of economic differentiation with regard to both the food and money sectors of the local economy. A decade ago, virtually all Clyde Inuit males were officially listed as employed, regardless of whether they held a wage position, were artisans or were harvesters. Only ten years ago, it was common to hear in the village how unfortunate it was that a man with a full-time job could go hunting. Today, productive, experienced hunters are officially classified in the government roles as unemployed.

7 IDEOLOGICAL RELATIONS AND HARVESTING

Introduction

No aspect of the northern seal debate provokes as much controversy as the ideological aspect of Inuit harvesting. Of particularly lively interest is whether any spiritual connection remains between Inuit and the seals they harvest. This question has been elevated recently to a level of special importance by environmental and animal rights advocates (see Regan 1982). Opponents of an Inuit seal hunting system that includes the sale of sealskins have argued that southern economic demands have dissolved all vestiges of the 'traditional' spiritual bond between hunter and animal. To critics like Smith (1988) and Livingstone (1989), the use of modern equipment to hunt seals and the selling of their skins for any reason are incompatible with presumed tenets of Inuit spirituality. To assert any deeper meaning to present-day Inuit seal hunting is to invoke what Livingstone (ibid.: 119) describes as 'neo-traditional' mysticism. Accordingly, *natsiq* represent no more to Inuit than the price Europeans attach to their pelts.

A spiritual bond between Native hunter and animals is certainly implied in the invocations and allusions made by many environmentalists (see, for instance, Udall 1962) to the deeper ecological understanding of Native Peoples. The best-known example of environmentalist-Native 'kinship' is found in the literature distributed by Greenpeace,

> An ancient North American Indian legend predicts that when the Earth has been ravaged and the animals killed, a tribe of people from all races, creeds and colours would put their faith in deeds, not words, to make the land green again. They would be called 'The Warriors of the Rainbow', protectors of the environment. (Greenpeace UK, *c.* 1984)

Some animal rights proponents like Maureen Duffy have even singled out Inuit to describe the depth of this relationship:

> Hunter gatherers, until they are ... corrupted by modern civilization, usually seem to show a rather different relationship to the other animals ... the same sort of kinship and near reverence ... as the Esquimaux. (Duffy 1984: 6)

Such views must necessarily be examined both as to their aptness and accuracy. Initially, such generalizations fail to recognize Inuit cultural heterogeneity (see Damas 1984b) in much the way that popular conceptualizations of 'normal' Inuit do. For instance, not all pre-contact Eskimos built snowhouses or lived on the sea ice for months at a time or depended on sea mammals year-round. This basic diversity makes southern expectations about the existence of a spiritual sameness extending from Bering Strait to East Greenland at least as unrealistic. The eastern and western ends of this world are separated by 10,000 km, major dialect differences, and a vast range of local environments.

No aspect of Inuit harvesting is as frustrating to systematic under-standing as the ideological connectivity between hunters and their prey. Often, well-meant analyses are too shallow, while the worst such attempts trivialize what they purport to analyse. Even in such a large and varied body of ethnographic and ethnological literature, the best works on Inuit–animal relations are limited.

A clue to the extent of these relations can be found in the work of Boas (1888) and other early northern visitors who recorded and reported many pre-Christian beliefs which allude to a cosmological link between animals and Inuit. Today, a number of scholars (see, for exam-ple, Hutchinson 1977; Saladin d'Anglure 1984; Sabo and Sabo 1985) have analysed such 'myths' as to their structural, cognitive, and ecological meanings.

Another approach to this area of investigation draws on observations in the ethnographic record of more overt spiritual actions by Inuit toward the animals they hunt, for example the act of 'offering' fresh water to a captured seal (Balikci 1970) so its spirit will tell other seals of how well it was treated. But Inuit rarely practice such 'traditional' actions today. Still, in Clyde and other communities, hunters of all ages know that water was once given to a newly killed seal, but also state that Christianity no longer makes this necessary.

Inuit traditional respect for animals is in fact often more subtle than brief casual observation can detect. Richard Nelson (1969) provides such an example in his description of Alaskan Inupiaq preparations for walrus hunting. Before embarking after an animal that Inupiaq consider to be the most dangerous in their environment, a boat crew offers a collective prayer for safety and success. While a Christian medium is employed today, it still indicates the respect and concern with which North Alaskan hunters had always approached walrus.

Sometimes such actions elude the most careful observation since spiritual preparation for hunting is often private and individual. Clyde harvesters often note that a man can harvest successfully only if he always seeks animals with the right thought (isuma) in his mind. By this they mean that the hunter must always think about the animal he hunts, speak correctly about it, never in a deprecating or negative way (see Wenzel 1983a), and be generous with the product of his efforts.

In the case of some species, behavior toward an animal may differ from one Inuk to another or be limited to the members of an ilagiit.

All Clyde River hunters actively seek bearded seal (ujjuk), which supply food and whose hide is used to make traditional sealskin rope (aklunak). But not every Clyde hunter will eat ujjuk because its meat 'is not good for them'. Even the everyday hunting of ringed seal may include special behaviors. Three brothers, who are among the most active young harvesters in the village, always move a fresh-killed natsiq a few metres away from its breathing hole before butchering it so that no blood will enter the water and offend other seals.

I cannot offer any deeper insight into Inuit–animal spiritual relations, but I should like to introduce another aspect of Inuit harvester ideology – the way hunting integrates the human and animal components of the arctic environment into a single shared community. These data were collected through long observation of Inuit actions and through conversations with Inuit from Clyde and other Eastern Arctic communities about the nature of animals.

While I believe this to be an important and often overlooked aspect of Inuit harvesting, I must admit to two scholarly and personal concerns. First, as an ecologically trained scientist, explanations based on the 'cognitive awareness' of others seem to me at times to be less than scientific. They are based neither on objective measurements nor, most times, on direct observation, but on the reporter's interpretation of Inuit discourse and behavior. Much more serious to me is the fear that I may not do justice to Inuit conceptions of wildlife and the natural environment, and that I run the risk of trivializing a vital part of Inuit identity and culture. Only a few Qallunaat like Brody (1975, 1987) and Fienup-Riordan (1983) strike me as having been able to avoid this pitfall. But the significance of these relations to the issue of Inuit sealing dictates the attempt for, as Fortes (1970: 27) has noted, 'an individual's social space is a product of that segment of the social structure and that segment of the habitat with which he or she is in effective contact'.

We are concerned with several levels of man–animal relations. The first is the way the social relationship between Inuit and animals is continually structured through niqituinnaq ('real' food). Second, how harvesting establishes a particularized relationship of the human community to the natural environment. Third, how the relationship between persons (inummariit) and this larger community are defined.

'Real food'

Brody (1987: 71) points out that the lives of Inuit hunters are intimately tied to that of animals. Apparent though this is, he (ibid.: 73) also notes that while Inuit must kill animals to live, they are also vulnerable to what are to us the vagaries of the natural world – animal movements, low points in biological cycles, and animal diseases. There is, therefore, an equality between the hunter and the hunted for animals, too, depend upon the hunt. According to Yu'pik Eskimos

(Fienup-Riordan 1983: 189), animals, like men, are renewed through hunting. Both Brody and Fienup-Riordan report that this perception is common to both Eastern Arctic Inuit and Bering Strait Yu'pik, that hunting is a contract between partners (see also Feit 1973).

My own research among Eastern Arctic Inuit (Wenzel 1986d) suggests that one way of understanding this belief is through Inuit perceptions of food. I shall show that Inuit harvesting is embedded in a network of social relations, a 'kinship' system, in which harvesting is not just the means by which food is extracted from the natural environment, but also the critical medium through which the human and animal communities are joined together.

Inuit catalyse that relationship through the harvesting and eating of *niqituinnaq* – foods that are 'real' – or as we often say, country foods. To Inuit, their culture is not just the sum of its material practices, but also a socially created cognitive model by which people actively and continually negotiate their identities. Ortega y Gasset's (1985) statement, 'I am I and the environment', synthesizes the kind of meaning Inuit impart when they speak about *niqituinnaq* – a unity of environment, community and human identity

The social integration of Inuit harvesting

We can think of Inuit subsistence as composed of two parts, resource harvesting and the distribution of these products. Harvesting is the ecological element and sharing the economic part of a single system. To understand this system, we must suppose that it is ordered and rational. Ethnological data from Alaska (Burch 1975; Fienup-Riordan 1983; Worl 1980) across the Canadian Arctic (Van de Velde 1956; Damas 1969a, b, 1972b, Wenzel 1981) to Greenland (Dahl 1990) support that assumption and demonstrate a clear association between the organization of Inuit interpersonal relations and the organization of Inuit ecological relations.

This association is consistent with Heinrich's (1963: 68) observation that, aside from technology, for Inuit 'kinship ... is the most important other adjustive mechanism since there is little else in the way of integration at a higher level than kinship'. Indeed, no other means is available to Inuit for the efficient and effective organizing and execution of the harvesting activities that underpin their day-to-day subsistence. Task group formation, decision making, resource choice, resource allocation and sharing, and hunting itself are and managed through behavioral constructs patterned after appropriate social conduct.

We have already seen that wildlife harvesting in a high-risk environment requires flexible deployment of personnel, equipment, and economic resources. In communities where individuals, households, and extended families are all joined into a single network of kinship, the application of the same rules that direct interpersonal cooperation

137

and intergenerational relations (see Wenzel 1981, 1986a, b) to harvesting forms a socially, as well as ecologically, efficient means of achieving material subsistence.

Inuit harvesting is a social endeavour, and a critical aspect of it is the role played by *isumataaq* - those trained and experienced elders - in nurturing the young in the social traditions of subsistence. Just as kinship socially attunes individuals to their society, it is the means by which new hunters are inculcated with the social meaning of wildlife for Inuit.

Attitude and intent

Since Inuit hunting is so focussed on the capture of large animals - walrus, seals, polar bears, caribou, even whales - it lends itself almost too well to statistical measurement. As was shown in earlier chapters, we can accurately estimate numbers of animals harvested, the frequency of harvesting success, returns in cash or calories on Inuit investment, and the character of hunting groups. All of this tells us about the material benefits of hunting.

But Inuit are critical of such interpretations and note that harvesting success cannot be evaluated solely in terms of energies and materials invested by hunters. In their own model of relations, the success of a harvester is indicative of that person's cognitive referencing to both the human and animal communities with which he interacts (see Wenzel 1983a; Brody 1987). Inuit emphasize that the core of any relationship between human beings and animals is the basic recognition that an equity exists with animals as sentient (see Dorais 1988) participating members in a shared environment. Where non-Inuit observers may attribute harvesting success to a combination of essential ingredients such as technology, knowledge of the local environment, accumulated skill, and luck, Inuit state that the critical elements in harvesting are proper attitude and intent toward animals.

Attitude is seen at Clyde as a reflection of the equal and joint roles of humans and animals in the ecosystem. Animals are to be 'respected' not because they are superior to humans, but because they, like us, are sentient beings (see Nelson 1969; Wenzel 1983a, 1986d). Being *silatu-juk* (intelligent), animals are aware of the thoughts, speech, and actions of hunters. This awareness provides animals with information so that they may choose to participate or not in encounters with hunters.

A hunter who seeks animals merely to demonstrate his prowess presents an attitude inconsistent with the situation of natural equality. It indicates a lack of seriousness toward the most serious relationship that exists between men and animals. Such a hunter, like one who denigrates animals or is immodest in his speech about them, will not be a successful harvester. Only a person whose thoughts are focussed on the relationship between himself and the animal he seeks demonstrates the correct attitude of a successful hunter.

Intent is explained by Clyde Inuit in two ways. The first is that a hunter must from the beginning of his actions have the intention of utilizing the animals he captures as fully as possible for food. While actual consumption may not always be possible, if, for example, the animal is diseased or a surplus supply of food is on hand, it is the intent of food use that is the essential and principal reason for harvesting.

There is a second aspect to intent. The food produced should not be kept for the exclusive use of the individual hunter. Animals, like land, are common property (see Berger 1977, 1985; Usher and Bankes 1986) and belong to no one person. Even after their capture, animals belong to all. The literature on Inuit harvester socialization (see Birket-Smith 1959; Fienup-Riordan 1983; Wenzel 1986a) and land occupancy and use (Freeman 1976; Brice-Bennett 1978) consistently reports the non-proprietary nature of relations practiced by Inuit toward animals and the environment. This, too, flows directly from the fact that animals possess awareness of human intent. Because animals and men form one community, a selfish or possessive hunter defeats himself.

Producing *niqituinnaq*, therefore, requires specific and essential cognitive ordering by Inuit with regard to animals and by animals to men. If an animal is to choose to participate in the food process, the Inuk harvester must approach the animal with an attitude of respect, and he must intend that the products of the animal's 'generosity' will be available to all.

Inummariit: being a 'real person'

While our discussion has dealt with the behavior of the individual harvester and animal, it must be extended to the groups to which each belongs – two intelligent, socially interacting communities of beings, one animal and the other human. For Inuit, it is important in any action or activity to be *inummarik*, literally a most genuine person. This quality is derived from full participation in the social image of his community. Brody (1975: 125) explains that a person can work, talk, and even walk *inummarik*, but most importantly he is being *inummarik* when he eats the meat of animals. It is *niqituinnaq*, real Inuit food, that conceptually and concretely integrates the human community through harvesting with the natural environment.

Discussions with Clyde Inuit about the essential qualities of a person who is *inummarik* pictured a person as being generous (*ilgasuuq*), patient (*qlinuituq*), obedient (*nalatuq*), and cooperative (*iikaiyuitatuq*). When Inuit spoke about these values, Clyde men and women identified these as being not just a part of hunting but as things learned through hunting. Production of *niqituinnaq* requires that people be imbued with these qualities. Generosity and cooperation are not simply forms of action but aspects of a genuine person's entire demeanor.

139

Graburn (1972), in his analysis of in-group classification among Quebec Inuit, was told by informants that sharing, especially of food (*niqituinnaq*), was a trait which distinguished Inuit from other men. And while in the northern Baffin Island settlement of Pond Inlet, Brody (1975: 136–7) found that elders often reminisced about the time when all Inuit were *inummariit*:

> The way we lived in camps was by living together . . . food - country food - was easy to share . . . it was always possible to share out game killed by one hunter, to share it out between all families.

Harvesters who are *inummariit* are, therefore, correct in their attitudes toward both animals and human beings, since the same social qualities pertain to both. Animals and people are perceived as responding to each other. This perception brings them together into a single cognitive community. The relationship between Inuit and animals rests on the same moral values which are the basis of human social interaction.

Continuity

The ethos of *inummariit* is critical to the successful continuation of relations between Inuit and seals, caribou, whales, and all animals. Fienup-Riordan (1983: 345), in her examination of the values the Yu'pik Eskimos of Nelson Island associate with traditional subsistence, reports

> when a person lives like his grandparents from the land and sea, he feels that those grandparents are still alive in him. I have also heard people say that if one lives off the land, one need never hoard money or even food . . . because each year the animals will return . . . Money can never be trusted like that. Thus, living off the land is the ultimate security at the same time that it makes possible . . . generosity.

Through a life that unifies the land, the animals, and the community past and present, harvesters acquire, reconstruct, and live out a world image which provides both a secure identity and behavioral direction. Inuit do not hunt only to eat, but also to structure the whole of their surroundings and to reproduce a rational cognitive model of the world. To be *inummarik* is to be actively engaged in a lifelong cycle of interaction with all that is living and has gone before (ibid.).

Hunting, sharing, and consuming animals is thus a necessary integrating act and the acquisition and utilization of food satisfies cognitive and social, as well as material, needs. Because generous exchanges among animals and men are inherent in *niqituinnaq*, they provide protection against any discontinuity between man and nature.

Most notable is the coincidence of values that humans and animals share in this socially formed community. A hunter's attitude and intent toward both the seal he awaits and the people with whom he lives directly influence whether a seal will come to that *aglu*. If the motivation to hunt is to share with others, then *natsiq* will choose to provide themselves to such a hunter. In so doing, in Fienup-Riordan's (ibid.: 345) words, a dual form of social reproduction occurs: the basis of human interdependence is reforged and the link between man and animal is continued.

The root of this common bond is first *niqituinnaq*, wild foods, and then *ningiqtuq*, the sharing that occurs from animal to man and from person to person. In this model of man–environment relations, the world image Inuit hold is not a static creation, but a construct that is undergoing constant transaction with all elements of the environment.

At Clyde, through the actions of wildlife harvesting and food sharing, of which seals form a most critical part, Inuit and animals join in forming and maintaining a shared social and ecological environment. While we have generally come to see (see Shweder and Bourne 1984: 193) cultural identity as separable into categories focussed either on self (egocentrism) or society (sociocentrism), it would seem (Stairs 1988, personal communication) that Inuit represent a third identity classification, that of ecocentrism.

Contradictory as it may appear to strangers, Inuit harvesting is an ultimate sign of respect for wildlife. It conserves animals by providing them with a means of renewal (see Fienup-Riordan 1983; Brody 1987), and it is a way of sharing with animals the qualities valued in human relationships through the demonstration of proper attitude and intent by harvesters.

For Inuit, hunting constantly reiterates the moral balance that constitutes the basic relationship between human beings and animals. The fundamental trait that underpins these relations is the belief of Inuit that a reciprocity exists between hunter and animal, between one person and another, and between the human community and the natural environment. Fienup-Riordan (1983: 175) has summarized the essentials of this relationship well.

> Power does not reside in the hunter himself. It resides in the context of his relationship with the seals. And this relationship, established outside the village, is the precondition for life inside the village.

8 THE SEAL PROTEST AS CULTURAL CONFLICT

In 1985, David Lavigne, a biologist studying harp seals, noted that the sealing controversy had reached a point in its evolution where it could no longer be resolved by scientific investigation.

The turning-point came in 1980 when the spearheads of the anti-sealing movement, Greenpeace and the International Fund for Animal Welfare (IFAW), made two fundamental changes in their strategy of protest. Instead of donning parkas and defending seals on the ice, they abandoned 'protest theater' to put on suits and lobby the halls of the European Parliament. More importantly, they withdrew from a losing battle on the ecological dangers of continued sealing to concentrate on an animal rights message.

The 1983 ban by the European Economic Community on commercial seal imports marks a watershed. Animal rights won a spectacular victory, the first of its kind, over industry and government. By translating its own moral concerns into political action directed at an environmentally sensitized public, it forced Canada to halt the world's most intensive commercial hunt of marine mammals. No environmental or animal rights campaign has since had such sweeping success.

The victory was, and still is, much celebrated, but the impact on Inuit has been less noted. As southern activists politicized their moral and ethical concerns about commercial sealing, they set Inuit seal hunting in that same negative framework. Inuit *natsiq* hunting was lumped with the European whitecoat hunt along Canada's eastern coast.

The devastating effects for Canadian and Greenlandic Inuit is disputed now by only the most obdurate members of the protest community (see Best 1986). The effects include reduction of access to the technical means hunters require for local food production, alienation of the traditional economy, growing socioeconomic differentiation in northern communities, and a weakening of the country food base on which Inuit communities depend.

It is not clear whether Inuit were an intended target of the initial anti-sealing campaign (see Foote 1967a; Wenzel 1978, 1986b; also Boe 1984). While the protest movement denies any such intent, it has since 1983 expanded its rhetoric (see, for instance, Best 1986; Smith 1988; Miller n.d.) into a much broader assault on nearly all aspects of Inuit wildlife use. The animal rights movement has questioned the fundamental economic context of contemporary Inuit wildlife use, not only with respect to *natsiq* but to other species used across the North. They have even questioned whether Inuit have any inherent right to the continued use of the animals upon which they have traditionally depended (see Greanville and O'Sullivan, respectively, in Bartlett 1988).

The depth of this cultural conflict is more difficult to document than measurement of the current Inuit economic situation can provide. Investigation must rest on an examination of the discourse and rhetoric that each side has applied to the situation. While by no means entirely unambiguous, this approach does suggest that the respective positions of both Inuit and the protest movement toward each other have undergone increasing polarization since 1983. The sympathetic and accommodating stance of Inuit toward the seal protest underwent considerable hardening after 1983 and the rhetoric employed by sealing's opponents has become more overtly hostile toward Inuit seal hunting and, increasingly, all consumptive uses of animals.

The shape of this side of the conflict has hinged on 'nuance'. Before 1983, protest spokespersons favoured Inuit sealing for traditional subsistence reasons, but at the same time qualified the selling of sealskins as being non-traditional and without subsistence benefit. Likewise, before the EC ban, Inuit went to great pains to sympathize with the seal protest's perspective on industrial sealing.

There has been little scholarly investigation (Foote 1967a; Wenzel 1978; Williamson 1978; more recently, Malouf 1986a) of the northern seal controversy as an event separate from the southern harp seal protest. This is especially the case with respect to the image which the anti-sealing movement has propagated with regard to Inuit culture and society. This aspect of the northern seal controversy is important to an understanding of present-day relations between Inuit and *Qallunaat*. Let us first examine the tenor of these exchanges before the boycott, and then look at changes since 1983.

Before the boycott

For over twenty-five years seal protesters rarely presented to the public any connection between their goal of ending commercial exploitation of seals and the implications of their campaign for Inuit subsistence hunters. Could the socioeconomic shocks that have struck Inuit be considered incidental, unexpected, and unavoidable byproducts of the movement's long effort? Could scientists, government, and the protesters have predicted and perhaps limited the effects on Inuit? The protest's appeal was to a literate, environmentally conscious Western public. How was information related to Inuit and seals presented to this audience?

Throughout the seal controversy, intensive scientific research was conducted on the biological health of the harp and hooded seal populations in the Northwest Atlantic area. These were the species sought in the southern commercial, or 'Newfoundland', seal hunt. So heated had the matter of this hunt become that some scientists, as Barzdo (1980: 4) notes, considered the modest monetary value of the hunt to be too low to justify the research investment. For most of this time, little similar research was directed at the ringed seals on which Inuit depended. The protest, according to its own literature and statements, was about the inhumane killing of harp seals. In Canada, the only interest in the northern seal research was concerned with the basic biology of *natsiq* (but see Smith 1973b).

Only occasionally during the two most successful southern protest episodes, in 1965-8 and 1976-8, did a few social scientists (Foote 1967a; Wenzel 1978; Williamson 1978) remark on the protest's indiscriminate approach to the sealing question and raise the spectre of intense economic consequences for Inuit. They argued that the campaign to end the 'baby seal' hunt would in no way be weakened by extending consideration to Inuit. But this advice had had little effect on either the protest's rhetoric or the news media, the two chief means by which information about the seal controversy was channeled to the general public.

To evaluate media reporting on Inuit and the seal issue, I surveyed the coverage provided by seven daily newspapers published in Canada, the United States, and Britain for selected years between 1970 and 1983. (These were the *New York Times*, the *Star* and *Globe and Mail* of Toronto, the *Montreal Gazette*, *The Times of London*, the *Vancouver Sun*, and the St. John's (Newfoundland) *Evening Telegram*.) Only twenty-four of 209 articles, editorials, and letters published on the sealing question made any mention of Inuit.

The greatest number of references (eight) to Native seal hunting were to be found in the *New York Times*, but six of these items actually discussed Aleut sealing in the Pribilof Islands and a seventh with public perceptions of consumptive use of wildlife, briefly mentioning use by Native Peoples. Only one item (21 March 1979) specifically addressed the implication of the controversy for Inuit, notably Greenlanders. Among Canadian papers, the *Montreal Gazette* carried five articles and letters about Inuit and seals and the Toronto papers, the *Globe and Mail* and *Star* carried four and three, respectively. The two papers either politically or geographically most associated with the hunt or the protest, the *St. John's Evening Telegram* and *Vancouver Sun* (Greenpeace at that time being headquartered in Vancouver) carried mention of Inuit three times and only once, respectively. No mention of Inuit appeared in *The Times of London* for any of the years surveyed.

In general, the media were riveted on the Northwest Atlantic harp seal hunt and the reaction it drew from protesters. Nearly one-quarter of all the articles reviewed had as their lead the protesters themselves, not the hunt or seals. Inuit were simply not a part of the reporting on the Canadian seal war.

The protest campaign itself set the tone and pace of coverage by the print and electronic media. Robert Hunter, in his description of the evolution of Greenpeace, describes a process which he calls (1979: 249) 'selective perception'. In this tactic, a single seal is identified as a symbol of all seals. Selective perception became a key element in the 'Save the Seals' publicity campaigns waged by Greenpeace and the International Fund for Animal Welfare, and this approach was accepted without comment by the media. Two pictorial images came to typify the seal controversy to the world – the face-front colour image of a white-coated harp seal pup and a man with upraised club looming over a whitecoat.

Selective perception accomplished two things. First, it made every seal small, a pristine white, and cuddly (Hunter 1979; see also Lamson 1979). Second, it planted the idea that all seals were killed brutally as part of a wholesale massacre. No attention was given to the conditions under which Newfoundland sealers lived (see Wright 1984), the differences that existed among various species of seals and their biological status (McLaren 1977), or the subsistence importance of seals to Inuit (Smith 1979–80).

An exception to this is an article that appeared in the *New York Times* on 24 March 1979, entitled 'The Wrong Seal Hunt', which discussed the economic realities faced by Greenland Inuit, and the hardship inflicted on them by a protest that did not distinguish Inuit harvesting from the industrial hunt. The article pointed out how the Inuit way of seal hunting differed from the 'ugly slaughter on the ice off the Canadian coast' and concluded with the statement that, while Inuit held little sympathy for the southern manner of killing seals, a 'mis-informed public' boycott was harming Greenlanders. Such in-depth analysis of effects on Canadian Inuit only appeared after the passage of the EC's seal ban (*Montreal Gazette* 22 October 1983: 8). Before 1983, the rule of thumb in protest rhetoric and media reportage appears to have been simply 'a seal is a seal'.

Anti-sealing rhetoric and Inuit

After 1983, when serious questions about how the protest campaign was waged made their way into public forums, anti-sealing advocates noted in their defense that Inuit subsistence hunting had never been the object of their efforts. Interviews I conducted with representatives of both Greenpeace (Boe 1984) and the IFAW (Best 1984) drew the response that neither organization saw any conflict between the aims of the protest and the Inuit way of life until after the Europeans had reached their decision. It must therefore be asked, was the movement so deeply ignorant of the Inuit situation? Were Inuit simply caught in an unforeseen backlash against all forms of sealing?

The most authoritative source in this regard from within the movement is Barzdo (1980), author of *International Trade in Harp and Hooded Seals*, a report prepared for and published jointly by the Fauna and Flora Preservation Society and the International Fund for Animal

Welfare. In it, he noted that scientists he interviewed had pointed out that anti-sealing protests had severely eroded the economic position of Canadian and Greenlandic Inuit subsistence hunters and that

In Canada the campaign is said to have damaged the Eskimo share of the market ... Greenland subsistence hunters have been so badly affected by the campaigns that the KGH is now subsidising them. (ibid.: 47)

Given the small catches of harp and hooded seals which he documents for Inuit (see below; also Barzdo 1980: 17, 30), the market damage he writes of must refer to sales of *natsiq*, the traditional food species hunted by Canadian and Greenland Inuit. He makes reference to the minor role of Inuit in the international commerce of harp and hooded sealskins and says with regard to Greenland that

Some skins enter commerce, but the hunters still live in a largely subsistence culture. Hunting communities rely on the cash from the seal trade to purchase their rifles, fuel and motor boats. Ringed seals are the primary catch. (ibid.: 5)

Barzdo is clear about the subsistence role of sealskin sales for Inuit, and he accurately represented the small role of Inuit in the harvesting of the two seal species protesters sought to protect. The report was co-sponsored and published without disclaimer by the International Fund for Animal Welfare, an organization which later orchestrated the strategy that led to Europe's seal ban.

This casts doubt upon later statements (Best 1984) from the IFAW. In 1984, Steven Best, then the IFAW's Canadian seal campaign coordinator, noted that the organization had been unaware of Inuit concerns about the protest until 1982 when they met Inuit accompanying an official Canadian delegation at the European Parliament in Strasbourg.

The same questions can be asked about the degree to which Greenpeace appraised the impact of its efforts on Inuit. Robert Hunter (1979: 368), the first executive director of Greenpeace, in his book *Warriors of the Rainbow: A Chronicle of the Greenpeace Movement*, makes important mention of Inuit only once. He reports that in 1977 Greenpeace, through its Seal Steering Committee, chose a most uncompromising course with regard to sealing: 'no seals were to be killed by anybody, not even by Eskimos or Indians.'

Hunter's statement contradicts later, post-EC boycott declarations of Greenpeace spokespersons (Boe 1984; Moore 1983, 1985; see also *Atuisoq* 1985) about the degree to which the organization considered Inuit concerns during the late 1970s. Vivia Boe (1984), seal campaign coordinator for Greenpeace International, has stated that Inuit reaction to the boycott and to Greenpeace's role in it took the organization by surprise. In 1984 Greenpeace was reported to be refashioning its seal policy in order to distinguish Inuit activities from those of European and Canadian sealers. Although its policy review was not yet complete, Boe stated in our interview: 'In principle, Greenpeace was not opposed to seal hunting if it provided food and skins that were for the family group or community.'

Less than a year later, another representative of Greenpeace International, Alan Pickaver, met with Inuit in Greenland. This was only the second such direct meeting between Inuit and protest advocates held in the North. At the meeting, representatives of Greenland's Home Rule Government asked Greenpeace to help them reverse the EC approach to Inuit sealing and to publicize the cultural and economic importance of sealing to Inuit (*Atuisoq* 1985: 4; Goddard 1986: 23–4). Pickaver demurred on these points, although Greenpeace shortly after acquiesced to the Greenlanders' request that it withdraw from a planned anti-trapping campaign. According to Goddard (ibid.: 24), Pickaver's response to the Greenlanders' requests regarding the seal campaign and boycott was that commercial sealing, even by Inuit, was not valid and he would not recommend any change in the organization's sealing policy.

Despite the contradictions, we can draw some conclusions. In the late 1970s, both Greenpeace and the IFAW were aware that their campaigns held serious socioeconomic consequences for Inuit. By the time these two major players adopted a boycott strategy (about 1980), they held internal information that Inuit were not seriously involved in the commercial killing of harp and hooded seal pups. Yet neither organization made any attempt in their public campaigns to differentiate northern aboriginal activities from those of southern commercial hunters.

The response that Greenpeace and IFAW received from Inuit even before the 1983 seal ban was unambiguous. To Inuit, the arguments which the campaign mustered against industrial sealing – that the whitecoat hunt was cruel and inhumane, that it endangered the long-term status of harp and hooded seals, and that commercial sealing was immoral because it sole market was luxury furs – all appeared to contrast their own subsistence harvest with southern commercial activities. Inuit, after all, harpooned or shot, not clubbed, ringed seals in order to provide their communities with food. Inuit even went as far as to express their own doubts about the nature of southern commercial hunting (*New York Times*, 21 March 1979).

The drastic fluctuations caused by the protest to the northern sealskin market were perplexing to Inuit. They saw clear differences between their own harvest and that done in Atlantic Canada, and the arguments which the protest mustered against commercial sealing seemed to support their own position. Inuit saw a simple answer to this problem: that the protest explain to other *Qallunaat* that Inuit sealed to live.

If the Inuit response in the 1970s to the protest seems naïve, several facts must be kept in mind. Before the summer of 1985, no representative of a major protest organization had held a face-to-face meeting with Inuit in the North. Physically isolated as they were, Inuit lacked the means of clarifying the position of the seal protest and so accepted the general rhetoric. This isolation extended to media coverage. Few villages received television before 1980 and radio broadcast news in Inuktitut was almost unknown. What Inuit learned about the protest before 1983 came to them through experiencing the drastic changes in the value of the *qlissiq* they sold to the local HBC or Co-op store. Unable to see and confront the theatrics of the seal campaign first-hand, as was the case in Newfoundland (see, especially, Lamson 1979), Inuit could only track events by the rise and fall of sealskin prices.

The only other source of information available to Northerners was publications produced by Inuit political and cultural organizations, principally Inuit Tapirisat of Canada (ITC), sometimes known as the Eskimo Brotherhood. Almost all of these were then based in southern Canada. They provide considerable evidence of how sympathetic and accommodative early Inuit reaction to the protest actually was. At the depth of the 1976–8 sealskin depression, ITC issued a press release, part of which declared (Inuit Tapirisat of Canada 977: 4):

> Inuit who rely on selling seal skins for their living are the victims of an international campaign to stop the spring harvest of seal pups off Newfoundland and in the Gulf of St. Lawrence. People all over the world are upset because they believe the hunting of seal pups is cruelty to cute little animals. So . . . they stop buying all furs, never bothering to stop and think that Inuit hunters take adult seals and rely on the skins for their income.

In a subsequent release, ITC (1978: 2) cited reports from Broughton Island that sealskin prices had dropped from $25.00 to $5.00 in the space of one year and that economic assistance was desperately needed in every Inuit hunting community.

That early published statement by ITC, interestingly, was in no way critical of the protest or its stated objectives. Rather, it concentrated on the relationship between sealing and Inuit well-being in a *Qallunaat*-dominated world. Despite the severe economic impact felt by Inuit, ITC attributed the conflict between Inuit and *Qallunaat* interests to misunderstanding and lack of information, not malevolent intent. A similar conciliatory perspective was voiced at the same time by other Native Canadian news outlets.

Greenland Inuit went even further in seeking accommodation with the protest. Speaking through both their own national press (*Atuagagdliutit/Gronlandposten* 22 January and 19 March 1981) and international sources (*New York Times* 21 March 1979; *Kristeligt Dagblad* 12 March 1981), Greenlanders emphasized that the problems they were experiencing were based mainly on misinformation and misunderstanding. They emphatically condemned the practices of the southern Canadian industrial seal hunt (*New York Times*, 21 March 1979: A23). As their own contribution to the information situation, the Greenland press (*Atuagagdliutit/Gronlandposten*, 19 March 1981) sought to clarify the relationship of the protest to Inuit, noting that 'Greenpeace . . . is *not* protesting against the Greenlandic seal hunt'.

The Greenlandic Inuit community also expressed a measure of sympathy with the seal campaign. For instance, Finn Lynge, an Inuk and Greenland's then representative at the European Parliament, as quoted in *Kriseligt Dagblad* (12 March 1981), said: 'I share the organization's misgivings as far as the large catches of hooded seals ... are concerned. We have always opposed hunting of baby seals and have never hunted them.' Lynge, according to the same article, also proposed a face-to-face meeting with Brigitte Bardot, the foremost public figure associated with the international seal campaign, to discuss the effect of the protest on Inuit. The meeting, however, never took place.

In the late 1970s and early 1980s, moderation, not conflict, motivated Canadian and Greenland Inuit responses to the seal protest. The moderate tone of Inuit protestations is especially evident when compared to the passionate rhetoric (see Lamson 1979) which southern sealers, shipowners, and fur manufacturers directed toward the protest. When it is remembered that it was the *natsiq* market, and not those for harp and hooded pup sealskins, that bore the economic brunt of the anti-sealing campaign before 1983, the continued Inuit attempt to explain the northern situation to protest activists is all the more remarkable.

1983: re-examining animal rights

Until the EC's boycott decision was finalized, Inuit continued to seek common ground with the anti-sealing movement. At that point, Inuit in Canada and Greenland began to re-evaluate their position on the seal protest (see Heinrich 1983; Peter 1983).

It became clear that they were observing a hardening attitude toward their concerns, although some elements, like Greenpeace Denmark (*Atuagagdliutit/Gronlandposten* 23 February 1983), advocated making an exception of some Inuit sealing. Certainly, some European parliamentarians (Royal Commission Hearings 1985a; Malouf 1986f: 68--9), while by no means unified as to the breadth or inclusiveness of boycott action, were, by the early 1980s, displaying various degrees of antipathy to the arguments which Inuit mustered. For example, Beate Weber (1982 personal communication), a West German member of the European Parliament, drew an extremely fine line between Canadian and Greenlandic Inuit hunting. She perceived Greenlanders' harvesting as more 'traditional' because they used dogteams and *qajaq*, but rejected the claims of Canadian Inuit who used snowmobiles. The fact that both groups ate the seals they killed figured not at all into her analysis.

Other European politicians were even more narrow. Hemmo Muntingh, a Dutch MEP, in an interview with Greenlandic journalists (reported in *Atuagagdliutit/Gronlandposten* 22 January 1981), reiterated his regret at the effects Holland's anti-sealing position might have on Inuit, but, apparently unaware of Inuit representations on the matter, suggested the Greenlanders direct their complaints to the commercial sealing countries, especially Canada and Norway:

> I know very well that the Greenlanders are not responsible for this situation. It is Canada and Norway which are to blame. And therefore the Greenlandic criticism must be directed against these countries and not against Holland.

The March 1983 decision to implement an EC-wide seal boycott in fact, if not in law, paralysed the Inuit sealskin economy, definitively altering Inuit perceptions of the protest and its relationship to them. Up to the passage of Directive 83/129/EEC, Inuit, in the words of Paul Okituk (1985, personal communication), looked at the protest as 'a problem between you white people. We are not part of your fight. To us, we are one with the land, we did not kill seals for money'. With official passage of the seal ban, Inuit statements on the sealing question shifted in emphasis from the difficulties created by *Qallunaat* misunderstanding to the matter of accusations of White hypocrisy (Peter 1983: 9-11).

Technically Inuit were represented in the Canadian and Danish delegations to the European Parliament because no other vehicle provided them with access to the European forum. But this curious participation may have done more harm than good and produced little real communication with anti-sealing advocates. For example, Steven Best (1984), IFAW's European campaign strategist, recalls how the several Inuit accompanying the Canadian delegation wore 'fancy suits and wristwatches' and blended with the government officials and industry spokespeople. To the best of his memory, these Inuit presented no arguments different from standard Canadian statements on the issue, and he perceived no Inuit position distinguishable from the official Canadian 'government-industry line'. What Inuit recall is that they were ignored and that they left Strasbourg feeling that Europeans had reached a negative decision on sealing long before Native delegates had an opportunity to state their case. Further such discussion was, in their eyes, pointless.

The years since the ban have done little to ease the tension – the Inuit sense of injustice arises from three things. First, despite repeated meetings, *Qallunaat* still hold the idea that Inuit hunt seals primarily for commercial purposes (see Goddard 1986: 33-4). So much does this rankle that in July 1989, the Inuit Circumpolar Conference (ICC), which politically represents the Eskimo and Aleut peoples of Canada, Greenland and the United States, for the first time made discussion of the animal rights movement a priority item on the agenda of its biennial meeting.

Beyond this persistent ignorance of Inuit cultural being, Inuit have begun to suspect they are victims of deliberate misrepresentation. Especially galling to Inuit are the patronizing, and even hostile, responses they have received from organizations formerly active in the seal campaign and who now disavow responsibility for the problems it has created. Inuit are asked to 'accept' the reality of a new southern consciousness about animals and to move on to other issues. Greenpeace is one such organization. The 1985 delegation from Greenpeace International to Greenland rebuffed Inuit requests for help and urged them to face historical reality (Atuisoq 1985: 4). Not surprisingly, Greenlanders found little satisfaction in this answer, so little that when the Greenpeace delegates, Alan Pickaver and Lorraine Thorne, arrived in one small West Greenland community they were greeted by a banner that welcomed 'Greenshit'.

Inuit are also patronized as innocent and unfortunate victims of a larger struggle. Patrick Moore, at one time a major figure in Greenpeace Canada and Greenpeace International, in response to an interviewer's question about the effects of his organization's campaign on Inuit (Moore 1983), replied:

> You have to look at the Native people that are taking seals in the Arctic, and those skins are going into the same fashion industry that the skins from the big commercial Newfoundland hunt are going to. And you have to make hard decisions there in the real world.

A vexing variant shifts responsibility for the impact of the protest and boycott to other shoulders. Vivia Boe (1984), of Greenpeace, and Steven Best (1984), then with the IFAW, have argued that the collapse of the world market for sealskins resulted not from the protest, but from the actions of an enlightened public in rejecting luxury furs. Boe and Best seem to suggest that the protest merely helped bring this rising sentiment to the surface more quickly.

More recently, members of the International Wildlife Coalition (Best 1986) have attributed the problems affecting Native communities to their association with the fur industry, past and present. He has compiled a catalogue of social pathologies affecting Native Canadians which, to him, are 'problems caused by the legacy of the fur fashion trade, from the disease, liquor and Christian missionaries it inflicted on the Native peoples ...' (ibid. 205). While Best acknowledges that Inuit and other Native Peoples have suffered badly in their relations with Whites, he absolves the 'animal rights movement' (ibid.) of any direct role. The seal protest, as he says, has merely exposed the fallacy of Natives turning, 'to the fur trade and animal-based resources as a form of economic and social salvation'. Best thus shifts social responsibility away from the movement and from Euro-Canadian conduct in the North.

Another point of friction is the persistence of campaigns that highlight sealing as a continuing issue. Both Greenpeace and the International Fund for Animal Welfare necessarily continue to use sealing as a 'hook' in their solicitations (see Allen 1979), and other organizations, like the World Society for the Protection of Animals (1990), have recently pressed the view that the current European seal boycott, last renewed in 1985, should not only be extended indefinitely but also broadened in scope. Although these groups consider Norwegian sealing to be the urgent problem, Inuit feel targeted by any continuation of the ban that does not recognise their activities as culturally rooted. (The EEC boycott was extended indefinitely in summer 1989.)

The 1986 success of the Humane Society of the United States (HSUS), Save the Seal Inc. and, especially, Greenpeace to restrict the use by Aleuts of fur seals in the Pribilof Islands (see Young 1981) is further perceived by Inuit as proof of the protest movement hypocrisy. On the one hand it says that it is not opposed to Native wildlife use and then, on the other, it continues to interfere with a critical element in the constricted food and money economy of the North. The Pribilof Islands episode was a repeat of their earlier experience, again suggesting that 'subsistence' can exist only when it conforms to a southern perception of what is traditional and necessary to Inuit 'Subsistence sealing means the taking of seal for survival, i.e., the consumption of the meat and the utilization of the pelt within the family group or community' (Dingwall 1986: 1).

Inuit see animal rights organizations orchestrating a new series of campaigns against other components of the northern Native economy. European protests against the leg-hold trap threaten Dene and Cree Indian, as well as Inuit; trappers and new groups like the Canadian-based International Wildlife Coalition (IWC) loudly protest almost every form of Inuit harvesting. They include caribou, because it fears that antlers may be sold to the Chinese and Korean pharmaceutical markets, small whale hunting because Inuit subsistence practice is mainly focussed on *muktaaq*, and even Inuit participation as guides and outfitters in sports hunting. In each of these situations, Inuit see the shadow of the seal protest.

The conflict crystallizes

How accurate, or paranoid, are Inuit perceptions of the animal rights movement's understanding and attitude toward their culture? Before 1983, the anti-sealing campaign consistently pled ignorance of any conflict between its own goals and the needs of Inuit. In the years since, such conflict appears to have become the norm. Is this new, or does it result from the movement, despite protestations of innocence, having ceased to present an appearance of even superficial concern for Inuit?

Since 1985, three forums, the 1985 public hearings of the Royal Commission on Seals and the Sealing Industry in Canada, the Canadian Arctic Resources Committee's (CARC) 1985 national symposium on northern wildlife management and the anti-harvest movement (Keith and Saunders 1989), and a 1988 *Animals' Agenda* (Bartlett 1988) roundtable on the fur issue, have provided insight into the animal rights position toward Inuit and other Native wildlife users. As we shall see below, the reports of these meetings present another side of the movement, one that perhaps indicates a growing negative view of aboriginal society.

A. The Royal Commission

The best-known and most extensive such discussion was the Royal Commission on Seals and the Sealing Industry in Canada, convened by the Canadian government in 1984–5 to investigate all aspects of the crisis affected by the protest and European sealskin boycott. The Commission was composed of four Canadian and three international members. After seven months of background study and extensive public hearings in Canadian, American and British cities, its findings were presented in a comprehensive three-volume report.

Although accused of anti-protest bias even before its first public meeting (see Mowat 1984: 402), the Commission served as a rare opportunity for both Inuit and anti-sealing activists to articulate their perceptions of the other's position. One-half of the more than fifty written or oral briefs submitted by boycott supporters touched, either directly or during commission questioning, on Inuit wildlife activities. All are available in the library of Fisheries and Oceans Canada in Ottawa.

These provide critical data on the range of views held within the protest movement at the time of Inuit. Even the most active protest organizations expressed general sympathy for Inuit sealing so long as it conformed to traditional patterns and was kept within bounds. Very quickly, however, what exactly such patterns and bounds are became an issue.

Typical of these briefs is the one submitted by Britain's Royal Society for the Prevention of Cruelty to Animals: it notes the fact that neither the seal protest nor the EC boycott took specific objection to seal hunting done for the purpose of subsistence. Stefan Ormrod, in presenting the RSPCA submission, in fact stated that neither he nor his organization could see any major grounds for conflict with Inuit, since EC Directive 83/129/EEC refers to harp and hooded seals alone and, because these species were known to be of little economic import to Inuit, the boycott directive could have 'only marginal economic impact on Inuit communities' (Royal Commission Hearings 1985a: 255).

Under Commission questioning, Ormrod (ibid.: 255) specified that he was referring to harp seal, but that his investigations into Inuit, mainly Greenlandic, harp sealing suggested that it was, in the main, 'quite clearly subsistence hunting'. Pursuing the question of subsistence, the following exchange occurred between Ormrod and Russel Barsh, the American representative on the Commission (ibid.: 256–7),

> (Ormrod) . . . we had a case . . . when Greenland did their tour of Europe, and there was much talk about subsistence hunting and we were considering the figures they were putting and of the people that could be termed aboriginal subsistence hunters. It worked out to about 2 per cent of the entire population, but in actual fact when we worked out the quota figures that were being put forward, it

was nine seals for every man, woman and child in Greenland. We would not consider that subsistence hunting.

(Barsh) You would not?

(Ormrod) No.

(Barsh) Why not?

(Ormrod) Because . . . only about 2 per cent were actually aboriginals, so if you were to say nine seals for every man, woman and child in Greenland, it would turn that into what would mean to the aboriginal people. It would be about 40 adult seals for every aboriginal. And we would consider that moving into the realm of the commercial.

(Barsh) Do you have any idea of about how many pounds of meat a family would take if it were primarily dependent on seals for food . . .

(Ormrod) . . . no, I would not want to guess that . . . But I would consider that 40 odd seals would be way above anything that would be needed for subsistence hunting.

The point which Barsh makes in this exchange is that a southern estimate of the number of seals adequate for subsistence might be arbitrary. Because the quantitative data exist to test the importance of seal at a survival level of human need, it is possible to improve on Ormrod's 'guesstimate' of what amount of seal is or is not necessary to Inuit.

To refine this estimate, we can take as test values the edible portion of a seal, 35–40 per cent of live weight (Foote 1967b), an individual seal meat consumption rate of 2.5 kg per day, and a daily individual metabolic requirement of 2,500–3,000 calories. Such values conform to field data collected by Kemp (1971) and Wenzel (1981) in two Baffin Inuit camp situations and relate only to bioenergetic, not nutrient or cultural, needs. Under these assumptions, an Inuk can subsist for approximately 6.5 days on a single seal before he or she incurs a bioenergetic deficit: before using more calories than are ingested. by day seven, another *natsiq* must be captured. By extrapolation, over a full year an individual human requires fifty-six adult seals for personal sustenance and the Greenland proposal of forty seals per harvester becomes not as far-fetched as Ormrod and the RSPCA supposed. If consumers include non-hunters – women, children, the aged and infirmed – the number put forward is too low, even in an environment that includes resources other than seal. Thus, what *Qallunaat* consider 'too much' in fact underscores the dimensions of southern misconceptions as to what constitutes reasonable subsistence.

In the same vein, the hearings elicited elaborations from within the protest community about the meaning of subsistence and the alternative economic options for Inuit. During its Vancouver hearing, Peter Hamilton, representing The Life Force Foundation, stated (Royal Commission Hearings 1985b: 16–17),

Tradition is the transmission of knowledge, opinions, practices, etc. from generation to generation by word of mouth and example. The current use of high-tech rifles, snowmobiles, and other equipment in hunt situations is not a transfer of knowledge and practice. In other words . . . tradition is disappearing in any case.

When queried by commission member Allen, Hamilton said (ibid.: 23-5):

killing seals to provide clothing and food for their families . . . is definitely a grey area. If they are killing to make a profit . . . we should find other less violent, safer ways for them to make money and subsist on.

Allen probed further

Inuit are using . . . some of the products of the animals they kill to buy the equipment . . . to go hunting for the animals they need for subsistence. Do you regard that also as a grey area?

In response, Hamilton stated

direct use for clothing and food could be a grey area if there isn't any other alternative. There may well be an alternative for Inuit . . . if one is making a profit in killing . . . that does start to get toward an area where we say lets develop some other way of bringing in that income . . . such as their art work or they have beautiful sculptures . . . and the tourism trade can be developed.

As to the economic options to sealing, W.G. Nettles (ibid.: 78-9) observed:

I suppose that if aboriginal people wish to hunt for meat that it could be a viable alternative to pushing a cart around the supermarket floor all day, but it seems that our modern advancement brings them food in cans and frozen . . .

Paradoxically, Vivia Boe of Greenpeace suggested (Royal Commission Hearings 1985c: 22) that Inuit 'accept a reality that is bigger than the both of us. A solution is that Inuit adopt a more traditional lifestyle'.

Some of these misperceptions can be set straight by the facts, as in the case of the bioenergetic needs for subsistence, but other statements have the ring of ideology.

Numerous protest speakers expressed the view that fashion trends and public sentiment, independent of the seal campaign, had caused rejection of Inuit sealskins. Mark Glover and Vivia Boe, both of Greenpeace International, presented this basic view at the hearings held in London and Washington. DC (Royal Commission Hearings 1985a,c). In response to a question from Commissioner Barsh about the relation between the European boycott and the collapse of the Inuit ringed seal market, Glover (Royal Commission Hearings 1985a: 334) replied, 'only the prices have dropped. Ring [sic] seals are still legal'. As to whether Inuit-hunted sealskins, as distant from commercially hunted skins, presented a problem, Glover (ibid.: 337) noted that the general public does not know the difference, 'There are seals and there are whitecoats'. Boe attributed the problem to the vagaries of fashion. As she saw it (Royal Commission Hearings 1985c: 122):

> Greenpeace does not have as much to say ... as fashion does ... No matter what Greenpeace does, people are starting to move away from wearing the furs of wildlife and fashion has a great deal to say about this.

Patrick Moore, Greenpeace spokesperson at the Vancouver hearing, likewise declined acknowledgment of any responsibility for that organization's past role in the collapse of the Inuit cash economy. Rather, in his eyes, the collapse had its roots in fur trade colonialism (Royal Commission Hearings 1985b: 39), and he blamed the Canadian government for consequences felt by Inuit:

> it is their fault and not the fault of the conservation and animal rights movement. It's been clear all along that the Native People who are engaged in a subsistence lifestyle were not the targets ... but it is also a fact that the spin-off of the protest was that consumers recognized sealskin(s) ... The government, instead of reacting positively and making a distinction of some kind and protecting the Inuit, used the plight of the Inuit to bash the environmental movement over the head ... by using the fact that Inuit had been caught between a rock and a hard place ... was immoral and unethical of the Canadian Government. (ibid.: 39-40).

Paul Watson, head of the Sea Shepherd Society, went even further (ibid.: 147). He argued that Inuit seal hunting was harmed because the existence of commercial sealing branded all seal products as unmarketable. If there were no commercial sealing in Canada, there would be no confusion over Inuit products.

The Royal Commission hearings elicited from the protest movement something that had occurred only rarely before: protestors stated explicitly their fundamental position for opposing Inuit sealing. Throughout the hearings, from London to Vancouver, opponents of sealing echoed Patrick Moore's views (Malouf 1986f: 72) on the fundamental issue at stake in the seal protest:

> It wasn't primarily a question of wildlife management or economics or politics or science or any of the other things they tried to argue their way around. It ... came down to a question of morality ...

Matters were helped little when Greenpeace's Boe (Royal Commission Hearing 1985c: 120-1), quoting Patrick Moore, went on to say

> We respect indigenous people as brothers and sisters, but we disagree with ... the international fur business. We ... will avoid confusing the public by refraining from confrontation in the press. Instead, we will try to work it out as if it were a family dispute, even though the conflict is apparently irreconcilable.

156

It was now fully evident to Inuit that the 'whys and hows' of northern subsistence sealing were being wholly misinterpreted. Throughout the Commission's hearings the protest movement seemed to make it clear that it was reserving for itself the right to evaluate Inuit tradition, that it refused any active role in correcting misinformation from earlier campaigns, and that its leadership had dismissed aboriginal sealing as an issue of mutual concern.

B. The Montreal CARC Conference

During 1986, the Canadian Arctic Resources Committee (CARC) hosted six national forums to discuss issues of political, socio-economic, and cultural importance to the North. The last meeting, held in Montreal in January 1987, had as its central theme the management and use of wildlife (Keith and Saunders 1989). Co-sponsored by the Fur Institute of Canada, its object was to bring together Native People, academics, government representatives, and critics of wildlife harvesting to discuss the present-day importance of animals in northern subsistence and their potential in the future.

As Keith and Saunders (ibid.: x) have noted, the Montreal conference centered on the relations of man and animal in the North and whether Native northerners possessed the right to use wildlife for subsistence and commercial purposes. Attention was focussed not on legal questions about aboriginal rights to animals, but on whether such rights and their exercise were 'moral'. Rather than pitting aboriginal interests against that of government and industry, as was usually the case, Montreal saw Native northerners and animal rights activists clash publicly.

While the CARC meeting was not intended to deal specifically with seal controversy, the debate took this turn for two reasons. First, the seal campaign had provided northern Natives with their main experience with animal rights concerns. And from the perspective of animal rightists, the seal campaign offered a successful model for broadening anti-fur efforts.

Peter Ernerk, of the Keewatin Wildlife Federation, in outlining the Native position toward animals (1989: 23), made it clear that the use of wildlife in the North remains firmly based in food production. He also emphasized that subsistence remains an essential component of Native cultural and economic life, as well as the critical link between Inuit and the environment, stating

> Subsistence is not an occupation in the conventional sense. It is a way of life. And, as a way of life, there are certain rules and guidelines in place to assist the hunter in his daily endeavors. These unwritten laws ... are the rules that assist us in our interaction with the environment ... we have always been taught that we cannot disassociate ourselves from our surroundings. We are always aware of the fact that we are merely a part of the natural scheme of things ... Dignity, respect, and ... self-interest guide us and act as our environmental ethics ... to clarify this last element of 'self-

interest'. I use the term to show ... that, for us to survive as a people, so must our land and our food supply.

He then went on to explain Inuit commercial involvement as an extension of subsistence in an environment modified by *Qallunaat* and specified the one overriding limitation Inuit recognize on harvesting (ibid.: 24):

no animal population must be placed in danger ... I emphasize that use and need must be legitimate. Wastage of any resource, including skins and meat, has always been considered criminal ...

Ernerk and other Native representatives to the conference (Gordon 1989: 116–17) refused to separate the three vital elements of the northern ecosystem – the animals, the environment, and their own cultures. Because *Qallunaat* – government, industry, or animal rights – all had a poor record in safeguarding this interconnection, Inuit could not depend on them to maintain wildlife and the environment as their cultural priority.

The animals rights activists at the meeting responded simply, stating that their job was not to assess the impact of their efforts on cultures. Rather, it is 'to protect animals' (Doncaster 1989b: 39), a point so fundamental and basic that 'there is no compromise' (ibid.: 40).

That single-minded and uncompromising position was a departure from the general tone of most protest supporters at the 1985 Royal Commission hearings. The newly aggressive animal rights stance clearly questioned the viability of subsistence in the modern Arctic and hammered repeatedly at the idea that subsistence harvesting could no longer continue as a way of life. Anne Doncaster alluded to this in the opening session of the meeting, and in her concluding statement (1989a: 21–2) noted:

If the Native people decide the fur industry does have a future, and they decide to train their children for a life on the trap-line, they will know that some of these children would have become doctors, lawyers, scientists, and, perhaps, trappers; but it would be a choice. Is it in the best interest of these children and the culture of the Native people to encourage them to trap, or to encourage them to get an education so that they can make their own choices in life?

In her eyes, continued fur harvesting would narrow the opportunities available to the next generation of Native society. Inuit who chose harvesting would be left behind.

Doncaster (ibid.: 21) and other activists rejected a definition of subsistence that included mechanized equipment and the sale of furs on the grounds that 'the public does not understand the "need" for cash to hunt'. Steven Best (1988), a year later, was even more blunt in this regard:

I own the Native culture. I bought it with my taxes. I own about two-thirds of it . . . That's how it survives. There would be no Indian culture today if it wasn't for the fact that southern Canadians pay for it.

With no apparent sense of contradiction, Best (ibid.) also put forward the suggestion that,

Native peoples have got to develop a culture that is sufficiently apart from southern interests, and they have to do it on their own terms. When they do, they will be able to call all their own shots.

More sophisticated than the arguments of either Doncaster or Best was the approach pursued by John Livingston (1989: 119) to demonstrate Inuit departure from 'tradition'. He argued that, prior to European contact, aboriginal subsistence was, by technological necessity, 'ecologically circumscribed'. Since then, the penetration of foreign artifacts and modes of exchange introduced 'a new way of life foreign to, and essentially antithetical to, aboriginal cultural traditions'. He refers to the application of the term subsistence to a harvesting system that includes the exchange of money for furs as a false 'neo-traditionalism', which 'guarantees that the natives are firmly anchored and contained, at the extractive level, in the service of the inter-national wholesale-retail industry'.

Livingston's argument has some merit. The fur industry is hardly altruistic, and few researchers are naïve as to its primary interest. But Livingston, in his contrast of pre-contact and modern subsistence, takes a narrow and non-systemic view of cultural adaptation. Dismissal of subsistence as a valid way of life in the North means advocating Native acceptance of cultural assimilation by southern society. Doncaster (1989: 43) phrased it this way:

We are saying, 'These are our values, this is the way we feel about it.' I don't tend to feel that Native people are a separate culture. I look at us as all Canadians.

Following up on this argument, John Grandy (1989: 44), of the Humane Society of the United States, explained his organization's objection to the Pribilof Islands fur seal hunt, in terms of Aleut hunters 'wanting to have it both ways'. 'Our definitions of subsistence', he explained, 'are written pretty clearly and thoughtfully in our Marine Mammal Protection Act.' In HSUS terms the Pribilof fur seal hunt 'was not what *we* [emphasis in original statement] mean by subsistence; that's not what the law means by subsistence'.

The proceedings of the Montreal meeting aptly bore the title *A Question of Rights*. Five years after the European boycott precipitated an economic crisis in Inuit villages, the spotlight had finally moved to the fundamental conflict between what southern activists called 'the rights of animals' and the rights of Inuit, as an aboriginal people, to define their own mode of subsistence and practice their own cultures.

Indeed, this was the point all along of Inuit concern about the protest.

Montreal made it clear that the protest movement's rejection of Native 'neo-traditionalism' was tantamount to the appropriation of their culture based on particular southern conceptions. Doncaster's reference to Inuit being 'Canadians like us' and Grandy's reliance on legal definitions of subsistence are nothing but articulations of a cultural perspective that is blind to other views. The moral focus of the movement on the rightness of sealing had now moved to an examination of Inuit culture itself. Best (1985: 11) summed up this perception when he put forward the assumption that 'Inuit kill for the same reasons as Newfoundlanders, as South Africans, as Scottish fishermen . . .' and answered it, 'to make some money'.

C. The Animals' Agenda

The following year, Native spokespeople and animal rights advocates again came together at a roundtable sponsored by the Animal Rights Network and published in *The Animals' Agenda* (Bartlett 1988). While the meeting was convened to examine the conflict over the use of leg-hold traps to capture wild furbearers, it provided a forum for animal advocates to expand upon their view of the nature of aboriginal cultures. Importantly, at this meeting, animal rightists for the first time attempted to tie the fur protest to the wider issues of concern to Native Peoples.

Technical debate over trapping opened up the larger issues. When the moderator (Cronon 1988: 16) initially posed the question of the moral acceptability of fur sales 'if it were to feed a Native village, and *only* to feed a Native village . . .', Michael O'Sullivan (1988: 16), of the World Society for the Protection of Animals, responded: 'No. The situation you're describing now no longer exists in Canadian society, so your question is so hypothetical that . . . It's unrealistic.'

Instead, Native spokespeople suddenly found themselves accused of exploiting 'subsistence activity' as a bargaining chip in the Canadian Native land claims debate. O'Sullivan introduced this new issue thus:

> Virtually all the land claim settlements under discussion in Canada right now have a heavy emphasis on traditional land use - hunting, fishing, trapping. Without that emphasis, from a legal standpoint, many of those land claims would not be successful. So there is a broader aspect of the trapping debate than has been focussed on so far in this discussion.

Patrice Greanville (1988: 16) then commented on the magnitude of the James Bay and Northern Quebec Agreement (JBNQA) as an example of land claims expediency, suggestive of 'the *de facto* alliance between the indigenous communities . . . and the fur industry'.

Before continuing, we must recall that 'land claims', to use the term by which aboriginal settlements with government in Canada are now known, arose as a Native political issue in the early 1970s when southern energy-related megaprojects, mainly dams and pipelines, threatened to dispossess Inuit, Cree and Dene of the lands and resources they had traditionally occupied and still used. After sixteen years, only two claims had been resolved. In the case of James Bay, the first modern land claim in the North, settlement was only reached after the Quebec government exercised 'gun to head' tactics on the Cree and Inuit (see Coates 1985; Salisbury 1986). To this day, many of the JBNQA's provisions have not been effectively implemented and still pose problems.

When the moderator asked whether the linking of land claims to subsistence activities was legitimate, Greanville (1988: 16) argued, 'the association of indigenous people today with the fur industry is predicated mostly on the validation of their ongoing claim', and challenged:

> If you come into sovereign rights in the near future, are you prepared to say that you will preserve the land for the traditional uses of fishing, hunting, and trapping only? That you will not sign leases for mineral exploration, gas pipeline exploration, or other commercial uses? (ibid.)

O'Sullivan pursued this matter, concluding that (ibid.: 17):

> while there will always be a segment of aboriginal society that will trap when land claims are settled ... the only way to have a financial basis for Native self-government in Canada is through land claims. The issues dovetail very closely. It is in the interest of aboriginal people to have a high profile that will bring attention not only to the trapping issues, but to other Native problems.

Thus, O'Sullivan and Greanville connected the most important issue in Native Canada, southern recognition of aboriginal rights to traditional lands and resources, to simple public relations and economic benefit. At the same time, they implied that now it was the broad conduct of Native Peoples that would be scrutinized by the movement.

In these exchanges, the Royal Commission's public hearings, CARC's Montreal conference and the *Animals' Agenda* roundtable, we can see that the animal rights movement not only stood by it original position on Inuit sealing, but also progressively intensified its opposition to include a broad range of Native wildlife activities. Then, as the moral power of the protest's stance on consumptive wildlife use was threatened by the opposition of Native Northerners seeking cultural sovereignty, the movement took aim at the very basis of this independence. We must now explore the question of why the protest rejected the Inuit claim of moral equality.

9 A BLIZZARD OF CONTRADICTIONS

Contrasting the past and the present

The gulf that separates Inuit from animal rights and seal protest activists has widened since 1983. Into the early 1980s, the protest had expressed some measure of understanding for Inuit dependence on the fur industry and, when closely questioned (see, for instance, Boe 1984) admitted ignorance of the ecological, social, and economic importance of ringed seals to Inuit. We have seen, however, that this innocence began to wane once the EC boycott had incorporated their own ideas. By the time of the Royal Commission in 1985, an inflexibility that still marks the Inuit seal controversy had become established.

The complicating feature of any analysis of the seal issue is the way the notion of subsistence has been interpreted by those opposed to seal hunting. Their apparent recognition of sealing as 'a natural and legitimate occupation' hinged on the way the term 'traditional' was applied in parts of Directive 83/129: sealing related to subsistence only if it formed 'an important part of the traditional way of life and economy' and, likewise, hunting was narrowly defined as the means 'traditionally practised by the Inuit people.'

The term *traditional* has been allowed to serve as a convenient reference to subsistence without any practical criteria or means for testing it. The *traditional* nature of Inuit interactions with seals was thus made a point of central importance: so much so that it now dominates the controversy.

The case that Inuit have generally presented for the wide significance of *natsiq* in their lives is well supported by current scientific data. To the surprise of all the parties, of anthropologists, biologists, planners and, most of all, Inuit, this straightforward appraisal of the continuing importance of seals in northern life has not been accepted by anti-sealers and has not elicited from them any counter-analysis of these data.

Instead, the movement has developed its own strategy of portraying Inuit life as being born of White contact, rather than flowing from indigenous tradition. That argument rests heavily on redefinition of Inuit culture solely in terms of materials and objects. Motorboats, snowmobiles, and firearms are continually contrasted with *qajaq*, dogteams, and harpoon hunting. Hence traditional Inuit culture became as frozen as Boas's description of Cumberland Sound in the 1880s.

162

Another feature of the protesters' strategy is to analyze the history of Inuit-*Qallunaat* contact in a selective way, emphasizing the dominant role of the fur trade in the early period. Negative aspects of modern Native life are attributed to these early influences (see Best 1986, 1989a) in what amounts to a worrying leap through history.

The picture of Inuit they paint is of a society that no longer retains any inner links to its own past. They argue, in the words of Dan Morast (1985, personal communication), that modern technology so distances Inuit 'from the way they lived 500 years ago' that the notion of tradition is indefensible. What Morast and others fail to recognize is that Inuit adopted these material changes under long and intense pressure from *Qallunaat* society – pressure that is still felt – in order to preserve other elements of their culture. Whose criteria should be used to identify the 'real' cultural traits that are Inuit tradition?

Analyzing the animal rights argument

Between 1982 and 1988, the animal rights movement developed three lines of argument within the broad strategy outlined above, and we shall see that they are often contradictory. The key features of the argument rest upon special conceptions of 1) the relationship of Inuit to the fur trade; 2) the role of new technologies in Inuit life; and 3) the degree of cultural assimilation that Inuit have undergone.

While these conceptions paint a dark picture of White intrusions on Inuit life and culture, they offer no basis for understanding the present situation in the North; they are presented only as reasons for rejecting Inuit arguments about the cultural importance of seal hunting. In them, Inuit are portrayed as a people who have lost all connection to their traditional culture and must therefore accept our definition of their future. Taking these lines of argument one by one, I shall show the fallaciousness of each.

I. The Inuit role in the fur trade

The first theme, and the most tenuous, concerns the degree to which Inuit have become willing accomplices in the exploitation of seals to fill the needs of European commerce. The argument surfaced in interview discussions and correspondence I had with representatives of the International Fund for Animal Welfare (Best 1984) and the Sea Shepherd Society (Watson 1985). While they acknowledge that Inuit were initially drawn unwittingly to participate in the fur trade, they argue that the role of Inuit in the industry is now voluntary.

Because they see the trade as antithetical to traditional Inuit values and culture, they regard the reasons Inuit might have for continued collaboration as suspect. They argue that Inuit have been seduced by what Best (1984) refers to as southern 'luxury imports – rifles, snowmobiles, washing machines, government-supplied houses, television

163

and modern health care. All those are offered (ibid.) as signs that Inuit are turning away from their traditional culture. In Paul Watson's words (1985, personal communication), Inuit chose to 'align' themselves with the 'enemy camp' and 'it is in the interest of the large fur companies ... to place the Native in the front lines'. In other words, Inuit know where these 'luxuries' come from, and the fur industry is more than happy to exploit the 'Nanook' image of the Inuk sealer.

Animal rightists presume that the ideology of Inuit seal harvesting has changed through participation in the fur trade. Their argument leans heavily on Calvin Martin's (1978) analysis of the role Native Peoples played in the early Anglo-French fur trade in eastern North America. Briefly, Martin (ibid.: 45–50) hypothesizes that depredations carried out by aboriginal peoples toward animals during the early fur trade (but see Krech 1984 and Tanner 1983 for counter-analyses of this hypothesis) were precipitated by Native belief that the devastating diseases they experienced through White contact came from animals. Tautologically, Martin (ibid.: 146) concludes that because Native Peoples believed that their animal partners had turned upon them for overhunting, they launched a human 'war of revenge' on wildlife.

Best (1984), for one, has suggested that Inuit attitudes toward wildlife have shifted from one of reverence to crass 'commoditization'. In his eyes, Inuit are now hostile toward animals for ideological and material reasons that have been institutionalized by the fur trade. In support of this view, he cites the lack of ritual Inuit display toward animals.

The flaw in both lines of the complicity argument lies in their ignorance of contemporary Inuit life. One seeks the safety of a single historiographic villain when the pattern of Inuit relations with the South has developed far more complexly than the argument identifies. The other, as Tanner (1983: 185–6) has pointed out, exemplifies the dangers of presumptively characterizing Native ideology.

II. New technologies in Inuit life

The most prominent argument made by the movement in the sealing debate is that Inuit culture has undergone such extensive technological change that it no longer resembles its traditional antecedents. The argument rests on the belief that the use of modern tools implies basic changes in Inuit adaptation. The presence of guns, snowmobiles and motor boats is used as evidence of an Inuit dependence on the South that goes far beyond these tools. It echoes Hantzsch's warning back in 1910 about Inuit developing a dependence on *Qallunaat* and their inability to survive without White assistance.

In making this argument, animal rights spokespeople rely on very selective evidence. In discussing Inuit culture change, they continually refer to the things that are new in Inuit communities, but they rarely note the many 'traditional' items which are still in use - from caribou parkas and sealskin boots to snowhouses and antler or ivory harpoon heads - nor do they note the modifications Inuit make to new goods to improve them for local use. Choosing only certain artifacts for inclusion in their critique, they conclude that these new tools lead Inuit to rely on southerners, pollute their environment, upset the natural ecological balance, and contribute little to the quality of northern life. While not disputing the truth within some of these examples (snowmobiles are deafening and noisome to anyone who follows too closely behind), a leap to the conclusion that Inuit are alienated from their traditions betrays the presence of considerable, and selective, 'cultural filtering'. Let us take some stock of the distortion that accompanies this filtering.

A wide range of 'traditional' artifacts - sleds, clothing, fishing and hunting equipment - are used daily by Inuit. Because some are restricted to circumstances away from the village, and others are made from non-indigenous materials, they are not recognized for what they are. The snowmobile is perhaps the best example of the problem of evaluating the effect of technological change on Inuit. One can too readily assume that a snowmobile is accepted by Inuit with the same motives and used for the same purposes as it is by Whites in southern Canada. In fact, as has already been explained, Inuit employ it in a novel manner that is faithful to the role once filled by dogteams.

The snowmobile, as we saw earlier, represents far more than the noisy recreational vehicle that it is taken to be by most southerners. To Inuit harvesters, it provides a mobility without which, in the current demographic circumstances, they could not sustain subsistence seal production. The *sikki*-doo, like certain other new tools, possesses a social history revealing of the whole fabric of Inuit–White relations. The cultural filtering that pervades the movement's understanding of Inuit use of this machine exemplifies the whole weight of modern colonial policy in the Canadian Arctic.

Instead of recognizing this situation, as the change argument is generally presented, it reduces these relations to the comic situation plotted in the popular movie *The Gods Must Be Crazy*. The snowmobile, the rifle, the television set, and the nurse's needle are presented like the empty Coca-Cola bottle found by a Bushman hunter in the film - as objects thoughtlessly interjected by Europeans into the North's environment that Inuit are powerless to understand or control.

Best (1984) and Smith (1988) treat artifacts such as the rifle as an inducement to Inuit to overhunt simply because the gun is a more efficient tool than the harpoon. They imagine that snowmobiles permit Inuit hunters to deplete the animals in one area and then leap to another without suffering the consequences. In their scheme, the adaptive advantages these tools may represent - enhanced mobility and harvesting effectiveness - to Inuit living under modern conditions negate what they imagine were the traditional ecological and cultural priorities of pre-European Inuit life.

Is it possible to thrust the whole responsibility of these 'cultural modifications' on to the shoulders of Inuit? Arguably, modern Inuit adaptation must be seen in the wider framework of modern southern intrusion into the North.

Snowmobiles, we recall, supplanted dogteams only when Inuit were removed from their traditional pattern of settlement in the 1950s and placed in large government villages, an event precipitated by the need for modern medical care in the face of endemic Inuit illness. To retain the advantage of health care, Inuit adopted the most effective technical means available to allow them to carry on their subsistence harvesting. The snowmobile provided the means for Inuit to use both *Qallunaat* medicine and traditional foods under the social conditions dictated by southern policy.

As the animal rights movement has promulgated its change argument (for instance, Best 1984), the only way for Inuit to reverse the process of loss of tradition is to abandon the artifacts - abandon, too, beneficial elements such as modern medicine - and dissociate themselves from *Qallunaat* policy. In this regard, the animal rights position conforms with that of Arctic 'rednecks' pressing development of oil, natural gas, and uranium. As a helicopter pilot once remarked to me if the Inuit I was with did not want a pipeline to disturb seals because they were a traditional food resource, 'they could damn well get off their snowmobiles and walk to and from the ice to prove their traditionalness. That was the way the old Eskimos did it.'

In the same vein, Greanville and O'Sullivan (in Bartlett 1988: 16-17) conclude that Canadian aboriginal emphasis on the role of animals in contemporary life stems more from a desire for a financial settlement of northern land claims than from a real attachment to or need for wildlife. As suggested by Greanville (ibid.: 16), the only way to prove otherwise is 'to say that you will preserve the land for the traditional uses of fishing, hunting, and trapping only'. Like the pilot, the animal rights representatives define the conditions of Inuit traditionalness in terms of identifiers from the past. This approach is justified, in Paul Watson's words (1985, personal communication), because:

> This is an era of changing social values . . . traditions will be broken, people on both sides will be hurt but it is a part of natural human evolution . . . should social change within the context of one social group be restricted by the result it will have on another social group, especially in light of the fact that such social change is perceived . . . as being progressive.

III. Inuit cultural assimilation

The third line of argument that animal rights advocates have developed centers on the degree to which Inuit society has accommodated itself to southern culture. The charge of sameness is in many ways only the logical end point of the movement's argument that Inuit culture has changed beyond ever being able to regain its former traditions. But there is another aspect to this argument that needs to be examined. It is that assimilation is an inevitable consequence of Inuit contact with a southern culture whose power to replace Inuit values with its own is equal to the voraciousness of its appetite for the furs Inuit can supply.

According to Steven Best (1985: 11)

All people are essentially the same ... Inuit kill for the same reasons as Newfoundlanders, as South Africans, as Scottish fishermen, to make some money. They may believe otherwise, but everyone believes otherwise.

As Best describes this condition, the way that seal harvesting has importance for Inuit differs not at all from statements heard in defence of southern industrial sealing – economic profit. He (ibid.) suggests that cultural considerations about Inuit hunting, whether for 'stories to tell, or for social interaction, or for gift-giving', should be put aside. To understand the importance of seals for Inuit, it is the relationship between Inuit and Europeans that needs to be examined.

Best (1986: 202–8) provides such an analysis. In it he makes such points as the fact that contact meant the introduction of pathogens formerly unknown to Inuit, and noting that European culture almost destroyed Inuit as a culture and a people he suggests but he also states that it was Europeans who recognized the effect they were having and moved to ameliorate it. He further points out that famine, epidemic infant mortality, and what he perceives as unacceptable forms of customary justice were eradicated through European and Canadian efforts. In summing up his points, he declares that 'life was short, often unpleasant and terrifying, and often painful'.

These points are made in support of one ringing conclusion: (Best 1989b: 149):

The Native people have got to become self-sufficient. They have got to have their own culture that is living. I own the Native culture. I bought it with my taxes. I own about two-thirds of it.

Best, (ibid.) is thus led to provide his final evaluation of the present state of Inuit relations with White culture 'Native peoples have got to develop a culture that is ... apart from southern interests, and ... on their own terms. When they do, they will be able to call all their own shots.'

Such statements are at the least startling, not only for their candidness, but because of the extreme ethnocentrism that the words carry. Best's avowal that 'Inuit kill for the same reasons' as Newfoundlanders, South Africans, and Scots, suggesting that the similarities he sees between Inuit and southern cultures is based solely on a willingness to kill for profit, might relate to the extreme distaste hunting evokes in him, but the suggestion that southern culture has taken over Inuit distorts the history and present state of Inuit relations with Euro-Canadian society.

Evidence from segments of the movement indicate that Best's perspective is not an isolated aberration, but one that is shared by a militant part of the animal rights movement. More and more, it appears that it is part of a strategy that does not simply seek to isolate in the public mind the present-day mode of Inuit life from *Qallunaat* notions of what authentic 'traditional' Eskimo culture was in an earlier time when it nurtured and maintained a 'natural' relationship with *natsiq*. To judge from more recent examples, its objective seems to be to question whether any of the value once attributed to traditional Native culture was ever present.

As recently as the Canadian seal commission hearings of 1985, testimony from many participants advocating an end to sealing focussed their presentations on whether Inuit were engaged in excessive exploitation of ringed seals. Since then, some animal rightists have made it clear that their critique of Native society is not limited to the use of animals, but is concerned with the wider values of indigenous cultures.

Anne Doncaster (in Keith and Saunders 1989: 21-2), for instance, suggests that Native harvesting, while it may have strong traditional roots, directly conflicts with 'the best interests of [Native] children'. She ends her thought with the hint that the continuation of such a tradition is distinctly detrimental to these children being able to make their own life choices in a complex world.

Even more pointed are the 'facts of life' enumerated in the *Ark II Activist* (Miller n.d.), an animal rights newsletter, about aboriginal traditional culture. Noting the dilemma which opposition of Indians and Inuit presents to the goals of animal liberation, the piece provides a singular examination of pre-European and fur trade era Native culture and society.

In it, Miller (ibid.: 1), while admitting that the known history of North American hunter-gatherers is fragmentary, writes that these peoples 'lived without the concept of hygiene ...', their 'meagre possessions' were carried by 'the chief beasts of burden ... women'. In times of hardship 'the weak were abandoned – the old, the sick and the women were jettisoned first' and female infanticide was widespread because girls 'were merely another mouth to feed, another low-status drudge who would be spared a lifetime of misery. Living with scarcity made the lives of all but the hunter dispensable'. In just a few pages, Miller points out that warfare was a blood sport, women were married in their early teens, and thereafter were virtually the property of men, and that life was lived 'in constant dread of the malevolent spirits' It is no wonder that Miller (ibid.: 2) concludes 'The reality of privation, hardship and misery shatter the mythological concepts of nobility and spiritual peace'.

Miller is no doubt correct in her assumption that aboriginal life entailed a degree of hardship that far exceeded what we imagine Inuit hunting to be even now. I suspect that this was also the case of our own pre-machine farmer forebears of a few generations ago. All evaluations of this kind are grounded in what we subjectively perceive as better, whether speaking of physical comfort or societal values. There is, therefore, little difficulty in construing another's culture and values as less inviting than our own.

There are more cogent grounds for criticizing Miller's rendition of traditional Native society. The first is that it represents little more than a catalogue of behaviors that our society has now generally rejected. The list is gratuitous as a means of explaining Native culture, good or bad, because her analysis points to the natural environment as the influencer of Native behavior. Such an environmental determinist argument is no more palatable as she uses it than it is when used to explain the temperments of Caribbean or Mediterranean cultures.

As to the overview's particulars, they are eclectic and random. Traits that are popularly, if not scientifically, attributed to a particular society are cast across all Native Canadians. The accusation of widely practiced infanticide is a case in point. Generally associated by anthropologists with one or two Inuit societies, its truth has in the last twenty years been the subject of wide scholarly debate (see Balikci 1967; Freeman 1971; Schrirer and Steiger 1974; Saladin d'Anglure 1984).

In the end, Native society from Mexico to the Arctic is tarred with the same brush, although Miller specifically identifies only two indigenous cultures in her review. Even the authority for these observations is doubtful; Miller cites only Anne Doncaster, also of Ark II, as her primary resource.

Contradictions

The animal rights movement finds itself in a dilemma. In Vicki Miller's (n.d.: 1) words, it seeks to 'fight for justice and reject oppression in any form regardless of whether it affects human beings, nonhuman beings or the Earth herself'. As part of its campaign, activists have pointed to Inuit (Duffy 1984: 6) as examples of harmonious natural living and harnessed Native oral tradition (Greenpeace UK 1984) to the support of the seal campaign. Now it is confronted by the same Inuit it appropriated and metaphorically idealized. What are the roots of this contradiction?

The first is that Inuit seal hunters present the movement with a brand of opposition that cannot be dismissed in the same terms activists have used to deal with the fur industry. This is because Inuit participation in the fur trade remains, as in the past, rooted in traditional ecological activity. Inuit take few species for their fur alone. *Natsiq* and polar bear are food species as important to Inuit today as they were before White contact. If any confirmation of this is needed, archaeology confirms this pre-contact use (see, for instance, Mohl 1979), while the role wild meat still plays in the contemporary diet (see Mackey 1984; Borre 1989) is evidence of the retention of this food tradition among Inuit.

Second, the manner in which harvesting is still done by Inuit remains as dependent on traditional ecological knowledge and skills as ever. Inuit winter seal hunting is the best example of this, but the importance of long-term training and association with animals that has been documented from Alaska (see Nelson 1969; Fienup-Riordan 1983) to Greenland (Born 1983; Dahl 1990) consistently reinforces the notion that technology only supplements this indigenous inventory.

The money Inuit receive as a byproduct of sealskin sales enables harvesters to operate as efficiently as they need in a changed northern economic environment. The snowmobiles that these sales produce allow Inuit to husband the traditional resources important to harvesting – time and energy – so that they can be used effectively. This harnessing of non-traditional technology with customary resources while a necessity in the modern North is consistent with the Inuit adaptive tradition.

Finally, it is clear that Inuit retain as strong a social ideology with regard to harvesting as ever. *Ningiqtuq* is so basic to Inuit social cohesion and so commonplace that it often is passed by us unremarked. It is the reason why Inuit villagers, while living in one of Canada's most economically depressed situations, never pass a day without food or unhoused. The social ethos that relates harvesting to Inuit society is literally as traditional an element of their culture as seal hunting.

To judge from protesters' statements during the Royal Commission hearings or 'The Warrior of the Rainbow' legend that Greenpeace flourishes, the central contradiction in the controversy seems to stem not from what Inuit do or say with respect to harvesting.

Instead, it seems to arise from the fact that the movement finally became aware of the everyday meaning of wildlife to Inuit and it did not conform to the image they themselves had built. Subsistence was more than a harmonious exchange between Eskimos and animals that took place without trauma according to an ethnographer's script. It included snowmobiles, ammunition paid for with sealskins, and Inuit living in hot, overcrowded government bungalows.

The discrepancy between the mechanized routine of modern harvesting and the ethnographic image of hunting suggests the reason for the movement's refusal to reject data that demonstrates that Inuit tradition lives on. The idea that Inuit can employ non-traditional technology that we associate with recreation and sell sealskins as a way of continuing their customary ecological and social adaptation as much threatens the picture activists have of themselves as it does the one of aboriginal culture.

To explain the difference, the movement, of necessity had to develop its own thesis about Inuit subsistence and culture. Without question, the fur trade has been a potent imperialist force in Inuit–White history. As we have seen, animal rights activists (Best 1986; Smith 1988; O'Sullivan and Greanville in Bartlett 1988; Miller n.d.) have used the historical factor to project why modern Inuit have 'lost sight' of their own traditions.

This 'historiographic' approach belies the fact that historical analysis of *Qallunaat*-Inuit relations, in the past and the present, means not only apportioning guilt; it also means accepting responsibility. Northern history did not cease when the Hudson's Bay Company held a vast monopoly on northern commerce. Change in the North has moved farther faster since the HBC's grip was loosened. More than some other agents, the movement seems unwilling to see the connection between achievement of its goals and this process of cultural erosion.

Acceptance of this connection does not absolve the fur trade, government, or science of the considerable role they have played among Inuit as agents of change. But the problems of contemporary Inuit or Indian society that Best (1986, 1989) has so extensively catalogued will not disappear because a finger has been pointed at the fur industry. When activists say they can see nothing different about present-day Inuit society from our own, they blatantly contradict nearly fifty years of Inuit experience with the South.

The process the movement has now embarked on of 'debunking' the myth of traditional aboriginal culture accelerates a descent into the realm of cultural imperialism (see Peter 1983). Miller's (n.d.) critique in *The Ark II Activist* is a potent example of this slide. Native cultures have been mythologized as 'natural ecologists', 'the original affluent society', and as 'pure' subsistence societies, and it must be remembered that animal activists have contributed to these images, too. Now, a new type of 'selective' image of Inuit is being constructed by the movement. Duffy's (1984) 'Esquimaux' no longer exemplify human partnership with animals. Instead, they now represent the hunter who has been 'corrupted by modern civilization'.

The last argument has developed in order to offset the moral paradox Inuit pose to the movement and its battle for the hearts and minds of the public. The earliest response of the movement to Inuit complaints about the effects of the sealskin protest and ban was to say that it was an inevitable consequence of Southern culture's historical and ethical evolution (see Watson 1985, personal communication). Inuit recognize this as the same reasoning used by other more obvious northern 'developers'. Now the argument seeks to dilute the socio-cultural link between traditional Inuit culture and the 'hybrid' of today (see Best 1986; Smith 1988; also Best and Livingston in Keith and Saunders 1989: 138–44 and 118–22, respectively) and to cast the whole image of what traditional culture represented into disrepute.

The reason for retrenchment by animal rightists from their early position is clear. Inuit have presented the animal rights movement with arguments that are as morally rooted and compelling to the southern public as the activists' own.

Why has the movement chosen this latest strategy? As the seal biologist, David Levigne, observed, the seal controversy revolves not around scientific data, but on politically translatable moral and ethical differences. Best (1984) says that politics is perception and, since very few people are in touch with the theory or philosophy of animal rights, politicization of the seal issue is the only way to mobilize them. In the latest stage of the Inuit seal controversy, the movement has chosen to make Native culture the issue.

10 THE CONTROVERSY TODAY

The Inuit situation

Knowledge of what life in Clyde River was like twenty years ago brings an important perspective to the present discussion. The many elements that are a part of the seal conflict's northern legacy come forward in ways that would otherwise be absent. Foremost, an understanding of how the protest, European sealskin ban, and even the post-ban actions of government have all worked radically to change the cultural environment of the North would be missed, even though these changes have touched all facets of modern Inuit culture, from the economic and material condition of daily life to the way social relations are structured in camp.

Nowhere is paradox more apparent than in the transformation the local economy has undergone. This is not so much because fresh southern foods and TV videos dominate the shelves of Clyde's much enlarged store; rather it is because the constant flow of hunters to and from the land is far less obvious now. In summer, boats sit along the beach for days without moving and the early mornings of winter now see little more than a handful of men out breathing-hole hunting. Food harvesting, the backbone of the Inuit economy only a few years ago, now gives the appearance of being diminished by the demands of local modernization. A hunter's time now seems as if it can be more fruitfully spent driving the water truck than waiting at an *aglu*.

The social discordance that accompanies rapid change now also appears to be a feature of small village life. At first glance, this tension may appear to be related to the unique dynamic Vallee (1962) called the 'Nunamiut-Kabloonamiut', the dicotomous pulls of acculturation (see also Honigmann and Honigmann 1965). To many *Qallunaat* observers, it is an obvious manifestation of the absorption process that Inuit subsistence adaptation began forty years ago when resettlement, southern health care and education and a cash-based economy were introduced as Canada's 'policy' for Inuit (see Duffy 1988). But, as long-term study in villages like Clyde River shows, these obvious answers are not as clear-cut as they appear.

Increased Inuit participation in the cash-economy has been stimulated less by the attractiveness of expanding wage opportunities than by the severe economic constraints under which subsistence production must now be practiced. The growth in the money sector of the economy in communities is less an indicator of Inuit socio-economic well-being or satisfaction than of concerted external pressure on the cash component of modern harvesting.

As has been described, the several-fold increase in the amount of money reaching Inuit hands in Clyde River during the last five years is not the product of any sustained or gradual expansionist trend in the social transfer and government-based employment systems of the community. It is, in fact, a response to catastrophic need. This need, in turn, relates directly to the loss of the chief indigenous means by which Clyde harvesters have supported local subsistence food production since the consolidation of the modern settlement, sealskin sales.

In this regard, an explanation of how money became an integral component of modern Inuit subsistence need is far from as simple as animal rights analysts like Best, Smith or Miller suppose. To understand this requires a systemic examination of *Qallunaat* policy, Canadian, American and European, in the formation of the post-war human environment in the Arctic. Such analysis brings to light two important elements about Inuit–Southern economic and social interaction.

The first is that after the Second World War the position held by the Hudson's Bay Company as the single significant source of southern economic influence reaching Inuit became diluted. New actors, mainly associated with the national government (Northern Affairs, National Defense), but, later, also territorial government and private agents, radically altered the composition of the Inuit economic environment. The labour Inuit could supply to these agents became a significant, if small by our standards, means of generating important amounts of cash income in every community. Inuit time and energy for use in non-hunting pursuits became part of the modern exchange economy.

The other is that non-economy-oriented aspects of post-war northern policy, like centralization, placed a variety of constraints upon local subsistence systems that, over time, were less amenable to solely indigenous solution. Hunter density and general demographic increase are examples of social policy decisions that affected local economic relations.

This is in sharp contrast, as Damas (1988: 106–8) and Goldring (1986: 171) both point out, to the situation that prevailed earlier. In the pre-war heyday of the arctic fur trade, Inuit living under traditional settlement and demographic circumstances pursued an economic regime that was far less dominated by exogenous influence than is often thought. It is ironic, therefore, that after the war the increased importance which imported technology offered Inuit as a means of ameliorating the problems attending resettlement made the Hudson's Bay Company an even larger factor in Inuit everyday life than previously. This enhanced influence arose from two simple facts. First, the HBC was already extensively situated throughout the North and, second, while a variety of agencies provided funding for Inuit, only the Hudson's Bay Company, with occasional exception, offered reliable opportunity for Inuit to obtain the technology settlement-based activities now required.

None of this is to say that the dynamics of the fur trade, examined from 1945 (and especially after 1960), are inconsequential. But this importance can only be appreciated in terms of the overall acceleration of change-related processes and events affecting Inuit. Indeed, with regard to Inuit sealskin use, two critical factors summarize the modern situation.

The first is that the opening of markets for *natsiq* pelts provided Inuit with a culturally coherent means of retaining control over the local economies of their settlements. As Damas and Goldring have described with regard to the fox trade, ringed seal harvesting allowed Inuit viably to participate both in the traditional food economy and the new cash one. At the same time, cash proceeds from an already highly profitable non-cash activity buffered Inuit from any need radically to conform to the main acculturation–assimilation mechanism of the post-war period, wage labour. Both the social and ecological relations that normatively define the Inuit subsistence universe thus remained intact.

The other important aspect of the sealskin 'story' relates directly to the political success of the seal protest in closing the international sealskin market. Like many analyses of the fur industry's role in the North, this, too, is all too frequently considered as a singular event, isolation from the larger context of Inuit–*Qallunaat* relations. The truth is that while the animal rights protest over sealing has a singular quality, it also falls fully within the pattern of Inuit experience with the southern world.

Its singularity revolves around two facts. The first is that the seal protest originated not through government policy, the usual effector of Inuit life, but with the selectively cultivated public perception of seals by a dedicated group of 'secular' activists. In this regard, the intent was single-purpose, to bring an end to commercial seal hunting. This was accomplished by projecting the image of a wide-eyed, snow white face of a harp seal pup as the image of all seals.

The other fact is that, at least from the time that the protest developed public momentum, around 1965-80, there was a growing awareness among scientists, government officials, and protest organizers that Inuit were innocently being drawn into the controversy's vortex. Contrary, however, to the reaction of many other southern-generated initiatives toward northern Natives during this time (the James Bay Project; the Mackenzie Valley and Polargas pipeline proposals; the Arctic Pilot Project), little effort was made (see Foote 1967a; Wenzel 1978; Williamson 1978) to make this development widely known. By and large, the extent of socioeconomic and ecological peril to the Inuit subsistence system remained confined to a few parties (Government of the Northwest Territories 1978; Barzdo 1980) directly concerned with the issue. While most other post-war actions that touched Inuit were linked to an overarching design of 'northern development', the seal protest occurred with barely a thought about its effects on them.

These singularities aside, the seal campaign conducted by the animal rights movement falls very much into the general pattern of all change-oriented policies so far imposed on the North. It is primarily motivated, at least in the eyes of its advocates, by the same rationales, discussed below, that have spurred most recent northern initiatives.

The first is that its success will improve the condition of Inuit. In the animal rights case this will be brought about by re-establishing the opportunity for Inuit to practice 'true' subsistence. The exact meaning of this is somewhat illusive, with suggestions ranging from the simple removal of sealskins from the cash exchange system (and, thus, Inuit complicity in the fur industry) to a return to some form of pre-contact lifestyle. The second is that southerners know, without the benefit of Inuit consultation (see Keith and Saunders 1989: 152–3), how best to improve the contemporary circumstances of Inuit life. This is an aspect of the seal protest that Inuit (Peter 1983) have long recognized as an attribute of the movement.

The worst effects of the result have fallen directly on the socio-economic stability of the traditional subsistence adaptation which Inuit, despite apparent deep changes related to technological innovation, have maintained through decades of intensive *Qallunaat* contact. Today, the human center of this adaptation, experienced adult harvesters, are able to contribute to the material and social needs of their communities with far less regularity than at any time in the post-war period. The reason for this is that they no longer share secure access to money, which because of southern-induced alterations to the demographic/economic environment of harvesting has now become as critical a resource to modern subsistence as time and energy.

As a result, the cultural focus of subsistence, sharing (*ningiqtuq*), based as it is on the customary social relations of production in harvesting, can be said to have begun to undergo a kind of 'fraying'. This relates, at the present time, not so much to any unavailability of traditional food than to the fact that production is increasingly becoming the province of those men who can successfully participate in the wage economy.

As heartening, and important, as this success currently is, there are strong suggestions that it offers few long-term solutions to the adaptational problem brought on by the northern seal protest. This is because, first, this relatively small cadre can only invest so much time, energy, and money to meet the needs of growing communities. Second, the employment prospectus for the Inuit North, without byproduct sales, remains, as it has been in the past, a limited one. Third, and most importantly, the sociology of work, as far as it can be analyzed in relation to the alternatives now being offered to harvesting (bureaucratization, non-renewable resource employment, tourism-related services), will offer little support (see Rinehart 1987; Ross and Usher 1986) to the social solidarity that is fundamental to *ningiqtuq* organization and adaptation.

At present, as data from Clyde River show, the chief socioeconomic accomplishment of the present sealskin ban among Inuit has been to create something disturbingly like Wilmott's (1961) dual economy situation. At Clyde, less than 10 per cent of the village population, those who have obtained full-time wage employment, provide at least 60 per cent of the monies reaching Inuit hands. The social consequences of such a dichotomous pattern of distribution, especially given the former circumstances of access, are only beginning to appear. As one Clyde Inuk, who works hard for the salary he earns, recently remarked: 'No matter how hard I work, I cannot give enough money to my relatives so they can hunt. Sometimes I cannot go [out] because I have no gas.' The same day, a middle-aged man, long regarded as one of the most reliable seal hunters in the village, ended the conversation we were having about his broken outboard engine by telling me: 'When you were here last year, I was away hunting. Then I was independent, now I take welfare.'

Both men's words underscore the present socioeconomic double-bind that the seal protest and perspective of the animal rights movement presents for Inuit (see also Smith and Wright 1989) in communities like Clyde River. Wage work, as presently estimated, carries with it the risk of alienating individuals from the social context which is the traditional centre of the subsistence system. Without money, however, the most skilled practitioners of harvesting are economically unable to contribute the non-cash wealth that provides the material substance of *ningiqtuq*.

The animal rights situation

The animal rights movement, for all the success achieved through the seal protest and European sealskin ban, presently also occupies a stance that is, at least, uncomfortable to maintain *vis à vis* Inuit. As has been noted throughout this work, during the movement's early days (pre-1985), animal rightists publicly portrayed themselves as being in fundamental sympathy with Native Peoples caught up in the seal protest. At the same time, as the 1985 exchange between Greenland Inuit and Greenpeace representatives (see Goddard 1986) and the experience of the Royal Commission on Seals demonstrated, the movement tried to maintain this sympathetic public face, while dismissing further dialogue with Inuit over seals as dwelling on past history.

The expansion of the seal protest into a much wider anti-wild fur/trapping campaign intensified, rather than relieved, the pressure the movement came to receive from Canadian aboriginal people. Indeed, the effect of this criticism about organizations' views of Native hunter-trappers led to the withdrawal of some seal protest members, notably Greenpeace International and Greenpeace Canada, from the fur campaign.

The fur campaign, which encompassed within its scope not just Inuit but all northern Natives, seems to have, in fact, galvanized a hardening of attitude among the protest groups that chose to persist. To Best (1986), the anomalous relationship that had punctuated Inuit-seal protest dialogue became clarified as a simple case of two political bodies openly in opposition to each other. Native People ceased to represent a moral counterpoint to the animal rights view, but rather, as Best (1985) has put it, have become 'a political problem'. The movement then began to 'test' arguments for offsetting Inuit critiques of their protest, so as at least to reduce it to a manageable political level.

These political counter-efforts, as they have been internally developed, have followed the same kind of selective perception process Hunter (1979) has described with regard to the early stages of the seal protest. In the seal campaign this included not only the strong anthropomorphization of individual seals, but also the creating of an image of sealers as an anonymous, emotionless entity. A powerful contrast was thus manufactured between a viewer's felt preference (see Norton 1984: 134–6) for baby seals and the 'abnormal' behavior, in terms of the general experience of the seal campaign's audience, of Euro-Canadian sealers.

Since 1985, it appears that a similar selective perception strategy has been adopted with regard to the political problem (Best 1986) Inuit and other aboriginal peoples pose to animal rights objectives. For instance, the term 'Natives' has been adopted by animal advocates to categorize the whole spectrum of aboriginal opposition to their program(s) and is applied to aboriginal critics whether they represent Indigenous Survival International or an ethnically identifiable aboriginal group. An example of this can be found in Miller's (n.d.) critical analysis of traditional Native culture, throughout which negative attributes are generally subsumed under the heading of Native. One of the few group-specific references appearing in her overview concerns the fight by the Northwest Coast Haida to protect their traditional lands from commercial lumbering (ibid.: 4), a positive aboriginal action within the Warrior of the Rainbow frame of reference.

From 1985 onward, the movement has increasingly oriented its rhetoric toward the 'demythologizing' of such concepts as tradition or subsistence with regard to contemporary Inuit and Indian culture. Livingston (in Keith and Saunders 1989: 119) has labelled the continued application of these terms to modern aboriginal consumptive activities like Inuit seal hunting and Cree trapping as the product of 'neo-traditionalism'. Likewise, Greanville and O'Sullivan (in Bartlett 1988) have conceptually linked present-day Inuit and Indian use of wildlife to the efforts of these Peoples to reach agreement with Canada on the issue of Native land claims. In so doing, animal rightists have interpreted Native subsistence activities to be mainly a tactic for exacting financial compensation from government and, in so doing, have lost sight of the larger issue aboriginal political, social and economic self-determination – which the term 'land claims' so poorly conveys (see Asch 1984; Berger 1985).

Within the scope of the widened confrontation that has occurred in the past five years between animal rightists and Native Peoples, the matter of sealing appears to have disappeared, lost among newer, bigger matters. In fact, this is not correct. Seals and sealing have stayed very much on the movement's agenda, so much so that Steven Best (*Montreal Gazette*, 19 March 1989) declared that 'We thought we had won in 1982 . . . But we didn't win, we lost. Now we've got to start all over again.'

The focus of Best's call for a new round of protests was the purported high level of sealing activity still conducted by Norway and southern Euro-Canadians. According to Best (*Montreal Gazette*, 18 April 1989), just the latter accounted for 240,000 animals still being killed in the region where the original harp seal protest was centered. When challenged, however, for data confirming a kill three times higher than that of Canadian government estimates, he noted (ibid.) that he held no firm information on the present state of Canadian seal hunting.

A more accurate reading of this upsurge in protest expression over an issue, declared by the movement with regard to Inuit concerns as moot, correlates to the 1989 expiration of the EC's official boycott (as set through Council Directive 85/444/EEC, Article 1). This is that the European Community, as of 1 October 1989, was to examine evidence regarding, among other things, the state of the 'market in seal skins derived from the Inuits' [*sic*] traditional hunting', as well as that of pelts derived from other non-excluded sources in the EC's original action. However, protest efforts persuaded the Community to renew its strictures of sealskin commerce in mid-summer of 1989, several months before its own stated review date.

The latest protest episode over southern sealing activity, intentionally or not, served to obscure the critical relationship that continues between Inuit and seals as a matter of cultural prerogative and economic need, just as it did in the early 1980s. Even more importantly, animal advocates, by presenting the continuation of the EC ban as the only means of morally sanctioning remanent non-Native sealing activity, prevented examination of ·the most important aspect of the seal issue today. This is the propriety of imposing a *Qallunaat* view of animals, whether it arises solely from within the movement or reflects a more generalized Western consciousness, on a people whose perspective has evolved in a considerably different cultural, ecological and historical setting.

The new Inuit-animal rights dynamic: speculations and conclusions

It is always very difficult to make definitive statements about conflicts when the issue discussed remains far from any conclusive resolution. This is certainly the condition that pertains between Inuit and the animal rights movement at present. Under the circumstances, it is, therefore, preferable to offer some speculations, judiciously mixed with the facts here presented, on the Inuit sealing controversy, especially if these are not interpreted as predictions or recommendations. I put

179

these forward as they relate to the main theme(s) of this study.

Briefly, this book has had two main objectives and concerns. The first was to place present-day Inuit use of seals, and other wildlife, in context to the internal and exogenous dynamics of contemporary northern life. The other was to examine the seal protest/animal rights movement in terms of its impact on and attitudes toward Inuit.

To the first end, considerable original and secondary information on the nutritional, ecological, and socio-cultural relations of Inuit harvesting has been presented. This was done not only in the hope of explaining why animals retain such continuing material importance for Inuit, but also to provide a more accurate appreciation of why Inuit statements about 'traditional subsistence' have little to do with the technology they use and much to do with the internal relations of their culture.

Likewise, considerable effort was devoted to examining the animal rights movement with regard to the Native wildlife issue. However, a careful reading will show that this was done neither to refute its basic moral–ethical datum or even its arguments about the conduct of the European fur trade in the North. Rather, the point of this critical examination was to place the movement within the spectrum of wider *Qallunaat*-Inuit relations, something that has so far rarely been done.

Inuit and other Canadian Native Peoples have argued that the animal rights movement, by refusing to acknowledge the particular cultural, ecological, economic and historical circumstances of aboriginal life and interaction with wildlife, has acted with little difference from earlier generations of southern imperialists. In essence, that it has acted with same ethnocentric *raison d'être* that has characterized all but perhaps the earliest moments of Inuit contact with Western culture.

To a large extent, that is the conclusion reached here, especially about the movement's behavior and attitude toward Inuit since the early 1980s. Like earlier missionaries, religious and secular, who have 'visited' themselves upon Inuit, the movement's advocates have followed a course of action based on the enlightened perspective from which *Qallunaat* culture has proceeded in its relations with Inuit.

Many feel, however, that the animal rightists, having been rebuffed, have accepted Inuit criticism with less grace than many of the southerners who preceded them. As the gap between Inuit and the movement has widened, it has become not uncommon to find Inuit seal hunting easily compared in some circles with East African ivory poaching. Moreover, this feat is accomplished with little, if any, reflection about the cultural and historical circumstances that might offer insight into the activities of Inuit or the African peoples whom we categorize as poachers (see Matowanyika 1989). The breadth of such generalization, in fact, makes it important to ask how it is achieved.

The link that permits such comparison is the way the movement defines wildlife and, especially, the lives of individual animals as an inherent 'Good'. While this perspective is, perhaps, a valid one within a strictly Western cultural context, its application to non-Western societies, without regard to either the specifics of culture or history, raises serious question about the way the movement substitutes action for responsibility as it pursues its objective. This is especially the case in the Inuit sealing controversy because the matter is not clouded by endangered species concerns or First versus Third World hostility as it is in many other areas of the world. (Indeed, the latter dynamic is so far absent in the North that some animal rightists have sanguinely declared that Inuit are, in reality, part of Euro-Canadian culture.)

The animal rights movement has long argued (see Peters 1971) that it is free of cultural constraint precisely because there can be no 'Good' equal in moral weight to the one it has accepted. If this is true, then Watson (1985) is correct in pursuing the universal establishment of animal rights as a general social philosophy. The fact, however, that the movement has taken upon itself the special task of 'demythologizing' Native culture(s) suggests that it feels the sting of the cultural imperialism accusation which Inuit have levelled at it and that the public upon whom it depends is aware of this.

Another important question which arises directly from the Inuit sealing situation concerns the appropriateness of the animal rights movement's attempts to reinterpret Inuit, Cree, or other Native cultures' traditions for its followers and the general public. This process, which includes not only demythologizing but also the appropriating of aspects of these traditions, has played an important role in the animal rights campaign regarding Native People.

Miller's (n.d.) purported critique of traditional and post-contact Native society provides a concise example of both of these actions. In her 'analysis', she provides the reader with a highly selective portrait of traditional aboriginal North American society and culture. In it, she suggests that infanticide, senilicide, gender discrimination and poor hygiene were not only endemic to all of the traditional cultures of North America, but that they were universally normative. She prefaces her critique, however, by quoting a 'Hopi Indian prophecy' about the coming of the 'Warriors of the Rainbow' as 'Protectors of the Earth' to provide proof of the rightness of animal rights objective, thereafter referring to movement activists as these Warriors (ibid.: 2, 4). (Parenthetically, the Warrior of the Rainbow metaphor was earlier used by Greenpeace (see Hunter 1979; Greenpeace UK 1984, who attribute it as originating in the oral tradition of Cree culture.)

While the appropriation of Native clothing and artifacts has long been the pleasure of hobbyists, the kinds of systematic appropriation of aboriginal cultural image and oral tradition, while rejecting any acknowledgement of Native cultural reality, has become a mark of the conflict dynamic between the movement and Native People. The only secure defense against the perpetuation of this kind of ethnocentrism in the northern sealing conflict is to allow Inuit the right to their own culture history and traditions.

This, in turn, must necessarily be accompanied by *Qallunaat* allowing Inuit the means to express their chief contribution to this history, the practice of their culture. The animal rights movement has, to date, been at best grudging in this regard. Instead, it has chosen to apply labels, like neo-traditional and speciesist, not analysis, to those practices which it finds not to its liking. At least until the time comes when animal rights advocates establish a valid, non-ethnocentric basis for their application of these labels to Native society, it must be recognized that the interest Inuit hold in this debate is deeply rooted in their traditional culture.

As the situation exists today, animal rightists seek to impose upon Inuit an atomistic form of anthropomorphism (see Scherer 1982), in which animals are individually idealized as each having inherent moral worth. This view is in contradistinction to that of Inuit for whom animals, through their meat and pelts, offer the means by which individual humans contribute to the collective security of the social group. The movement, however, summarily rejects the proposition that Inuit perception and behavior toward animals can be rooted in anything more complex than a desire to obtain the imported goods that sealskins can provide (Best 1984, 1985: 12).

In adopting this stance toward what is, in fact, a well-considered ecosystemic cultural adaptation, the movement rejects not only the practices by which Inuit sustain themselves, but also the right of Inuit to any course of action which it does not validate. Recently, this view appears to provide a license through which all aspects of contemporary Inuit culture, from seal harvesting to the settlement of aboriginal title to traditional land and resources, can be placed in a negative perspective.

The Inuit seal controversy is far from over despite the renewal of the European sealskin ban. This is because, first, Inuit, despite protest denials to the contrary, must adapt to a unique phase in their experience with southern society. It is the 'animal rights phase', just as there were the fur trade and government phases. It is marked, however, by the first deliberate attempt by *Qallunaat* to systematically alienate Inuit from the resources they have customarily depended on for their cultural independence. The solutions to the problems that this has created are much further away than the simple return to the winter *aglu* with harpoon in hand that the animal rights movement suggests.

As has been mentioned already, such a hope on the part of animal rightists is unrealistic, but not because Inuit have for too long succumbed to the lure of modernity. Rather, the problems that modern life in the North presents to Inuit require more than a return to the material condition of an idealized past can accomplish. They require an appreciation on the part of Inuit and Euro-Canadians of just how complexly the interactions of both cultures have changed the human environment of the North.

Continuation of the northern seal controversy as it is presently being conducted does not bode well for either of the parties involved. Inuit remain faced by the prospect of reassembling the stability that seal, caribou, and other species offered the traditional subsistence system. In this regard, the solutions that are currently being imported, adventure tourism, commercial food harvesting and further bureaucratization, are far from the mark. All are the product of non-Inuit imagination. Past experience with externally developed strategies for Inuit cultural 'development' (see, for instance, Duffy 1988) suggests that even the best ideas, proposed without indigenous input, invariably produce little else but greater change.

As for the movement, every escalation in the rhetoric it directs toward aboriginal peoples multiplies the risks it runs for itself and its message. For instance, the Inuit seal controversy, and, now, Native trapping, have brought the most uncompromising exponents of the animal rights philosophy to the fore of the public's attention. To date, the differences that exist in the public persona of groups like the International Wildlife Coalition or Ark II and their internal attitudes toward Inuit and Indians have received little attention. The risk, however, is that the rigid dogmatism this wing represents regarding Native society and culture may, as it receives greater exposure, weaken the important larger social influence the movement has obtained over non-Native issues.

Acrimonious debate with Inuit and Indians, who are themselves equally worthy objects of empathy, has already become an important matter of concern, affecting both the internal and external relations of the movement. So much so that, in the first case, some original seal protest actors, like Greenpeace, have chosen to disassociate themselves from further conflict with Inuit.

With regard to the movement's external relations, the arguments that animal rightists have flung back at Native critics, regarding economic complicity and cultural assimilation, have not served it well. Although the Native community (including sympathetic social scientists) was initially stunned by statements that linked the problems of modern aboriginal society exclusively to the fur trade and its own weakness (see Best 1986; also, for reactions, Green and Smith 1986), the past several years have shown Native Peoples to be both a resilient and powerful opponent.

These declarations have precipitated two unfortunate results. The first is that they have caused Inuit increasingly to reject parts of the movement's message with which they were once in sympathy. Inuit initiatives for compromise have been, and remain, based on the appeal that some aspects of this message holds for them.

Second, the movement's own dogmatic stance provided the basis for Inuit joining the fur industry and government in the countercoalition activists now face. In this regard, and as much as the movement may point an accusing finger (see Best 1984; Watson 1985; Miller 1989) at such an 'alliance', it was its uncompromising and culturally biased interpretation of what constitutes traditional aboriginal subsistence, its ethos of shared social solidarity, that led to the gulf that now exists between Inuit and animal rightists.

It is impossible to predict what the final effects of the northern seal debate will be on Inuit or the animal rights movement. For Inuit culture, the past five years have meant exposure to one of the most intensive periods of externally directed change that it has experienced at the hands of *Qallunaat*. At the moment, there is little prospect for the weight of this pressure for culture change, whether unintended or deliberate, to abate. As for the animal rights movement, as long as it ignores the traditional socio-cultural relevance of the modern Inuit subsistence adaptation, it will remain a victim of the parallax view of Native culture that it has created for itself, at times a noble remanent of some hunter-gatherer ideal (Duffy 1984) and others a social artifact perceived to be without contemporary merit (Miller 1989).

In closing, it is useful to note the words of Schirer (quoted in Headland and Reid 1989: 2) regarding the image of Native Peoples that is often held by scientists and the public: 'Modern foragers tend still to be viewed in most of the current anthropological literature as sequestered beings . . . They are depicted as quintessential isolates.'

Inuit remain very much a traditional people living in the modern world. A part of this modern reality is the technology that has accompanied *Qallunaat* into the North. The animal rights movement has misconstrued, as others have, the presence of these new tools as reflecting the substance of contemporary Inuit life. In fact, it is *ningiqtuq* which is this substance.

In discussing Inuit tradition, hunting, and subsistence, consideration of artifacts often clouds cultural understanding. It is Euro-Canadian contact history which makes the snowmobile a useful tool in modern Inuit harvesting. It is the continuing social relevance of traditional *ningiqtuq* practice that makes seal harvesting a valid component of contemporary Inuit subsistence culture.

APPENDIX

Notes On Inuktitut

Inuktitut is the language or dialect formally denoted by Woodbury (1984: 49) and other linguists as Inuit-Inupiaq. Over most of the Northwest Territories and Nouveau-Quebec, Inuktitut is written using syllabic symbols, although the Roman alphabet is used in some portions – Greenland, Labrador, the Mackenzie Delta – North Alaska – of the Inuktitut language area.

The Inuktitut terms that are used in the text are from the North Baffin-Iqlulingmiut sub-dialect spoken by the Clyde Inuit. These are transcribed and presented in their romanized forms for the convenience of the reader. These terms, arranged in alphabetical order, are presented below.

Inuktitut terms	English meaning
aglu	seal breathing hole (pl. *agluliit*)
akpaallugiit	a form of extra-family sharing
angajuqqaaq	an elder
angiukaaq	leader; also 'boss', foreman
ataata	father
igunaaq	fermented meat
iikaiyuitatuq	cooperation
ilagiit	extended family
ilgasuuq	generosity
illu	a dwelling, snowhouse (igloo)
ilniq	son
ilniriit	father-son relationship
inuk	an Eskimo (sing.)
inuit	Eskimo (pl.)
inummarik	a person possessing Inuit values
inummariit	the plural form of *inummarik*
isuma	idea, thought
isumataq	elder (lit. one who thinks)
isumataaq	plural form of *isumataq*
ivvik	walrus (*Odobenus rosmarus*)
kamik	sealskin boot (pl. *kamiit*)
kaiyukquiyuk	a form of extra-family sharing
mauluktuk	winter seal hunting method
minatuq	commensal sharing practice
miut	being of a place (suffix)

muktaaq	whale skin
mungii	a term describing a certain food
nalatuq	obedience
nanuk	polar bear (*Ursus arcticus*)
natsiaq	ringed seal pup
natsiariit	ringed seal birth lair
natsiq	adult ringed seal (*Phoca hispida*)
natsiavinnik	yearling ringed seal
nattiaminikiq	a pregnant ringed seal
ningiqtuq (*ningiq*)	to share (v.)
niqi	meat; food
niqiliriiq	those who share; 'neighbors'
niqisutaiyuq	a form of commensal sharing
niqitatitanaq	a modern form of non-kin sharing
niqituinnaq	country food; 'real' food
nirriyaktuktuq	commensal meal
nitsik	gaff, hook
nuna	land, place
nunariit	co-residents, companions
payuktalik	a form of commercial sharing
piksuktuk	wind-blown snow; a white-out
qajaq	kayak, small skin boat
Qallunaat	a non-Eskimo person (European)
qamutiik	a sled
qillilungaaq	narwhal (*Monodon monocerus*)
qlissik	a sealskin
qlinuituq	patience
quaktuq	something frozen
quaktuaktuq	a form of commensal sharing
sikkidoo	snowmobile, Ski-doo
siku	sea ice
sikkuak	newly formed sea ice
silatujuk	intelligence
tigutuinaaq	a form of extended family sharing
tiluaaq	a white cloth used as camouflage
tugaluk	a local Clyde term for narwhal
tukkak	harpoon head
tuktu	caribou (*Rangifer tarandus*)
tuqagaujuq	a form of extended family sharing
ujjuk	bearded seal (*Erignatus barbatus*)
umiak	large open skin boat
umiaqqatiqiit	the crew of a boat; crewmen
uuttuq	a seal atop the spring ice
uuyuk	boiled meat

BIBLIOGRAPHY

Allen, Jeremiah (1979) 'Anti Sealing as an Industry' *Journal of Political Science* 87(2): 423-28.

Ames, R., D. Axford, P. Usher, E. Weick, and G. Wenzel (1988) *Keeping on the Land: A Study of the Feasibility of a Comprehensive Wildlife Support Programme in the Northwest Territories*, Ottawa: Canadian Arctic Resources Committee.

Anonomous (1977) 'Anti-Sealing Lobby Severely Hurting Inuit' *The Native Perspective* 2(7): 8.

Asch, Michael (1984) *Home and Native Land: Aboriginal Rights and the Canadian Constitution*, Toronto: Methuen.

Atuagagdliutit/Gronlandposten (1981a) 'Holland Aiming At Canada and Norway But Hitting Greenland'. 22 January, (reprinted in *Greenland Press Review 1981*).

—— (1981b) 'Many Inquiries About Greenlandic Seals.' 23 February, (reprinted in *Greenland Press Review 1981*).

—— (1981c) 'Boat Carrying Activists On Its Way To Canada To Stop Seal Hunt'. 19 March, (reprinted in *Greenland Press Review 1981*).

—— (1983) 'Many Inquiries About Greenlandic Seals'. 23 February, (reprinted in *Greenland Press Review 1983*).

Atuisoq (1985) 'Piniarneq Inuuniutigaarput Kultureralugulu'. p. 4.

Baffin Regional Inuit Association (1982) 'Summary of Harvests Reported by Hunters in the Baffin Region, Northwest Territories, During 1981' unpublished report, Iqaluit, N.W.T.

—— (1983) 'Summary of Harvests reported by Hunters in the Baffin Region, Northwest Territories, During 1982. unpublished report, Iqaluit, N.W.T.

—— (1984) 'Summary of Harvests Reported by Hunters in the Baffin Region, NWT, During 1983'. unpublished report, Iqaluit, N.W.T.

—— (1985) 'Summary of Harvests Reported by Hunters in the Baffin Region, Northwest Territories', in 1984. unpublished report, Iqaluit, N.W.T.

Balikci, Asen (1964) 'Development of Basic Socioeconomic Units In Two Eskimo Communities', *Bulletin 202*. Ottawa: National Museum of Canada.

—— (1967) 'Female Infanticide on the Arctic Coast', *Man* 2(4): 615-25.

—— (1968) 'The Netsilik Eskimos: Adaptive Processes', In *Man the Hunter*, ed. by R. Lee and I. DeVore. Chicago: Aldine. pp. 78-82.

—— (1970) *The Netsilik Eskimo*, New York: American Museum of Natural History Press.

Bardot, Brigitte (1978) *Noonoah: Le Petit Phoque Blanc*, Paris: Grasset and Fasquelle.

Barnard, Alan (1989) 'The Lost World of Laurens van der Post', *Current Anthropology* 30(1): 104-113.

Bartlett, Kim (ed.) (1988) 'A New Ethic or an End to a Way of Life?' *The Animals' Agenda* VIII(9) 18pp.

Barzdo, Jon (1980) *International Trade in Harp and Hooded Seals*, London: Fauna and Flora Preservation Society and the International Fund for Animal Welfare.

Beardsley, T. and J. Becker (1982) 'Who's Cooking What Books?' *Nature* 300: 674.

Bentham, Jeremy (1789) *The Principles of Morals and Legislation*, New York: Haffner.

Berger, Thomas R. (1977) *Northern Frontier, Northern Homeland: The Report of the Mackenzie Valley Pipeline Inquiry*, 2 Vols. Ottawa: Supply and Services Canada.

—— (1985) *Village Journey: The Report of the Alaska Native Review Commission*, New York: Hill and Wang.

Berkes, F., D. Feeny, B.J. McCay and J.M. Acheson (1989) 'The Benefits of the Commons', *Nature* 340: 91-93.

Best, Steven (1984) Taped Interview (24 September), Toronto, Canada.

—— (1985) 'God, Culture, and Women' a paper presented to the McGill Symposium on the Sealing Controversy, 15pp.

—— (1986) 'The Animal Rights Viewpoint' in *Native Peoples and Renewable Resource Management*, Ed. by J. Green and J. Smith, Edmonton: Alberta Society of Professional Biologists, pp. 197-213.

—— (1988) Presentation to the Concordia Animal Rights Association (CARA), 4 February, Concordia University, Montreal.

—— (1989a) Roundtable discussion on 'Aboriginal Societies and the Animal Protection Movement: Rights, Issues, and Implications', in *A Question of Rights: Northern Wildlife Management and the Anti-Harvest Movement*, ed. by R. Keith and A. Saunders, Ottawa: Canadian Arctic Resources Committee, pp. 138-44.

—— (1989b) Floor discussion, in *A Question of Rights: Northern Wildlife Management and the Anti-Harvest Movement*, ed. by R. Keith and A. Saunders Ottawa: Canadian Arctic Resources Committee, pp. 145-61.

Bicchieri, Marco G. (ed.) (1972) *Hunters and Gatherers Today: A Socio-Economic Study of Eleven Such Cultures in the Twentieth Century*. New York: Holt, Rinehart and Winston.

Birket-Smith, Kai (1959) *The Eskimos*, London: Methuen.

Boas, Franz (1888) 'The Central Eskimo', *Sixth Annual Report of the Bureau of American Ethnology for the Years 1884-1885*, Washington, DC: The Smithsonian Institution, pp. 399-669.

Boe, Vivia (1984) Taped interview (10 December), Vancouver, Canada.

Boles, B., L. Jackson, and M.G.A. Mackey (1983) *Breaking the Ice: Seal and Seal Harvesting Patterns and Benefits in Relation to Navigational Ice Breaking in Lake Melville, Labrador*, Goose Bay, Labrador: Labrador Institute of Northern Studies.

Bonner, Nigel (1982) *Seals and Man: A Study of Interactions*, Seattle: University of Washington Press.

Born, Erik (1983) *Havpattedyr og Havfugle i Scoresby Sund: Fangst og Forekomst*, Hellerup, Denmark: Danibu ApS.

Borre, Kristen (1986) *Dietary and Nutritional Significance of Seal and Other Country Foods in the Diet of the Inuit of Clyde River, NWT*, Technical Report No. 11, Royal Commission on Seals and the Sealing Industry in Canada, Montreal.

—— (1987) *'Without Seal I Will Die': The Animal/Human Relation, Ethnicity and Diet Among North Baffin Island Inuit*, unpublished paper presented at the 85th Annual Meeting of the American Anthropological Association, Philadelphia.

—— (1989) 'A Bio-Cultural Model of Dietary Decision Making Among North

Baffin Island Inuit: Explaining the Ecology of Food Consumption By Native Canadians', unpublished PhD. dissertation, Department of Anthropology, University of North Carolina.

Borre, K. and G.W. Wenzel (1988) 'Seals and Snowmobiles: Inuit Solutions to Subsistence Problems in a Cash Economy, paper presented to the 1988 Meeting of the Society for Economic Anthropology, Knoxville.

Brice-Bennett, Carol (1978) *Our Footprints Are Everywhere: Inuit Land Use And Occupancy in Labrador*, Nain: Labrador Inuit Association.

Bruemmer, Fred (1977) *Life of the Harp Seal*, Montreal: Optimum.

Brody, Hugh (1975) *The Peoples' Land: Eskimos and Whites in the Eastern Arctic*, London: Penguin Books Ltd.

—— (1987) *Living Arctic: Hunters of the Canadian North*, Vancouver: Douglas and McIntyre Ltd.

Burch, Ernest S., Jr. (1972) 'The Caribou/Wild Reindeer as a Human Resource', *American Antiquity* 27(2): 339-68.

—— (1975) *Eskimo Kinsmen: Changing Family Relationships in Northwest Alaska*, Monograph No. 59, American Ethnological Society, Minneapolis: West Publishing.

—— (1977) 'Muskox and Man in the Central Canadian Subarctic, 1689-1974' *Arctic* 30(3): 135-54.

Burton, J.A. (1978) 'Why the Seal Cull?', *New Scientist*, 28 September, p. 16.

Busch, Briton Cooper (1985) *The War Against the Seals: A History of the North American Seal Fishery*, Montreal: McGill-Queen's Press.

CBC (1985) *All Things Bright and Beautiful*, video aired 10 February 1985, Toronto: Canadian Broadcasting Corporation.

Chafe, L.G. (1923) *Chafe's Sealing Book*, St. John's: The Trade Printers and Publishers.

Chance, Norman A. (1984) 'Alaska Eskimo Modernization' in *Handbook of North American Indians, Volume 5: Arctic*, ed. by D. Damas, Washington, DC: The Smithsonian Institution, pp. 646-56.

Clancy, Peter (1987) 'The Making of Eskimo Policy in Canada, 1952-62: Life and Times of the Eskimo Affairs Committee', *Arctic* 40(3): 191-7.

Coates, Kenneth (1985) *Canada's Colonies: A History of the Yukon and Northwest Territories*, Toronto: James Lorimer and Company.

Coish, Calvin (1979) *Season of the Seal: The International Storm Over Canada's Seal Hunt*, St. John's: Breakwater Books.

Colman, J.S. (1937) 'The Present State of the Newfoundland Seal Fishery', *Journal of Animal Ecology* 6: 145-59.

Cornell, George L. (1985) 'The Influence of Native Americans on Modern Conservationists', *Environmental Review* 9(2): 104-117.

Dahl, Jens (1989) 'The Integrative and Cultural Role of Hunting and Subsistence in Greenland', *Etudes/Inuit/Studies* 13(1): 23-42.

Dalton, George (1968) 'Introduction', in *Primitive, Archaic and Modern Economies: Essays of Karl Polanyi*, ed. by G. Dalton, Boston: Beacon Press, pp. ix-liv.

Damas, David (1963) *Igluligmiut Kinship and Local Groupings: A Structural Approach*, Bulletin No. 196, Ottawa: National Museum of Canada.

—— (1969a) 'Environment, History, and Central Eskimo Society', in *Contributions to Anthropology: Ecological Essays*, ed. by D. Damas, Bulletin 230, Ottawa: National Museum of Man, pp. 40-64.

—— (1969b) 'Characteristics of Central Eskimo Ban Structure', in *Contributions to Anthropology: Band Societies*, ed. by D. Damas Bulletin 228,

Ottawa: National Museum of Man, pp. 116–34.

—— (1972a) 'The Structure of Central Eskimo Associations', in *Alliance in Eskimo Society* ed. by L. Guemple, Seattle: American Ethnology Society, pp. 40–55.

—— (1972b) 'Central Eskimo Systems of Food Sharing', *Ethnology* 11(3): 220–40.

—— (1975) 'Three Kinship Systems from the Central Arctic', *Arctic Anthropology* 12(1): 10–30.

—— (1984a) *Handbook of North American Indians, Volume 6: Arctic*, ed. by D. Damas, Washington, DC: The Smithsonian Institution.

—— (1984b) 'Introduction', in *Handbook of North American Indians, Volume 5: Arctic*, ed. by D. Damas. Washington, DC: The Smithsonian Institution, pp. 1-7.

—— (1988) 'The Contact-Traditional Horizon of the Central Arctic: Reassessment of a Concept and Reexamination of an Era', *Arctic Anthropology* 25(2): 101–38.

Davies, Brian (1970a) *Savage Luxury: The Slaughter of the Baby Seal*, London: Souvenir Press.

—— (1970b) 'A Lonely Place', *Defenders of Wildlife News*, October–December, pp. 357–62.

Davis, Rolph A., Kerwin J. Finley, and W. John Richardson *The Present Status and Future Management of Arctic Marine Mammals in Canada*, Yellowknife, N.W.T.: Science Advisory Board of the Northwest Territories.

Degerbol, Magnus and Peter Freuchen (1935) Zoology I: Mammals, *Report of the Fifth Thule Expedition, 1921-24*, V.II, No. 4-5, Copenhagen: Gyldendalske Boghandel.

de Groot, Govert (1986) Correspondence, 5pp.

Deloria, Vine, Jr. (1970) *We Talk, You Listen: New Tribes, New Turf*, New York: Macmillan.

Descartes, R. (1960) *Discourse on Method and Meditations* New York: Bobbs-Merrill.

Devall, William (1980) 'The Deep Ecology Movement', *Natural Resources Journal* 20(1): 299–322.

Devall, William and George Sessions (1985) *Deep Ecology: Living as if Nature Mattered*, Salt Lake City: Gibbs M. Smith, Inc.

Dingwall, Anne (1986) 'The Sealskin Trade', Greenpeace, (mimeo).

Donaldson, Judith L. (1988) *The Economic Ecology of Hunting, A Case Study of the Canadian Inuit*, unpublished Ph.D. dissertation, Department of Organismic and Evolutionary Biology, Harvard University.

Doncaster, Anne (1989a) Presentation in the session on 'Environmental Ethics and Wildlife Harvesting', in *A Question of Rights: Northern Wildlife Management and the Anti-Harvesting Movement*, ed. by R. Keith and A. Saunders, Ottawa: Canadian Arctic Resources Committee, pp. 17–22.

—— (1989b) Floor discussion, in *A Question of Rights: Northern Wildlife Management and the Anti-Harvest Movement*, ed. by R. Keith and A. Saunders, Ottawa: Canadian Arctic Resources Committee, pp. 39-51.

Dorais, Louis-Jacques (1988) 'Inuit Identity in Canada', *Folk* 30: 23-31.

Draper, H.H. (1977) 'The Aboriginal Eskimo Diet in Modern Perspective', *American Anthropologist* 79(2): 309-16.

Duffy, Maureen (1984) *Men and Beasts: An Animal Rights Handbook*, London: Paladin Publishing.

Duffy, R. Quinn (1988) *The Road to Nunavut: The Progress of the Eastern*

Arctic Inuit Since the Second World War, Montreal: McGill-Queen's Press.

Dunbar, Maxwell (1968) *Ecological Development in Polar Regions: A Study in Evolution*, Englewood Cliffs: Prentice-Hall.

Dyson, John (1979) *The Hot Arctic*, Boston: Little, Brown.

Ellen, Roy (1982) *Environment, Subsistence and System: The Ecology of Small-scale Social Formations*, Cambridge: Cambridge University Press.

England, George A. (1969) *The Greatest Hunt in the World*, Montreal: Tundra Books.

Emerk, Peter (1989) Presentation in the session 'Environmental Ethics and Wildlife Harvesting', in *A Question of Rights: Northern Wildlife Management and the Anti-Harvest Movement*, ed. by R. Keith and A. Saunders, Ottawa: Canadian Arctic Resources Committee, pp. 22-5.

European Community (1983) *Council Directive of 28 March 1983 Concerning the Importation into Member States of Skins of Certain Seal Pups and Products Derived Therefrom*, (83/129/EEC).

―――― (1985) *Council Directive of 27 September 1985 Amending Council Directive 83/129/EED*, (85/444/EEC).

Evernden, Neil (1985) *The Natural Alien: Humankind and Environment*, Toronto: University of Toronto Press.

Feit, Harvey (1973) 'The Ethno-Ecology of the Waswanipi Cree: Or, How Hunters Can Manage Their Resources', in *Cultural Ecology: Readings on Canadian Indians and Eskimos* ed. by B. Cox, Toronto: McClelland and Stewart, pp. 115-25.

Fenge, Terry (1988) 'The Animal Rights Movement: A Case of Evangelical Imperialism', *Alternatives* 15(3): 69-71.

Fienup-Riordan, Ann (1983) *The Nelson Island Eskimo: Social Structure and Ritual Distribution*, Anchorage: Alaska Pacific University Press.

Finley, Kerwin J. and Gary W. Miller (1980) *Wildlife Harvest Statistics From Clyde river, Grise Fiord and Pond Inlet, 1979*, Toronto: LGL Limited.

Foote, Don (1967a) 'Remarks on Eskimo Sealing and the Harp Seal Controversy', *Arctic* 20(4): 267-8.

―――― (1967b) *The East Coast of Baffin Island, N.W.T.: An Area Economic Survey, 1966*, Ottawa: Department of Indian Affairs and Northern Development.

Forde, C. Daryl (1934) *Habitat, Economy and Society: A Geographic Introduction to Ethnology*, New York: Methuen.

Fortes, Meyer (1970) *Time and Social Structure and Other Essays*, New York: Humanities Press.

Freeman, Milton M.R. (1971) 'Social and Ecologic Analysis of Systematic Female Infanticide Among the Netsilik Eskimo', *American Anthropologist* 73(5): 1011-18.

―――― (1976) *Report of the Inuit Land Use and Occupancy Project*, 3 Vols, Ottawa: Department of Indian and Northern Affairs.

―――― (1984) 'Arctic Ecosystems', in *Handbook of North American Indians, Vol. 5: Arctic*, ed. by D. Damas. Washington, DC: The Smithsonian Institution. pp. 36-48.

Geist, Valerius (1988) 'How Markets in Wildlife Meats and Parts, and the Sale of Hunting Privileges, Jeopardize Wildlife Conservation', *Conservation Biology* 2(1): 15-26.

Gilberg, Rolf (1974-5) 'Changes in the Lie of the Polar Eskimos Resulting from a Canadian Immigration in the Thule District, North Greenland in the 1860's', *Folk* 16-17: 159-70.

—— (1984) 'Polar Eskimo', in *Handbook of North American Indians Vol. 5: Arctic*, ed. by D. Damas. Washington, DC: The Smithsonian Institution, pp. 577–94.

Gilbert, Joan (1985) 'John Woolman and Animals', *Friends Journal*, December pp. 11–12.

Girard, Andre (1985) Inuit Tapirisat of Canada's Statement on Sealing, *Tagralik*, February, p. 31.

Goddard, John (1986) 'Out for Blood', *Harrowsmith* X(6): 29–37.

Godlovitch, Rosalind (1971) 'Animals and Morals', In *Animals, Men and Morals: An Enquiry into the Maltreatment of Non-Humans*, ed. by S. and R. Godlovitch and J. Harris, London: Victor Gollancz Ltd. pp, 156–72.

Godlovitch, Stanley and Rosalind, and John Harris (eds) (1971) *Animals, Men and Morals: An Enquiry into the Maltreatment of Non-Humans*, London: Victor Gollancz Ltd.

Goldring, Philip (1986) 'Inuit Economic Responses to Euro-American Contacts: Southeast Baffin Island, 1824–1940', *Historical Papers/Communications Historiques*, pp. 146–72.

Gordon, Mark R. (1989) 'Roundtable on Aboriginal Societies and the Animal Protection Movement: Rights, Issues, and Implications', in *A Question of Rights: Northern Wildlife Management and the Anti-Harvest Movement*, ed. by R. Keith and A. Saunders, Ottawa: Canadian Arctic Resources Committee, pp. 116–7.

Government of the Northwest Territories (1978) 'Sealing Conference, August 1–3', unpublished transcript.

Graburn, Nelson H.H. (1969) *Eskimos Without Igloos: Social and Economic Development in Sugluk*, Boston: Little, Brown and Co.

—— (1972) *Eskimos of Northern Canada*, 2 Vols, New Haven: Human Relations Area Files.

Grandy, John (1989) 'Floor Discussion', in *A Question of Rights: Northern Wildlife Management and the Anti-Harvest Movement*, ed. by R. Keith and A. Saunders, Ottawa: Canadian Arctic Resources Committee, pp. 39–51.

Green, Jeffrey and Judith Smith (eds) (1986) *Native People and Renewable Resource Management*, Edmonton: Alberta Society of Professional Biologists.

Greenpeace (UK) (1984) *Greenpeace*, 8pp.

Gubser, Nicholas (1965) *The Nunamiut Eskimos: Hunters of Caribou*, New Haven: Yale University Press.

Guthrie, Daniel A. (1971) 'Primitive Man's Relationship to Nature', *Bioscience* 21(13): 721–3.

Hall, Sam (1988) *The Fourth World: The Heritage of the Arctic and Its Destruction*, New York: Knopf.

Haller, A., P. Cove, and G. Anders (ed.) (1967) *Baffin Island – East Coast: An Area Economic Survey*, Ottawa: Department of Indian Affairs and Northern Development.

Hammond, Marc M. (1984) 'Report of Findings On An Alleged Promise of Government To Finance the Return of Inuit At Resolute and Grise Fiord To Their Original Homes At Port Harrison (Inukjuak) and Pond Inlet', unpublished report (84–099) to Indian and Northern Affairs Canada.

Hantzsch, Bernard (1977) *My Life Among the Eskimos: Baffinland Journeys in the Years 1909 to 1911*, L.H. Neatby, ed. and trans., Saskatoon: University of Saskatchewan.

Harper, Kenn (1984) '*Narwhal Tusk Market*', (mimeo) 2pp.

Harris, John (1971) 'Killing for Food', in *Animals, Men and Morals: An Enquiry into the Maltreatment of Non-Humans*, ed. by S. and R. Godlovitch and J. Harris, London: Victor Gollancz Ltd., pp. 97–110.

Headland, Thomas N. and Lawrence A. Reid (1989) 'Hunter-Gatherers and their neighbours from prehistory to the present', *Current Anthropology*, 30(1): 43–66.

Heinrich, Albert (1963) 'Eskimo-Type Kinship and Eskimo Kinship: An Evaluation and a Provisional Model for Presenting Data Pertaining to Inupiag Kinship Systems', unpublished Ph.D. dissertation in anthropology, University of Washington, Seattle.

Heinrich, Ole (1983) 'The Greenland Sealskin Campaign in Europe', *Inuit: ICC-Arctic Policy Review*, 1/83: 18–19.

Herscovici, Alan (1985) *The Animal Rights Controversy*, Toronto: CBC Enterprises.

Hickey, Clifford (1984) 'An Examination of Processes of Culture Change Among 19th Century Copper Inuit', *Etudes/Inuit/Studies* 8(1): 13–36.

Holt, S. and D. Lavigne (1982) 'Seals Slaughtered-Science Abused', *New Scientist* 93: 636–9.

Honigmann, John and Irma Honigmann (1965) *Eskimo Townsmen*, Ottawa: Canadian Research Center for Anthropology.

House of Commons (1986) *Minutes of Proceedings and Evidence of the Standing Committee on Aboriginal Affairs and Northern Development*, Issue No. 24 (27 May), Ottawa.

Hudson's Bay Company (n.d.a.) *Clyde River Post Diary* (unpublished), B403/a/3, Winnipeg: Manitoba Provincial Archives.

—— (n.d.b.) *Clyde River Post Diary* (unpublished), B403/a/4, Winnipeg: Manitoba Provincial Archives.

—— (n.d.c.) *Clyde River Post Diary* (unpublished), B403/a/5, Winnipeg: Manitoba Provincial Archives.

Hughes, Charles Campbell (1963) 'Review of James Van Stone: Point Hope: An Eskimo Village in Transition', *American Anthropologist* 65(2): 452–4.

Hunter, Robert (1979) *Warriors of the Rainbow*, New York: Holt, Rinehart and Winston.

Hutchinson, E. (1977) 'Order and Chaos in the Cosmology of the Baffinland Eskimo', *Anthropology* 1(2): 120–38.

International Council for the Exploration of the Seas (1983) 'Report on the Meeting of an Ad Hoc Working Group on Assessment of Harp and Hooded Seals in the Northwest Atlantic', *ICES Cooperative Research Report 121*.

Inuit Tapirisat of Canada (1977) *News Release* (File No. 20-040).

—— (1978) 'Fisheries Minister Orders Board to Study Low Seal Skin Prices', *ITC News* (January/February) p.4.

Jelliss, Arvin D. (1978) *Report on the impact of Depressed Sealskin Prices in the Northwest Territories*, unpublished report, Economic Analysis Division, Department of Indian Affairs and Northern Development, 14pp.

Jenness, Diamond (1922) 'The Life of the Copper Eskimos', *Report of the Canadian Arctic Expedition 1913-18*, Vol. XII, Ottawa: F.A. Acland.

Jochim, Michael (1981) *Strategies for Survival: Cultural Behavior in an Ecological Context*, New York: Academic Press.

Kapel, F.O. and R. Petersen (1982) *Subsistence Hunting: The Greenland Case*, report to the International Whaling Commission (Special Issue 4) London.

Keith, Robert and Alan Saunders (eds) (1989) *A Question of Rights: Northern*

Wildlife Management and the Anti-Harvest Movement, Ottawa: Canadian
Arctic Resources Committee.
Kellert, Stephen R. (1981) 'Trappers and Trapping in American Society',
Proceedings of the Worldwide Furbearer Conference, ed. by J. Chapman and
D. Pursley. Frostburg, Maryland: pp. 1971-2003.
Kemp, William B. (1971) 'The Flow of Energy in a Hunting Society', *Scientific
American* 225(3): 105-115.
—— (1976) 'Inuit Land Use in South and East Baffin Island', in *Inuit Land
Use and Occupancy Project*, ed. by M.M.R. Freeman, Vol. 1, Ottawa: Indian
and Northern Affairs.
—— (1984) 'Baffinland Eskimo', in *Handbook of North American Indians*,
V.5, The Arctic, ed. by D. Damas. Washington, DC: The Smithsonian Institu-
tion, pp. 463-75.
Kemp, W.B., G.W. Wenzel, E. Val, and N. Jensen (1977) *The Communities of
Resolute Bay and Kuvinaluk: A Socioeconomic Baseline Study*, Toronto:
Polargas.
Krech, Sheperd (ed.) (1984) *The Subarctic Fur Trade: Native Social and
Economic Adaptations*, Vancouver: University of British Columbia Press.
Kristeligt Dagblad (1981) 'A Different Kind of Seal Hunt: No Protest to the
Greenland Seal Hunt.' 12 March (reprinted in *Greenland Press Review
1981*).
Kroeber, Alfred (1939) *Cultural and Natural Areas of North America*, Univer-
sity of California Publications in American Archeology and Ethnology. Vol.
38, Berkeley: University of California Press.
Lamson, Cynthia (1979) '"Bloody Decks and a Bumper Crop": The Rhetoric of
Sealing Counter-Protest', *Social and Economic Studies* No. 24 St. John's:
Institute of Social and Economic Research.
Langdon, Steven (1981) 'Part I: Anthropological Economics', in *Distribution
and Exchange of Subsistence Resources in Alaska*, in S. Langdon and R.
Worl, Division of Subsistence Technical Paper No. 55, Anchorage: Alaska
Department of Fish and Game, pp. 1-54.
—— (1984) 'Alaska Native Subsistence: Current Regulatory Regimes and
Issues', brief presented to the Alaska Native Review Commission, 101pp.
Lantis, Margaret (1957) 'American Arctic Populations: Their Survival
Problems', in *Arctic Biology*, ed. by H.P. Hansen, 18th Annual Biology Collo-
quium, Corvallis: Oregon State College.
Lavigne, David (1976) 'Counting Harp Seals with Ultra-Violet Photography',
Polar Record 18(114): 269-77.
—— (1978) 'The Harp Seal Controversy Reconsidered', *Queen's Quarterly* 85:
377-88.
Leacock, Eleanor and Richard Lee (1982) *Politics and History in Band
Societies*, Cambridge: Cambridge University Press.
Lecky, William E.H. (1911) *History of European Morals from Augustus to
Charlemagne*, London: Longmans, Green and Company.
Lee, John Alan (1988) 'Seals, Wolves and Words: Loaded Language in
Environmental Controversy', *Alternatives* 15(4): 21-29.
Lee, Richard B. (1968) 'What Hunters Do for a Living, or How to Make Out
on Scarce Resources', in *Man the Hunter*, ed. by R.B. Lee and I. DeVore,
Chicago: Aldine. pp. 30-43.
—— (1979) *The !Kung San: Men, Women, and Work in a Foraging Society*,
Cambridge: Cambridge University Press.
Lee, Richard B. and Irven DeVore (1968) *Man the Hunter*, Chicago: Aldine.

Lentfer, Jack (1974) 'Agreement on the Conservation of Polar Bears', *Polar Record* 17(108): 327-30.

Lister-Kaye, John (1979) *Seal Cull: The Grey Seal Controversy*, London: Penguin Books.

Livingston, John (1989) Roundtable discussion on 'Aboriginal Societies and the Animal Protection Movement: Rights, Issues, and Implications', in *A Question of Rights: Northern Wildlife Management and the Anti-Harvest Movement*, ed. by R. Keith and A. Saunders, Ottawa: Canadian Arctic Resources Committee, pp. 118-22.

Lonner, Thomas D. (1980) *Subsistence as an Economic System in Alaska: Theoretical and Policy Implications*, Division of Subsistence Technical Paper No. 67, Anchorage: Alaska Department of Fish and Game.

—— (1983) 'Subsistence as an Economic System in Alaska: Theoretical Observations and Management Implications', in *Contemporary Subsistence Economies of Alaska*, ed. by S. Langdon, Fairbanks: Alaska Department of Fish and Game, pp. 41-74.

Lopez, Barry (1986) *Arctic Dreams: Imagination and Desire in a Northern Landscape*, New York, Scribners.

Low, A.P. (1906) *The Cruise of the Neptune, 1903-4*, Ottawa: Government Printing Bureau.

Lust, Peter (1967) *The Last Seal Pup: The Story of Canada's Seal Hunt*, Montreal: Harvest House.

Mackenzie Valley Pipeline Inquiry (1976) *Transcripts of Oral Testimony*, Vol. C44.

McCartney, Allen P. (ed.) (1979) *Thule Eskimo Culture: An Anthropological Retrospective*, Archaeological Survey of Canada Mercury Paper No. 88, Ottawa: National Museums of Canada.

McGhee, Robert (1978) *Canadian Arctic Prehistory*, New York: Van Nostrand, Reinhold.

McLaren, Ian A. (1958a) *The Biology of the Ringed Seal* (Phoca hispida Schreber) *in the Eastern Canadian Arctic*, Bulletin 118, Ottawa: Fisheries Research Board of Canada.

—— (1958b) *The Economics of Seals in the Eastern Canadian Arctic*, Arctic Unit Circular 1, Ottawa: Fisheries Research Board of Canada.

—— (1977) 'The Status of Seals in Canada', in *Canada's Threatened Species and Habitats: Proceedings of the Symposium on Canada's Threatened Species and Habitats*, ed. by T. Mosquin and C. Suchal, Ottawa: World Wildlife Fund, pp. 71-8.

Mackey, Mary G.A. (1984) *Country Food Use in Selected Labrador Coast Communities Comparative Report*, 5 Vols, St. John's: Extension Service and Faculty of Medicine, Memorial University of Newfoundland.

Mahoney, Patrick (1979) *Reasons for Judgement Between the Hamlet of Baker Lake and the Minister of Indian Affairs and Northern Development*, Federal Court of Canada, T-1628-78.

Malaurie, Jean (1973) 'Le Peuple Esquimau Aujourd'hui et Demain', *Quatrième Congrès International de la Fondation Française d'Etudes Nordiques*, Paris: Mouton.

Malouf, Albert (Chair) (1986a) *Seals and Sealing in Canada: Report of the Royal Commission*, 3 Vols, Ottawa: Supply and Services Canada.

—— (1986b) 'The Atlantic Sealing Economy' in *Seals and Sealing in Canada: Report of the Royal Commission*. Vol. 2, Ottawa: Supply and Services Canada, pp. 295-340.

—— (1986c) 'The Benefits and Costs of the Seal Hunt', in *Seals and Sealing in Canada: Report of the Royal Commission*, Vol. 2. Ottawa: Supply and Services Canada, pp. 341-416.

—— (1986d) 'The History of Sealing', in *Seals and Sealing in Canada: Report of the Royal Commission*, Vol. 2, Ottawa: Supply and Services Canada, pp. 15-39.

—— (1986e) 'Should Seals Be Killed?', in *Seals and Sealing in Canada: Report of the Royal Commission*, Vol. 2, Ottawa: Supply and Services Canada, pp. 191-203.

—— (1986f) 'The Campaign Against Sealing', in *Seals and Sealing in Canada: Report of the Royal Commission*, Vol. 2, Ottawa: Supply and Services Canada, pp. 65-101.

—— (1986g) 'The Importation Ban of the European Communities', in *Seals and Sealing in Canada: Report of the Royal Commission*, Vol. 2, Ottawa: Supply and Services Canada, pp. 104-48.

—— (1986h) 'Sealing in Northern Communities', in *Seals and Sealing in Canada: Report of the Royal Commission*. Vol. 2, Ottawa: Supply and Services Canada, pp. 219-85.

Martin, Calvin (1978) *Keepers of the Game: Indian-Animal Relationships and the Fur Trade*, Berkeley: University of California Press.

Mathiassen, Therkel (1928) 'Material Culture of the Iglulik Eskimos', *Report of the Fifth Thule Expedition 1921-24*, Vol. VI, No. 1 Copenhagen: Gyldendalske Boghandel.

Matowanyika, Joseph Z.Z. (1989) 'Cast Out of Eden: Peasants Versus Wildlife Policy in Savannah Africa', *Alternatives* 16(1): 30-9.

Maxwell, Moreau S. (1974-5) 'An Early Dorset Harpoon Complex', *Folk* 16-17: 125-32.

—— (1985) *Prehistory of the Eastern Arctic*, New York: Academic Press.

Mighetto, Lisa (1988) 'Wildlife Protection and the New Humanitarianism', *Environmental Ethics* 12(1): 37-49.

Miller, Vicki (1989) *The Ark II Activist: Canadian Animal Rights Network*, 4pp.

Mohl, Jeppe (1979) 'Description and Analysis of the Bone Material from Nugarsuk: An Eskimo Settlement Representative of the Thule Culture In West Greenland', in *Thule Eskimo Culture: An Anthropological Retrospective*, ed by A.P. McCartney, Archaeological Survey of Canada Mercury Paper No. 88, Ottawa: National Museums of Canada. pp. 380-94.

Montreal Gazette (1983) 'Sealskin Boycott is Crippling Inuit Hunters Lifestyle', 22 October.

—— (1989a) 'Seal Slaughter Growing Demonstrators Say', 19 March.

—— (1989b) 'Seal Hunt Resurfaces As Issue During Newfoundland Elections', 18 April.

Moore, Patrick (1983) Taped interview with Alan Herscovici.

—— (1985) Telephone interview, 20 January.

Morantz, Toby (1980) 'The Fur Trade and the Cree of James Bay', in *Old Trails and New Directions: Papers of the Third North American Fur Trade Conference*, ed. by C. Judd and A. Ray. Toronto: University of Toronto Press, pp. 39-58.

Morast, Dan (1985) Telephone interview.

Morgan, Katherine B. (1983) 'An Overview of Animal-Related Organizations, With Some Guidelines for Recognizing Patterns', *Community Animal Control*, March/April, 2pp.

Mowat, Farley (1952) *People of the Deer*, Boston: Little, Brown.
—— (1959) *The Desperate People*, Boston: Little, Brown.
—— (1984) *Sea of Slaughter*, Toronto, McClelland and Stewart.
Muller-Wille, Ludger (1978) 'Cost Analysis of Modern Hunting Among Inuit of the Canadian Central Arctic', *Polar Geography* II(2): 100-14.
Naess, Arne (1973) 'The Shallow and the Deep. Long Range Ecology Movements', *Inquiry* 16(1): 95-100.
Neatby, L.H. (1984) 'Exploration and History of the Canadian Arctic', in *Handbook of North American Indians, Vol. 5: The Arctic*. ed. by D. Damas, Washington, DC: The Smithsonian Institution, pp. 377-90.
Nelson, Richard (1969) *Hunters of the Northern Ice*, Chicago: Aldine.
Nelson-Smith, A. (1978) 'Cull Again', *New Scientist*, Vol. 89: 14.
New Scientist (1982a) 'Join the Club', Vol. 93: 214.
—— (1982b) 'Scientists Disagree and the Seal Hunt Goes On', Vol. 2 93: 547.
—— (1982c) 'Ministers to Try Again for Seal Ban', Vol. 93: 627.
—— (1982d) 'Temporary Ban on Seal Skins', Vol. 93: 781.
—— (1983a) 'Canada Denies Arm-Twisting Over Seal Trade', Vol. 94: 7.
—— (1983b) 'Market for Baby-Seal Skins Dries Up', Vol. 94: 570.
New York Times (1979) 'The Wrong Seal Hunt', by Lars Toft Rasmussen, 21 March, p. 23.
News of the North (1984) Untitled editorial, 20 July.
Nooter, Gert (1976) *Leadership and Headship: Changing Authority Patterns in an East Greenland Hunting Community*, Mededelingen Van Het Rijksmuseum Voor Volkenkunde, Leiden: Brill.
Norton, Bryan G. (1984) 'Environmental Ethics and Weak Anthropocentrism', *Environmental Ethics* 6(2): 131-48.
O'Bryan, Deric (1953) 'Excavation of a Cape Dorset Eskimo house Site, Mill Island, West Hudson Strait', *Annual Report of the National Museum of Canada for 1951-52*, Bulletin 128, Ottawa: Government of Canada, pp. 40-57.
Ortega y Gasset, Jose (1985) *Meditations on Hunting*, New York: Scribner's.
Parry, William Edward (1821) *Journal of a Voyage for the Discovery of a Northwest Passage from the Atlantic to the Pacific: Performed in the Years 1819-20*, London: John Murray.
Peter, S. (1983) European Hypocrisy is Alive and Well, *Inuit Ublumi-Inuit Today* 1(2): 9-11.
Peters, Michael (1971) 'Nature and Culture', in *Animals, Men and Morals: An Enquiry into the Maltreatment of Non-Humans*, ed. by Stanley and Rosalind Godlovitch and John Harris, London: Victor Gollancz Ltd., pp. 213-231.
Peterson, Everett (1976) 'Biological Productivity of Arctic Lands and Waters: A Review of Canadian Literature', in *Inuit Land Use and Occupancy Project*, Ed. by M.M.R. Freeman, Vol. II, Ottawa: supply and Services Canada, pp. 85-100.
Plumet, Patrick (1979) 'Thuleens et Dorsetiens dans l'Ungava (Nouveau-Quebec)', in *Thule Eskimo Culture: An Anthropological Retrospective*, ed. by A.P. McCartney, Archaeological Survey of Canada Mercury Paper no. 88, Ottawa: National Museum of Man, pp. 110-21.
Polanyi, Karl (1968) 'The Economy as Instituted Process', in *Primitive, Archaic and Modern Economies: Essays of Karl Polanyi*, ed. by G. Dalton, Boston: Beacon Press, pp. 139-74.
Quigley, N.C. and N.J. McBride (1987) 'The Structure of an Arctic

Microeconomy: The Traditional Sector in Community Economic Development', *Arctic* 40(3): 204–11.

Rasmussen, Knud (1929) 'Intellectual Culture of the Iglulik Eskimos', *Report of the Fifth Thule Expedition 1921-24*, Vol. VI, No. 1 Copenhagen: Gyldendalske Boghandel.

—— (1931) 'The Netsilik Eskimos: Social Life and Spiritual Culture', *Report of the Fifth Thule Expedition 1921-24*, Vol. VIII, No. 1-2, Copenhagen: Gyldendalske Boghandel.

Regan. Tom (1982) 'Environmental Ethics and the Ambiguity of the Native Americans' Relationship with Nature', in *All That Dwell Therein: Animal Rights and Environmental Ethics*, Ed. by T. Regan, Berkeley: University of California Press, pp. 206-39.

—— (1983) *The Case for Animal Rights*, Berkeley: University of California Press.

Regan, Tom and Peter Singer (eds) (1976) *Animal Rights and Human Obligations*, Englewood Cliffs, N.J.: Prentice-Hall.

Remmert, Hermann (1980) *Arctic Animal Ecology*, New York: Springer-Verlag.

Riches, David (1982) *Northern Nomadic Hunter-Gatherers: A Humanistic Approach*, New York: Academic Press.

Riewe, Roderick R. (1977) 'The Utilization of Wildlife in the Jones Sound Region by the Griese Fiord Inuit', in *Truelove Lowland, Devon Island, Canada*, ed. by L.C. Bliss. Edmonton: University of Alberta Press, pp. 623-44.

Rinehart, James W. (1987) *The Tyranny of Work: Alienation and the Labour Process*, Don Mills: Harcourt Brace Jovanovich Canada.

Roff, Derek A. and W.D. Bowen (1983) 'Population Dynamics and Management of the Northwest Atlantic Harp Seal *(Phoca groenlandica)*', *Canadian Journal of Fisheries and Aquatic Sciences* 40(7): 919-32.

Rosenfeld, Leonora (1968) *From Beast-Machine to Man-Machine*, New York: Columbia University Press.

Ross, David P. and Peter Usher (1986) *From the Roots Up: Economic Development as If Community Mattered*, Croton-On-Hudson: Bootstrap Press.

Ross, W.G. (1979) 'Commercial Whaling and Eskimos in the Eastern Canadian Arctic 1819-1920', in *Thule ESkimo Culture: An Anthropological Retrospective*, ed. by A.P. McCartney, Archaeological Survey of Canada Mercury Paper No. 88, Ottawa: National Museum of Man, pp. 242-66.

—— (1985) *Arctic Whalers, Icy Seas: Narratives of the Davis Strait Whale Fishery*, Toronto: Irwin Publishing.

Royal Commission Hearings (1985a) *Transcripts of Public Session, London, England 9-10 April*, 2 Vols.

—— (1985b) *Transcripts of Public Session, Vancouver, Canada, 4-5 February*, 2 Vols.

—— (1985c) *Transcript of Public Session, Washington D.C., USA., 17 April*.

—— (1985d) *Transcript of Public Session, Toronto, Canada, 28-31 January*, 4 Vols.

Sabo, George III and Deborah Rowland Sabo (1985) 'Belief Systems and the Ecology of Sea Mammal Hunting Among the Baffinland Eskimo', *Arctic Anthropology* 22(9): 77-86.

Sahlins, Marshall (1968) 'Notes on the Original Affluent Society', in *Man the Hunter*, ed. by R.B. Lee and I. DeVore. Chicago: Aldine, pp. 85-9.

—— (1972) *Stone Age Economics*, Chicago: Aldine.

Saladin D'Anglure, Bernard (12984) 'Inuit of Quebec', in *The Handbook of*

North American Indians, Vol. 5: The Arctic, ed. by D. Damas, Washington, DC: The Smithsonian Institution, pp. 476-507.

Salisbury, Richard (1986) *A Homeland for the Cree: Regional Development in James Bay, 1971-81*, Montreal: McGill-Queen's Press.

Salt, Henry (1894) *Animal Rights: Considered in Relation to Human Progress*, New York: Macmillan.

Schaefer, Otto (1971) 'When the Eskimo Comes to Town', *Nutrition Today*, November/December, pp. 8-16.

Scheffer, Victor B. (1958) *Seals, Sea Lions and Walruses. A Review of the Pinnipedia*, Palo Alto: Stanford University Press.

―――― (1974) 'Killing for Subsistence', in *A Voice for Wildlife*, New York: Charles Scribner's Sons, pp. 50-72.

Scherer, Donald (1982) 'Anthropocentrism, Atomism and Environmental Ethics', *Environmental Ethics* 4(2): 115-23.

Schneider, Lucien (1985) *Ulirnaisigutit: An Inuktitut-English Dictionary of Northern Quebec, Labrador and Eastern Arctic Dialects*. Quebec: La Presse de l'Université Laval.

Schrire, Carmel and William Steiger (1974) 'A Matter of Life and Death: An Investigation into the Practice of Female Infanticide in the Arctic', *Man* 9(2): 161-84.

Shweder, R. and E. Bourne (1984) 'Does the Concept of the Person Vary Cross-Culturally? In *Culture Theory: Essays in Mind, Self, and Emotion*', ed. by R. Shweder and R. Levine. New York: Cambridge University Press.

Singer, Peter (1975) *Animal Liberation: A New Ethics for Our Treatment of Animals*, New York: Avon.

―――― (1985) *In Defense of Animals*, ed. by P. Singer, New York: Perenial Library.

Smith, Eric A. (1980) Evolutionary Ecology and the analysis of Human Foraging Behavior: An Inuit Example from the East Coast of Hudson Bay Ph.D. dissertation in anthropology, Cornell University.

Smith, James, G.E. (1981) 'The Chipwyan', in *Handbook of North American Indians, V. 6: The Subarctic*, ed. by J. Helm, Washington, DC: The Smithsonian Institution, pp. 271-84.

Smith, Lorne (1972) 'The Mechanical Dog Team: A Study of the Ski-doo in the Canadian Arctic', *Arctic Anthropology* 9(1): 1-9.

Smith, P.A. (1977) *Résumé of the Trade in Polar Bear Hides in Canada*, 1975-76, Progress Note 82, Ottawa: Canadian Wildlife Service.

―――― (1978) *Résumé of the Trade in Polar Bear Hides in Canada, 1976-77*, Progress Note 89, Ottawa: Canadian Wildlife Service.

Smith, P.A. and C. Jonkel (1975a) *Résumé of the Trade in Polar Bear Hides in Canada, 1972-73*, Progress Note 43, Ottawa: Canadian Wildlife Service.

―――― (1975b) *Résumé of the Trade in Polar Bear Hides in Canada, 1973-74*, Progress Note 66, Ottawa: Canadian Wildlife Service.

Smith, P.A. and I. Stirling (1976) *Résumé of the Trade in Polar Bear Hides in Canada, 1974-75*, Progress Note 66, Ottawa: Canadian Wildlife Service.

Smith, Thomas G. (1973a) *Population Dynamics of the Ringed Seal in the Canadian Eastern Arctic*, Bulletin 181, Ottawa: Fisheries Research Board of Canada.

―――― (1973b) 'Management Research on the Eskimo's Ringed Seal', *Canadian Geographic Journal* 86(4): 118-25.

―――― (1979-80) 'How Inuit Trapper-Hunters Make Ends Meet', *Canadian Geographic* 99(3): 56-61.

—— (1987) *The Ringed Seal*, Phoca hispida, *of the Canadian Western Arctic*, Canadian Bulletin of Fisheries and Aquatic Sciences 216, Ottawa: Department of Fisheries and Oceans.

Smith, Thomas G. and Ian Stirling (1975) 'The Breeding Habitat of the Ringed Seal *(Phoca hispida)*: The Birth Lair and Associated Structures', *Canadian Journal of Zoology* 53(9): 1297-1305.

Smith, Thomas G. and Deborah Taylor (1977) *Notes on Marine Mammal, Fox and Polar Bear Harvests in the Northwest Territories 1940 to 1972*, Technical Report No. 694, Ottawa: Department of Fisheries and the Environment.

Smith, Thomas G. and Harold Wright (1989) 'Economic Status and Role of Hunters in a Modern Inuit Village', *Polar Record* 25(153): 93-8.

Smith, Tony (1988) 'Is Furwearing an Act of Philanthropy?' *Alternatives* 15(3): 67-8.

Spencer, Robert F. (1959) *The North Alaskan Eskimo: A Study in Ecology and Society*, Bureau of American Ethnology Bulletin 171, Washington, DC: The Smithsonian Institution.

Stefansson, Vihjalmur (1913) *My Life With The Eskimo*, New York: Macmillan.

Steward, Julian (1955) *Theory of Culture Change: The Methodology of Multilinear Evolution*, Urbana: University of Illinois Press.

Tanner, Adrian (1979) *Bringing Home Game: Religious Ideology and Mode of Production of the Mistassini Cree Hunters*, New York: St. Martin's Press.

—— (1983) 'End of Fur Trade History', *Queen's Quarterly*, 90(1): 176-91.

Taylor, William E. Jr. (1960) 'A Description of Sadlermiut Houses Excavated at Native Point, Southampton Island, N.W.T.' Bulletin 162, *Anthropological Series 45*, Ottawa: National Museum of Canada. pp. 53-100.

Testart, Alan (1988) 'Problems in the Social Anthropology of Hunter-Gatherers', *Current Anthropology* 29(1): 1-31.

Thomas, Keith (1983) *Man and the Natural World: A History of Modern Sensibilities*, New York: Pantheon.

Udall, Stuart (1962) *The Quiet Crisis*, New York: Holt, Rinehart and Winston.

Usher, Peter (1976) 'Evaluating Country Food in the Northern Native Economy', *Arctic* 29(2): 105-20.

Usher, P., D. DeLancey, G. Wenzel, M. Smith and P. White (1985) *An Evaluation of Native Harvest Survey Methodologies in Northern Canada*, ESRF Report No. 004, Ottawa: Environmental Studies Research Fund.

Usher, Peter and Nigel Bankes (1986) *Property, The Basis of Inuit Hunting Rights: A New Approach*, Ottawa: Inuit Committee on National Issues.

Usher, Peter and G.W. Wenzel (1987) 'Native Harvest Surveys and Statistics: A Critique of Their Construction and Use', *Arctic* 40(2): 145-60.

—— (1988) 'Socioeconomic Aspects of Harvesting', in *Keeping on the Land: A Study of the Feasibility of a Comprehensive Wildlife Harvest Support Programme in the Northwest Territories*, ed. by R. Ames, D. Axford, P. Usher, E. Weick, and G.W. Wenzel, Ottawa: Canadian Arctic Resources Committee, pp. 1-52.

Usher, Peter, G.W. Wenzel, and Peter Jull (1987) *The Inuit of Canada*, Reference Series No. 38, Ottawa: Department of External Affairs.

Vallee, Frank G. (1962) *Kabloona and Eskimo in the Central Keewatin*, N.C.R.C.-62-2, Ottawa: Department of Northern Affairs and National Resources.

Vallee, Frank G., Derek G. Smith, and Joseph D. Cooper (1984) 'Contemporary Inuit of Canada', in *Handbook of North American Indians, V. 5: Arctic*, ed.

by D. Damas, Washington, DC: The Smithsonian Institution, pp. 662–75.

Van de Velde, Frans (1956) 'Rules for Sharing the Seal Amongst the Arviligjuarmiut Eskimo', *Eskimo* 41: 3-6.

Vibe, Christian (1967) 'Arctic Animals in Relation to Climatic Fluctuations', *Meddeleser om Gronland* 170(5), Copenhagen.

Watson, Paul (1985) Correspondence (1 March), 3pp.

Watson, Paul and W. Rogers (1982) *Sea Shepherd: My Fight for Whales and Seals*, New York: W.W. Norton and Co.

Weber, Beate (1982) Untaped interview (14 May), Montreal, Canada.

Weetaluktuk, Jobie (1985) 'It's Time for This Endangered Species to Fight Back', *Taqralik* (September), pp. 3-4.

Wenzel, G.W. (1973) *The Ecology of a Central Eskimo Hunting Group: Clyde River, N.W.T*, unpublished report to the Carnegie Museum, Pitsburgh, 95pp.

—— (1978) 'The Harp Seal Controversy and the Inuit Economy', *Arctic* 31(1): 3-6.

—— (1979) 'Analysis of a Dorset-Thule Structure from Northwestern Hudson Bay', in *Thule Eskimo Culture: An Anthropological Retrospective*, Archaeological Survey of Canada Mercury Paper No. 88. ed. by A.P. McCartney, Ottawa: National Museum of Man, pp. 122-33.

—— (1981) *Inuit Ecology and Adaptation: The Organization of Subsistence*, Canadian Ethnology Service Mercury Paper No. 77, Ottawa: National Museum of Man.

—— (1983a) 'Inuit' and Polar Bears: Cultural Observations from a Hunt Near Resolute Bay, N.W.T.', *Arctic* 36(1): 90-5.

—— (1983b) 'The Integration of "Remote" Site Labor into the Inuit Economy of Clyde River, N.W.T.', *Arctic Anthropology* 20(2): 79-92.

—— (1984a) 'Archaeological Evidence for Prehistoric Inuit Use of the Sea Ice Environment', in *'Sikumiut': The People Who Use the Sea Ice*, ed. by A. Cooke and E. Van Alstine, Ottawa: Canadian Arctic Resources Committee, pp. 41-60.

—— (1984b) *Kinship as a demographic and Ecological Integrator Among Inuit of the East Baffin Island Coast. Circa. 1920-1960*, unpublished report to the Canadian Ethnology Service, National Museum of Man, Ottawa, 57pp.

—— (1985a) 'Marooned in a Blizzard of Contradictions: Inuit and the Anti-Sealing Movement', *Etudes/Inuit/Studies* 9(1): 77-91.

—— (1985b) 'Subsistence, Cash and the Mixed Economy: Adaptation Among Baffin Inuit', unpublished report (No. SC 257400) to the Department of Economic Development and Tourism, Government of the Northwest Territories, Iqaluit, 28pp.

—— (1986a) 'Resource Harvesting and the Social Structure of Native Communities', in *Native People and Renewable Resource Management*, ed. by J. Green and J. Smith, Edmonton: Alberta Society of Professional Biologists, pp. 10-22.

—— (1986b) 'Canadian Inuit in a Mixed Economy: Thoughts on Seals, Snowmobiles, and Animal Rights', *Native Studies Review* 2(1): 69-82.

—— (1986c) *The Ecology and Organization of Inuit Sealing Activities at Clyde River, N.W.T.*, Technical Report 10, Royal Commission on Seals and the Sealing Industry in Canada, Ottawa, 99pp.

—— (1986d) '"I Am I and the Environment": Inuit Wildlife Harvesting and Community", paper presented at the 85th Annual Meeting of the American Anthropological Association, Philadelphia.

—— (1989) 'Sealing At Clyde River, N.W.T.: A Discussion of Inuit

Economy', *Etudes/Inuit/Studies* 13(1): 3-22.

n.d.a. Unpublished Clyde Field Notes, 1971-74.

n.d.b. Unpublished Clyde Field Notes, 1978.

n.d.c. Unpublished Clyde Field Notes, 1988-89.

Weyer, Edward (1932) *The Eskimos: Their Environment and Folkways*, New Haven, CT: Yale University Press.

Williamson, Tony (1978) 'Inuit: The Innocent Victims', *Decks Awash* 7 (11): 60.

Wilmott, William E. (1961) *The Eskimo Community at Port Harrison, P.Q.* N.C.R.C.-61-1, Ottawa: Department of Northern Affairs and National Resources.

Winterholder, Bruce and Eric A. Smith (1981) *Hunter-Gatherer Foraging Strategies: Ethnographic and Archeological Analysis*, Chicago: Aldine.

Wolfe, Robert (1979) *Food Production in a Western Eskimo Population*, unpublished Ph.D. dissertation, Department of Anthropology, U.C.L.A.

Woodbury, Anthony C. (1984) Eskimo and Aleut Languages. In *Handbook of North American Indians. V. 5: Arctic*. Ed. by D. Damas. Washington, D.C.: the Smithsonian Institution. pp. 49-63.

Worl, Rosita (1980) 'The North Slope Inupiat Whaling Complex', in *Senri Ethnological Studies 4: Alaska Native Culture and History*, ed. by W.B. Workman and Y. Kotani, Osaka: National Museum of Ethnology, pp. 305-20.

—— (1986) *Sociocultural Values of Clyde River Inuit*. Technical Report No. 18, prepared for the Royal Commission on Seals and the Sealing Industry in Canada, Ottawa. 17pp.

World Society for the Protection of Animals Information Bulletin, 2pp.

Wright, Guy (1984) *Sons and Seals: A Voyage to the Ice*, St. John's: Institute for Social and Economic Research.

Wright, Robert (1990) 'Are Animals People Too?' *New Republic* 202(11): 20-7.

Young, Oran (1981) 'The Political Economy of the Northern Fur Seal', *Polar Record* 20(128): 407-16.

Zaslow, Morris (1988) *The Opening of the Canadian North: 1914-1967*, Toronto: McClelland and Stewart.

INDEX

aboriginal peoples *see* Native peoples
aglulitt 64, 66, 83, 84, 85-6
Aleuts 152, 159
Anglican Church 31
animal rights movement 1, 3, 50
  and seal hunting 4-6, 45-55, 142-3,
    149-52, 158-9, 163-72, 177-84
  background 37-41
  Euro-strategy 48-9
  pictorial images 35-6, 46-7, 48, 145
  tactics 35, 48-9
Animal Rights Network 160
Animal Welfare Trust 49
Animals' Agenda 152, 160-1
anthropology
  in Inuit 6-9, 24-5
anti-sealing campaign *see* animal rights
  movement
Aquinas, Thomas 38
Arctic fox 32-3, 50-1, 69-70
  see also fox trapping
Ark II Activist 168, 171

Bardot, Brigitte 48, 52, 54, 149
barter 110-11
Barzdo, Jon 145-6
bearded seals 22, 136
  see also seals
Bentham, Jeremy 40
Best, Steven 8, 59-60, 146, 151, 158-9,
  164, 165, 167-8, 171-2, 177-8,
  179
blubber 43, 44
Boas, Franz 6, 29, 30, 69, 75, 84, 100,
  103-4
Boe, Vivia 146, 151, 155-7
breeding 66, 89-90
bricolage see mixed economies
Busch, Briton Cooper 44

Canada 1, 31
  and seal controversy 48-9, 54
  government policies 109-10, 111
  see also Inuit
Canada Audubon 47
Canadian Arctic Resources Committee
  152, 157-60
caribou 94-5, 132

Cartesianism 38-9
Cartier, Jacques 42-3
cash economies 98-9, 110-12, 113, 122-3,
  129-30, 132-3, 173-5
casual labour 113
Catholic Church 31
Clyde River Inuit *see* Inuit
colonialism 4, 5
Comité d'Action 49, 51
commensal sharing 103-4, 105
communal meals 103-4
community dynamics 101-4, 105
complicity arguments 163-4
conservation interests 36-7, 46, 47
  species conservation 47, 48
continuity 140-1
Cousteau, Jacques 48
cultural assimilation 166-9, 173-84
cultural dependence 30-1
  see also Inuit culture
cultural issues 142-61
cultural modifications 165-6
cultural survival 1-2, 134-5
Cultural Survival Inc. 8

Damas, David 100-1
Davies, Brian 3, 4, 47
deep ecology 40-1, 50
Denmark 49
Descartes, Rene 38-9
DEW Line 33
diet *see* food supplies
disease 30-1, 33
disequilibrium systems 94-5
dogteams 84-5, 86, 87, 91, 122
Doncaster, Anne 158-9, 160, 168
Dorset Culture 26, 30
Duffy, R. Quinn 112, 113
dyed pelts 52
  see also fur trade

ecological concerns 7, 46-7, 54, 61, 74-96,
  97-8
  deep ecology 40-1, 50
  see also subsistence cultures
economic structures 97-133
economic survival 1, 2, 3, 32-3, 51-4,
  109-23

EEC
  and conservation 1-2
  ecological concerns 1
  import bans 1-2, 34, 49, 54, 123, 128-9,
    150
employment levels 129
environmental conditions 15-23, 64, 76
  ice seasons 64, 66
  spring season 89-92
  summer season 16, 20-3, 79, 92-4
  temperatures 15, 16, 89, 93
  white-outs 84
  winter season 15-16, 17-20, 78, 84-9
epidemics see disease
equipment depreciation 116
Ernerk, Peter 157-8
Eskimos see Inuit
equilibrium systems 94
Eskimo Brotherhood see ITC
European Economic Community see EEC
Europeans
  missionaries 27, 31-2
  relations with Inuit 8, 11, 13, 27-34
explorers 26, 27-33

Fauna and Flora Preservation Society
  145-6
firearms 29, 30, 51, 90-1, 95-6
fishing 23, 83, 96
floe edge sealing 91-2
food sharing 101-4, 105, 132
food supplies 80-3, 104, 136-7
  imported 118-19
  seals 3, 18-19, 42, 80-3, 119-23, 125-6
Foote, Don C. 52, 53
formal economic structures 98, 99
fox trapping 106-8
  see also Arctic fox
Franklin, Sir John 26, 27
Frobisher, Martin 26
The Front 45
Fur Institute of Canada 157
fur seals 42, 52
  see also seals
fur trade 28-9, 31-3, 36, 44, 52-3, 69-70,
  106-23, 163-4, 174-5
  Arctic fox 32-3, 50-1
  dyed pelts 52

Glover, Mark 155-6
Grandy, John 159, 160
Greanville, Patrice 160, 161, 166, 178
Greenpeace 3, 36, 41, 48, 52, 142, 145,
  146-53, 155-7, 181
Greenpeace Canada 53, 177
Greenpeace Denmark 149

Hall, C.F. 11

Hamilton, Peter 154-5
harp seals 1, 22, 35-6, 42-3, 44-5, 47, 51,
  143-4
  see also seals
harpoons 87-8, 93
harvesting see seal hunting
Heinrich, Albert 100
hooded seals 1, 143-4
  see also seals
Houston, James 13
Hudson's Bay Company 27, 28, 29, 31-2,
  36, 50-1, 69, 106-9, 174
Hughes, Charles C. 6
Humane Society of the United States 152,
  159
Hunter, Robert 144-5, 146-7, 178
hunting 18, 21, 77-81, 83, 98, 132
  attitudes to 4, 5-6, 7
  prime species 77
  secondary species 77
  see also seal hunting
hunting cultures 24-5, 56-63, 166

ice seasons 64, 66
ideological issues 134-41
IFAW 3, 4, 36, 47, 48-9, 52, 142, 145-52,
  163
import bans
  effects of 128-33
  on sealskins 1-2, 34, 49, 54, 123, 128-9,
    150
imported food supplies 118-19
imported goods 163-4
informal economic structures 98, 99-105
International Fund for Animal Welfare see
  IFAW
International Polar Bear Convention 74
International Wildlife Coalition 8, 36, 49,
  151, 152
International Work Group on Indigenous
  Affairs 8
Inuit 11-34
  and seal controversy 1-4, 50-5, 123-33,
    142-4
  anthropology 6-9, 24-5
  as subsistence hunters 57-63
  economic structure 97-133
  economic survival 1, 2, 3, 32-3, 51-4,
    109-23
  history 11, 13, 24-34
  kinship 62-3, 99-105, 137-8
  Nunavut 55
  relations with Europeans 8, 11, 13,
    27-34
  seal hunting 1-2, 4-6, 18-19, 21-2, 50-5,
    64-96
  Thule Culture 26-7, 30
  victimization 52

Inuit boats 92, 114-15
Inuit children 117, 131
Inuit communities 11-15, 32, 33, 109-10, 127
Inuit culture 1-2, 27, 29-31, 34, 54, 134-5, 162-3, 170-2
Inuit life style 17-23
Inuit Tapirisat of Canada *see* ITC
inummarik 139-40
ITC 148

Jeffords, James 48

Keewatin Wildlife Federation 157-8
kinship 62-3, 99-105, 137-8

land claims 160-1
Lavigne, David 142, 171
Life Force Foundation 154-5
Livingstone, John 159, 178
Lopez, Barry 14
Lynge, Finn 149

market economics 114-23, 124-8
Martin, Calvin 164
mauluktuk hunting 84, 91, 131
mechanized harvesting 115-16, 117, 131
media attitudes 144-5
Miller, Vicki 168-9, 178, 181
minimax strategy 28, 30
missionaries 27, 31-2
mixed economies 113, 114-23
modern technology 7-8, 29-30, 33-4, 53, 94-6, 115-16, 164-6
money-flow cycle 115-16
Moore, Patrick 151, 156
Moravian Church 31
Mowat, Farley 13, 95
Muntingh, Hemmo 149-50
mythology 13

nalartuk see kinship
narwhal 93, 132
Native peoples 41, 54, 56-63, 97, 157-8, 160-1, 168-9, 178-9
see also Inuit
natsiq see ringed seals
natural environment *see* environmental conditions
Nature 54
New Scientist 54
ningiqtuq see sharing economies
North Pacific Fur Seal Convention (1911) 42
Norway 1, 45, 51, 151
Nunavut 55

oil industry 33

Ontario Humane Society 47
open water sealing 92-4, 96
O'Sullivan, Michael 160, 161, 166, 178

Pacific area 45
Parry, William 66, 69, 97-8
Peary, Robert 11, 13
Peters, Michael 181
Pickaver, Alan 147, 151
pictorial images
emotive use of 35-6, 46-7, 48, 145
place names 65, 68
polar bears 70, 74
political concerns 54, 142
see also EEC
population decline 30
prime species 77

qajaq see open sealing
Quallunaat see Europeans

Regan, Tom 38-40
religious attitudes 38, 132
relocation programs 33, 66, 69-70, 95, 110-11, 116-17
resource allocation 98-105
ringed seals 2-3, 21-2, 32, 42, 44, 51-3, 64, 66-9
see also seals
Ross, John 11
Royal Canadian Mounted Police 26, 32, 69, 108
Royal Commission on Seals (Canada) 1-2, 152, 153-7, 168, 177
RSPCA 36, 37, 153
Ryan, Leo 48

Salt, Henry 37, 40
Save the Seal Inc. 152
sculps 44
sea ice 64, 66
Sea Shepherd Society 156, 163
seal hunting methods 84-93
seal controversy 41-9
and Canadian government 48-9, 54
and cultural issues 142-61
and Inuit 1-4, 50-5, 58-63, 123-33, 142-84
background 4-6, 35-41
seal hunting
and animal rights 4-6, 45-55, 142-3, 149-52, 158-9, 163-72, 177-84
and EEC 1-2, 34, 49, 54, 123, 128-9, 150
attitudes to 3-4, 134-41
commercial 52
for food 3, 18-19, 42, 80-3, 119-23, 125-6
history 41-4

images of 35-6, 46-7, 48, 145
importance 2-3, 42, 43
Inuit 1-2, 4-6, 18-19, 21-2, 50-5, 64-96
mauluktuk 84, 91, 131
mechanized 115-16, 117, 131
open water 92-4, 96
· prime species 77
seal pups 66, 89-90
seal strikes 87-8
sealing cycle 74-94
seals 42
    bearded 22, 136
    fur 42
    harp 1, 22, 35-6, 42-3, 44-5, 47, 51,
        143-4
    hooded 1, 143-4
    ringed 2-3, 21-2, 32, 42, 44, 51-3, 64,
        66-9
sealskin prices 51, 70, 71-3, 111, 114-15,
    116, 124-6
sealskin rope 136
sealskins 42, 114-15, 175
    import bans 1-2, 34, 49, 54, 123, 128-9,
        150
    preparation of 19-20
seasons *see* environmental conditions
secondary species 77
selective perception 145
sharing economies 98-105, 114, 132-3,
    139-40, 176
Smith, Tony 58, 59, 165
snowmobiles 34, 84, 85, 91, 95, 115, 165-6
social transfer payments 115, 131
socioeconomic concerns 62, 98-105,
    128-33, 137-8, 176-7
Soviet Union 45

species conservation 47, 48
    see also conservation interests
spring season 89-92
subsistence cultures 24-5, 56-63, 97-105,
    176
summer season 16, 20-3, 79, 92-4, 127-8

tanning 51, 70
technology *see* modern technology
temperatures 15, 16, 89, 93
    see also environmental conditions
Thorne, Lorraine 151
Thule Culture 26-7, 30
    see also Inuit
trading 27, 28-9, 69, 106-8
    fur 28-9, 31-3, 36, 44, 50-1, 69-780,
        106-23
    whaling 22-3, 27, 28-9
traditional artifacts 164-5
transport 34

utilitarianism 40

walrus 93-4
Watson, Paul 53, 156, 181
Weber, Beate 149
whaling 22-3, 27, 28-9, 95
white-outs 84
Wilderness Society 36
wildlife 16, 32-3
winter season 15-16, 17-20, 78, 84-9
Woolman, John 40
World Society for the Protection of
    Animals 151, 160
World Wildlife Fund 47, 52